WAFFLE HOUSE DIARIES

WAYNE SMITH

Bluehotel Press
Chattanooga
Tennessee

Cover art by Patty Maroney
from oil painting "At the End of the Day"

Author photograph by Thomas Ware

A few names have been changed, a few people and events are composites, and all
have been filtered through time and imagination.

Bluehotel Press

ISBN-13: 978-0615610542
ISBN-10: 0615610544

FOR JOE

Acknowledgments

My thanks to all the law enforcement personnel, both federal and local, who worked with me during my thirty years with the Department of Justice. The joint efforts and the camaraderie made a difficult job rewarding.

I am grateful to those who read earlier drafts of chapters of the book and gave me encouragement to finish it.

I am especially grateful to my family, who were always there for me even though I missed countless holidays, soccer games, birthdays, school events, and other important parts of their lives.

Contents

Jacked

Chattanooga, 1998

I T WAS WEIRD. I had just gotten a call from an agent in New York and then another from an agent in El Paso about the same investigation. Neither knew the other was going to call, so when I talked with the guy from El Paso, I already knew more about the case than he had planned to tell me.

Seems the El Paso office was listening to the pagers of a group of coke brokers, and the New York office had a wiretap on a bunch that apparently wanted to do business with the hombres from El Paso. Turned out that somehow little old Chattanooga was in the middle of the deal, and we had become very popular in a hurry.

The boss was getting ready to go on annual leave, so when I ran it down to him, I got a somewhat disinterested go ahead.

My team located the motel where the two truck drivers were staying, and it was a dump. Situated in an area of town known for truckers' lodgings and whores, it was not a place one would willingly take one's family. Since our information was skimpy and we didn't really know what we were going to do, we just set up surveillance on the front of the building and tried to figure out which room the bad guys were renting.

The simple thing would have been to drive over, walk in, and ask the front desk crew about our friends, but this motel was not one where that was possible. The group of locals working with me had just cleaned out a crack dealing prostitution outfit operating out of this same dump, so I didn't think we'd get any cooperation from the front desk. They sure as hell hadn't helped us last time, and this was too big a deal to risk.

Besides, it wasn't our case. Messing up one of our own cases was bad, but screwing New York and El Paso in one shot might be a career ender.

I stationed one of our cars west of the motel, in a small business lot across Orchard Knob from the Army Reserve, and I then sat east near the Burger King. I had two other cars in the area, just in case.

We sat.

The New York agent had said that there was a shipment coming from El Paso via tractor trailer rig and that the current thinking was the two mopes in Chattanooga were relief drivers who would take the truck on to the Big Apple.

It seemed a little strange, changing drivers in the middle of a run, especially with the cargo that had been described to me. Two thousand kilograms of cocaine was a bit much to turn over to relief drivers in the middle of the night on a handshake, but nobody ever said the dope business was supposed to make sense.

"Fourteen Zero Five to Fourteen Zero Two."

"Two. Go ahead."

"I got the west end covered. You got a clue on the room number yet?"

"Waiting on the call from New York."

All we had to roll on was the name of the hotel, and the guys on the phone were supposed to give us more information when they got it. We were, as the military likes to call it, pre-positioned, and waiting. The summer day was not too humid, and it was a pleasant way to spend a few hours, even if it was in an undesirable neighborhood.

"Fourteen Zero Two to Seven and Eight."

"Fourteen Zero Eight. Go ahead, Two."

"Both of y'all stay away for the time being. We got the eyeball for now, so don't let's burn all our cars right away."

"Eight. We got it. We be way out of sight."

△ △ △ △ △ △ △ △ △ △

MY CELL PHONE was both a blessing and a curse. I started the job when there were no pagers, no car phones, and the crude radio system didn't work outside major cities. Now with a digital messaging pager, a cell phone, and two car radios, it was almost impossible to hide from the office and do a little personal business.

The pager started squawking, and the display showed an El Paso number. I punched the digits into the cell phone and got through immediately.

"El Paso District Office, how may I direct your call?" At least they didn't yet have one of those electronic call directors.

"I need to speak to Agent Ramirez in Group Two."

"Ramirez. Is this Chattanooga?"

"Yeah, this is Smith. I just got your page. What you got?"

"Our clone pager just showed a New York number. Our guys in the motel should be walking out to a pay phone in a short. This bunch don't ever use motel phones."

"Great, maybe we can get a look at them now. We still don't have a hint of the room number. You got any description of possibles?

"Don't have a clue. All we got is the pager number here, and we haven't figured out who the group has out your way. Give me a shout back when you spot them, and maybe we can tell you who you got."

A little small talk about El Paso, my home for six years a few years ago, and I got off the phone.

△ △ △ △ △ △ △ △ △

"FOURTEEN ZERO TWO to surveillance. We've got a call coming in a short. Be eagle eyed for one or two guys leaving the motel and going to a pay phone. Should be happening now. "

In a few minutes, two males, one gringo and one Hispanic, left the motel property, crossed 23rd Street, and started walking toward the Army Reserve center. There was a large parking lot in a common area between the center and its neighbor, and at least two pay phones hung on utility poles in the parking lot. Lots of folks used the phones while sitting in cars there. Sort of a redneck car phone.

"Anybody get a look at where these mopes came from?"

"Fourteen Zero Five to Fourteen Zero Two. They came out of a room on the top floor at the back. I got it marked. We can get the number later."

The suspects dutifully walked to a pay phone, dialed in a very long string of numbers, and started talking. The tall gringo was on the phone, while the other leaned against the booth, listening. The call lasted about four minutes. Then the two sauntered back toward the motel.

Before they could get there, my cell phone shrilled. Since I had tinnitus from years of qualifying on the range, high pitched sounds sometimes escaped my notice. So I kept the volume turned all the way up and had it set on the most annoying ring possible. The caller ID on the cell showed a New York number.

"Smith here. Whatcha got?"

"Hey, Wayne. This is Jerry from the New York Group. We just had an incoming call from a number in Chattanooga. Suppose you can get us a location and subscriber on the number?"

"Hell, Jerry, I can do better than that. I got one pretty decent picture of the two guys on the pay phone just across the parking lot from me. We got a hint from El Paso on the call, and saw them come out and dial up. From the punching the guy gave the dial, I think they're using calling cards. You get any decent overheards on the call?"

"The guys up here were asking them when they might be coming up. Real vague, but they didn't get any better than they gave. We don't know a damned thing more than we did before the call."

"Oh, hell yeah, we do. This dump has exterior entrances. I got an eyeball on the room now, and I got half-assed descriptions on these two mopes. It wasn't a complete loss."

△ △ △ △ △ △ △ △ △ △

THIS WAS BEGINNING to look like a long, boring overnight job. I halved up the troops, sending three home to get some sleep. Two of us would stay out here till midnight, sitting in the smelly cars. Jeff was

5

parked in a decent spot where he could see the room door, and my car was where I could eyeball the payphone they had used.

The afternoon droned on, turning into evening. The same working girls were circulating around the block where I was sitting. By now they had begun to pay a little more attention to me than I needed. One strolled over and asked if I might be interested in a date, adopting a more than usually circumspect manner.

I got the message. They thought I was a local cop, maybe vice, and just had to size me up. No one sat in a car for hours in this neighborhood without some ulterior motive. Hookers watch people, notice what is going on around them. Their survival depends on staying out of the cars of cops and sadists.

With Jeff down west, I had the east covered. I figured we could hold out till the midnight relief and then grab a few hours of sack time before the suspects started rolling in the morning. The late dark crept on in, and the night life around the BK picked up markedly.

Slow drivers eased through the lot, then detoured into the lot of the strip mall with the Dollar Store anchor just behind and to the east of the BK. That lot was the home office for most of the prostitutes working the corner at Kelly and 23rd. The blocks between Kelly and Willow off 23rd housed them, crack dealers, burglars, and a whole host of other unsavory inhabitants with the honest folks living in fear behind locked doors. As usual, the crooks roamed free, and the citizens were locked in.

A few more calls to and from both New York and El Paso yielded little or nothing. We had the guys described to El Paso, but they weren't able to put names with the faces. Since we were hesitant to approach the motel management, we had no idea how long they had rented the room, or whether they were making any local calls.

Intelligence is great, but there is never enough of the right kind to allow a reliable decision. The good news was that this wasn't our baby — all we had to do was babysit the brat.

A couple of cheeseburgers and a cup of really bad coffee had come and gone, and the dinner hour was giving way to bedtime for ordinary folks.

Jerry called from New York and relayed some more useless info about a phone call the guys up there had gotten from El Paso. The gist was that the truck was somewhere, moving in some direction, and would arrive sometime.

I was all set to tuck in for the night when another one of the hookers came over to the car. It was a cool evening, and I had rolled the windows down so that I wouldn't have to run the engine and the AC. She wanted to know if I was lonely, and did I need some company, and was I interested in a date.

This attention was getting out of hand, and I was getting a little tired of shooing the ladies off. I wasn't so sure the last one was a lady. Sort of looked like a tossup.

When I looked around for a less popular location, I saw a pay phone directly behind the BK, at the side of a parking space facing onto Willow.

I rolled around the block, feeling the night air flow through the windows, airing out the cheeseburger aroma, the smell of sweat and boredom as well. I pulled back into the lot, rolled up to the pay phone, pulled the handset off the hook, and dangled it inside the car. My Dodge Intrepid was new, with all the conveniences — power windows, power seats — a comfortable ride. Not at all like my first G-car, a 1965 Ford pickup with a three speed manual transmission and miserable steering.

Figured if I pretended to be making a call I would look less out of place here and blend in with the crowds a little better.

"Fourteen Zero Two to Fourteen Zero Five."

"Five. Go."

"Five, I've moved to the back of the BK, sitting at a pay phone on Willow if you need me."

"Two. Why would I ever need you?"

"Smartass."

I could see only a small bit of the motel, relying on Jeff to cover the actual room. As I sat, I began to look around at what was in my area. I always look for things out of place, cause you never know what might be happening in a spot like this.

A small white compact drove down Willow to 23rd, turned east and left.

I had seen the same car driving around slowly earlier and had marked it as a john looking for a special friend. Seemed a little strange that he was back so soon. Otherwise, the lot was quiet.

A few working girls were standing along the front of the Dollar Store, and occasionally one would walk to the pay phone mounted on the wall of the building, directly behind me, and make a call.

△ △ △ △ △ △ △ △ △ △

LOOKING BACK IN the mirror, I saw something that piqued my interest, something out of place. Two young black males, not unusual, dressed in what appeared to be school uniforms, most unusual for 10:30 at night in this neighborhood. They were walking west along the front of the strip mall with the Dollar Store on the corner, white long sleeved dress shirts with tails out in the breeze, khaki pants. Not the low rider khakis with crotch at knee level, but more traditional slacks.

Why school uniforms that late at night? My kids could never wait to get home and shuck the Catholic school uniforms they wore. Some of the public schools in the city had instituted the white shirt and khaki pants uniforms recently, but I was surprised to see them at night.

The two strolled directly down the front of the building, walking purposefully, but not in a hurry.

"Fourteen Zero Five to Fourteen Zero Two."

"Two. Go ahead, Five."

"I'm gonna pull off and hit the head."

"Two to Five. Can you hold it for a few, and I'll drive down and take your eyeball."

"Five to Two. Don't leave me hanging for long."

I looked back in the rearview, saw the two kids had reached the corner and stopped. One reached out and took the handset of the payphone on the wall, put it to his ear, and then dropped it in what appeared to be disgust. The same phone that had been working well for the prostitutes.

Both then stepped off the curb and started walking directly toward my car. Their line of travel would take them between my car and the utility pole on which my payphone was mounted.

△ △ △ △ △ △ △ △ △ △

THIS WAS A minor job, just a routine surveillance for other offices, and I hadn't brought all my usual gear. My SIG .45 was locked in the trunk, and a small five shot .38 in an ankle holster was my only available weapon.

I may never know why I did it, but I reached down, pulled the Centennial from the elastic sheath, and held it inside the hiking vest I was wearing. The two kept walking, approached the rear of the car.

The lead YBM said something to me as he moved to the front of my open window.

Damn these electric windows, you can't close them with the ignition off like the old roll up kind!

I assumed he wanted to use my pay phone, but then I saw what was really going on.

A small blue steel automatic handgun appeared, as if by magic, at the upper rear corner of my open window. It looked a lot like a Spanish Llama .380. Amazing what can go through your head, besides the ninety-grain jacketed bullet in the .380.

I dropped back onto the console between the bucket seats, trying to lie as flat as possible. My revolver came up to the window, and I screamed.

"I'LL KILL YOU MUTHERFUCKER!"

Nice talk for a Federal Agent!

The kid with the pistol was slightly behind me, and the wide center pillar of the car blocked any shot I might have had. It seemed like minutes went by before the two began to run.

I jumped out of the car, screaming epithets of various kinds, raging in the dark. I came around the front of the car and looked north on Willow. The two white shirts stood out in the center of the street. I went into a perfect combat stance, putting the front sight blade right in the middle of one of the retreating white blobs.

I could have easily made the shot, but my brain began to tell me what not to do.

Which blob had the gun? The internal debate over dropping the shot down range was going furiously in my head.

I could see headlines: "Narc Murders 15-year-old Black Youth." We had just undergone a revision to our shooting policy, written by the Attorney General.

Ms. Reno had taken a very simple subject, one paragraph in the Agent's manual, and muddled it up so much that I, in that split second, had no idea as to whether I was allowed to shoot in such a situation. Her fifteen-page epistle made little sense, but as with most documents written by lawyers, it was designed to cover the agency's ass, not mine.

Good sense overtook me. I stuck the piece in a vest pocket and got back into the car.

"Fourteen Zero Two to Fourteen Zero Five."

"Five. Go."

"Come up here."

"Two, I thought you were going to relieve me to go pay a water bill."

"Two to Five. Get your ass up here. Some turd just tried to shoot me!"

△ △ △ △ △ △ △ △ △ △

JEFF CAME SCREECHING into the lot, the cavalry riding to the rescue. He jumped out, Glock in hand.

"What the hell are you talking about?"

I told Jeff the story, or started to, when the cell phone screamed again. The display showed a New York number, and I answered in a rush.

"Hey, Wayne, how's it going?"

11

Just what I needed right now, a New Yorker with an urge to shoot the shit. Jerry began to talk, but I wasn't making out the words. It was like an auditory blur. I held the phone to my ear and looked at Jeff. He was hopping up and down, impatient to hear what I had started.

"Jerry, some turd just stuck a gun to my head and tried to carjack me. I gotta go. I'll call you back."

Jerry would not be brushed off so easily, and I had to tell him the story.

△ △ △ △ △ △ △ △ △ △

THUS BEGAN A cycle that continues. The telling of the story. I have told it way more times than I cared to.

Jeff stood as I spoke with New York, and when I had finished the call, he demanded that I tell it again. When I had given him every detail I could remember, he suggested that I should call the cops.

"Hell, we *are* the goddamned police. I don't need to call 'em!"

Jeff calmly explained that maybe if we called the city, they might get some cars in the area and actually find the creeps.

Feeling it was totally useless, I called. As I finished the call, Jeff began to laugh.

"Man, you were whiter than a sheet when I got here. You're looking a little better now, but you were fucked up big time."

△ △ △ △ △ △ △ △ △ △

IN A MUCH shorter time than I had anticipated, a city car rolled into the lot. The young officer got out and walked to my car, where Jeff and I were standing.

"Mr. Smith, how you doing? Haven't seen you in forever."

The young officer was a kid I had encouraged to come to work for the department. His name was Bobby, and he had clerked in a gun shop where I did business, and I had always had great expectations for him.

My mouth was dry and I was faced with telling the story again. I just stood, saying nothing.

"So you saw a stickup. Where's the victim, and why the hell didn't you shoot the bastard?"

△ △ △ △ △ △ △ △ △ △

I TOLD IT again. This telling was wearing me down. Bobby listened in what appeared to be awe and then got on the radio. Within minutes, there were a half dozen cars flooding the area, riding the streets between Willow and Kelly with spotlights glaring.

No luck.

The white shirts and khakis were gone for the evening.

An old homeless guy sidled up to the city car and spoke with Bobby. Bobby came over and asked if I had seen a white compact car earlier.

When I replied in the affirmative, I learned that the homeless guy had seen my two bandits get dropped off on Kelly by the white car.

△ △ △ △ △ △ △ △ △ △

THE FUROR WAS over, and we went back to the night's work. Very quickly it became midnight, and the relief crew arrived. I called everyone together in the lot behind the Army Reserve.

"Look, I'm only gonna tell this story one more goddamned time."

In the Beginning
Atlanta, 1969

I WAS NOT even sure I wanted to be an agent with BNDD. It sort of happened, rather than being planned. I had read an article in a national magazine about the Agents of the Bureau of Drug Abuse Control, BDAC, and then tried to find them. The number listed in the Atlanta phone book was answered Bureau of Narcotics and Dangerous Drugs when I called, and I assumed I had made a mistake in dialing.

When I eventually got an agent on the phone, we talked for a few minutes. He sounded interested in my interest in the Bureau, and after a while we agreed to meet. Strangely enough, he lived near the K-Mart where I worked unloading fertilizer for the spring planting season.

The meeting place must have been prophetic. Waffle House. How many hours, how many meetings in these small places over the next thirty years?

The most anonymous place in America. Almost everybody goes there at one time or another. At any hour, truck drivers rub elbows with late night hookers, wannabe playboys, drunks, college students, narcs and snitches. No one is dressed incorrectly. No one is out of place.

I sat in a booth, waiting for the agent to show up.

He said he'd be there around six, that he was wearing a blue plaid shirt and green pants. Sounded like a fashion plate.

I sat there drinking a Coke, since I hadn't gotten hooked on coffee yet. That would come with time, and the job.

He slid in, dressed like he said, but wearing a pair of expensive western boots.

△ △ △ △ △ △ △ △ △

"YOU WAYNE?"

"Yes. Mr. Joseph?"

"Mr. Joseph is my dad. I'm Joe."

And he was always Joe. My first partner, my second boss, and the man who taught me everything I really needed to know about being a narc. We talked for a while. Then he went back to the parking lot, came in with a stack of paper and an envelope.

"Fill out this SF-171, and make yourself a copy. They use it for the application, but it also generates your security clearance. You're gonna have to answer these same questions a million times in the next twenty or thirty years, and the answers have to be the same. New birth date for your mama and the world will fall in on you."

Special Agent Marion A. Joseph was so sure of himself, so sure I was right for this work. I was amazed. I had hoped this meeting would lead to a job, but talking with him made it seem more like a religious calling.

16

We talked about what he had done, where he was going. A Captain in the Georgia National Guard, a P-51 pilot in Korea with the Texas Guard. He was larger than life.

I was impressed and would stay that way for a long time. It was hard to reconcile the physically slight, self deprecating man with the image that formed in my mind.

△ △ △ △ △ △ △ △ △ △

WE LEFT THE Waffle House, and over the next months, I took tests, mailed in paperwork, and waited for a phone call.

None came.

My wife, Joyce, and I drove to Florida with her family for a short vacation. When we returned to Conyers, a series of notes was stuck behind the screen door of our apartment.

Looked like someone was trying to get in touch with me.

When I called the office on Monday, I was told it "looked good."

On Wednesday, Joe called.

"You had better get ready. I think they're going to give us the word by tomorrow. You'll have to be in Washington by Sunday."

"By Sunday? That doesn't give me much time. Do they usually give so little notice?"

"Hell, you've got two or three days. It doesn't get much better than that. If this goes like it looks, you'll have to come in on Friday to get sworn in, and do some payroll paperwork. Leave Friday open."

Open? I was currently unemployed, having left the wonderful position at K-Mart in hopes of landing this job. I was so available that it hurt.

Friday came quickly. I was sworn in, given an airline ticket to D.C., a few hundred dollars in expense money, and sent home that afternoon.

By Monday morning, I was learning how to be an Agent.

△ △ △ △ △ △ △ △ △ △

AT THE END of training, we were to get our assignments. I had had no contact with the Office in Atlanta, and had no idea where I was going.

Since my roommate had left the academy already, Joyce was able to come spend the last week with me at the Hotel Sonesta. We were scheduled to graduate, have our badges and credentials presented by the Director on September 19.

On the 17th, they started giving out station assignments. The first day, we got the divisional assignment. In my envelope a slip of paper said, "MIAMI REGION." In 1969 the drug wars in Miami were not yet underway, and the city sounded like fun and sun.

The next day we were called in individually and told the specific assignment within the Division. The Deputy shook my hand, and congratulated me on going back to Atlanta. I had become so accustomed to the idea that I was going to Miami it had not occurred to me that the Atlanta District Office was in the Miami Region.

As I had been looking forward to a change of scenery, I was a bit disappointed.

△ △ △ △ △ △ △ △ △ △

WE DROVE BACK to Atlanta, and on Monday, I reported in to the Office. After a briefing by the boss, I was told that I was to be the junior partner of S/A Marion Joseph. I walked into the squad bay and over to the desk where Joe was sitting.

Joe looked up, shoved some paper across the messy desk, locating a set of keys. He tossed the keys generally in my direction.

"You'll be driving. That desk over in the corner's yours. Get with Alice Lee, and get the stuff you'll need — paper, pens and other stuff."

Joe had been pecking out a document on a green portable typewriter, and he went back to it as soon as I walked to the front office to get my stuff. I got issued all the things I needed, as Alice Lee saw the need.

I got daily report forms, stacks of carbon paper, and stacks of thin paper with a sheet of carbon paper bonded at the top. I got SF-1012s, Car Report forms, Report of Investigation forms, Purchase of Evidence forms, Lab Report forms, a stack of return receipts for mailing.

I got a handful of the shiny black ball point pens with "Property of the U.S. Government" stamped on the side, paper clips, a stapler, a two hole punch, some green folders, and a stack of forms that I did not recognize at all.

Alice Lee continued to order me around like an office boy, and I was afraid to talk back. I just kept getting what she told me and doing what she said. I ended up with enough to stock a small office supply store.

One of the other agents came over after a while, and said, "Where did you get all this? I been trying to get a new ball point for a week," as he took one of mine and put it in his shirt pocket.

When I explained the source of my luxuries, he just grinned.

"She'll treat you like gold now, but just you wait. You'll piss her off soon enough, and she'll make your life as miserable as everybody else's. She always spoils the new guys. Just wait!"

19

I had no idea what I was to do with most of Alice Lee's bounty. I spent the next few hours organizing my desk for the first, and probably last, time in my career. From that point on, my desktop would get worse and worse, a sea of misplaced stuff.

I glazed over, trying to figure out just where to put what. The grey metal desk was old. I was maybe the hundredth or so inhabitant, and it was not very clean inside. I took hand towels from the men's room and cleaned it as best I could. I got everything in the desk, and I sat.

I had no idea what I was to do, and I was damned sure not about to ask.

At lunch, we all went next door to the Italian restaurant. I had been there before. During the hiring process, I had to be fingerprinted, and when the time came, they took me next door to the Italian place, where I was introduced to Russ Jessup.

Russ had been a crusty old Federal Bureau of Narcotics Agent, one of only two in the office. The merger between BDAC and FBN had created BNDD, and it wasn't a happy or cozy marriage.

When Jess had been summoned from the restaurant, he had already vanquished at least one, and I later guessed more than one, pitcher of beer. He did my fingerprints in a precise manner, though, and I always appreciated his art.

I came to learn that he did all the fingerprints for the office, as no one else could match his skill. Later I made it my business to do the best fingerprints ever taken, and my skill became a secret pride for me.

△ △ △ △ △ △ △ △ △ △

WE ATE LUNCH, and I pretended to be less than hungry, as I had only a couple of dollars. During the afternoon, Joe and his former

20

partner, Luther Cooke, huddled, and talked at length about something that I assumed I was supposed to remain ignorant of.

"Hey, Wayne. Let's go."

I looked up. Joe was standing there, looking down at me. Joe was all of five foot nine, and weighed about a hundred and a half on a good day. He seemed impatient to be on the way, and I assumed we were finally going to go and do some of the agent shit I had been so keenly trained for.

I had worn a sport coat, with tie and slacks, to work. I got up, put the issued revolver in the issued holster, and went to get my jacket off the rack. It was about four in the afternoon, and I was ready to go do something.

We walked out the back door of the office and across the paved lot to a small enclosed space.

"We park the G-cars in here. Last one out at night has to lock the lot. I hope Alice Lee gave you a key with all that other shit she piled on you."

She had indeed given me a key to the lot, along with keys to the front door, the back door, a gun locker, a clothes locker, and combinations to the ADT alarm system. I was going to have to develop a method to keep up with all the keys, as they all looked more or less the same.

△ △ △ △ △ △ △ △ △ △

JOE WENT AND stood next to a dark blue, 1965 Pontiac GTO convertible. The scoop on the hood bore the legend TRI-POWER. I felt like I was shaking in my Hush Puppies. A tri power goat!

I was a car nut, but an impoverished one. I had dreamed of a car like this, but never actually saw myself pumping fuel through the three two barreled-carbs sitting on top of a 389 cubic inch engine.

Joe looked at me, and then just stood. I stood.

"Is this your car?"

A stupid question is better than nothing at all, I guess.

"Belongs to the G, and we'd be in it driving off if you'd unlock the door."

Suddenly it dawned on me that he was waiting for me to open the door and drive. I was really shaking now.

Where had I put the keys he had given me? I didn't want to start patting pockets, acting like a fool, but I couldn't remember where I had put them. Both hands slowly descended into my pockets, and the keys were at the bottom of my right front pants pocket.

I unlocked the door, and slid in, or tried to. The seat was jammed up as far as it would go to the dash, and my six foot seven frame wouldn't fit in.

I eased out, slid the seat to the rear and then re-entered the car. I reached across and unlocked the passenger's door to let Joe get in.

"Christ, we look like Mutt and Jeff."

I wasn't sure whether that was criticism or just comedy. There wasn't anything I could do about being tall. He was stuck with my size, and I was afraid he was going to palm me off on somebody else as a partner.

In the basic training school, I had heard horror stories about senior partners who had their juniors wash the G-Car, pick them up in the morning, type reports, and go get their laundry. I was more than willing to do all that, as I was hooked on the idea of Joe as a partner. He had hired me, and now I was going to work with him. He had been partnered with Luther, and now I had broken up that team.

"Get us on the connector southbound, toward the airport. We're going to check on a surveillance."

I cranked the goat, shifted the Hurst four-speed into reverse, and then headed out onto Peachtree Street going in front of the BNDD office. The glassed front, street level office building had once housed an A&P grocery store. There was no sign visible, and from the street it was all but impossible to tell it was a government office.

I headed south, got onto the I-75/I-85 downtown connector, and headed toward the airport. Then I was directed to get off at the Virginia Avenue exit and go to the Holiday Inn at the airport.

△ △ △ △ △ △ △ △ △ △

THE RIDE WAS short, and I got the first of many blunt lectures from Joe. It set the tone for our partnership, and my career. Straight to the point, no holds barred, and very colorful.

He carefully listed every agent in the office. He then plainly told me the work habits, the personal life story, and the trustability factor for each one. He prefaced the lecture with a standard warning that this was off the record, not to be repeated, and not to be questioned unless I was able to prove he was wrong.

I soon learned that I was not working with a group of supermen. I began to think maybe I had made a mistake in coming into this little family. One was a narcoleptic who fell asleep in meetings, one was a career drunk, one was a prematurely senile guy who could not be trusted to carry out the simplest task, and one was so concerned about his appearance that he spent several hours a week of duty time at the hairdresser's. One was so full of plans and alternatives that he never seemed to get anything done, and one was almost as good an agent as Joe.

Oh, great!

Learning the Job
Washington, D.C., 1969

WE HAD BEEN married just a bit under three years when I got the call from BNDD. Joyce went with me to the office downtown, as I plowed through the necessary paperwork, and then to the United States Commissioners Office, where I was sworn in as a Special Agent.

They don't do it that way anymore. Hardly anyone around even remembers when there were U. S. Commissioners, or even just what they were. When we got back to the office, I was given a one way ticket to Washington and $500.00 in cash for expenses.

"Wayne, make us proud of you in Washington."

Marion Allen Joseph, the agent who recruited me, walked me through the process and got me hired, was now sending me off with a guilt trip on my shoulders.

I still had absolutely no idea what this job entailed. Oh, I had the general idea. We arrested bad guys, sent them to prison. That I knew. It was just how that process actually got done that I was perfectly unclear about. But I was going to learn.

On Sunday, I had packed the clothes I thought would be appropriate for the basic training school. They had told me it was a coat and tie deal, and I was still green enough to figure that was the way it was going to be for my whole career.

After we put my luggage in the back of the Dodge Dart, Joyce drove me to the Atlanta Airport. This was the first time since we had married that we would be apart for any length of time, and we were both quiet on the drive. I was afraid to be too eager to go for fear of making her think I was looking forward to being away.

What I didn't realize was that this would be the first of way too many separations instigated by the government. If I had had good sense, I'd have thrown the ticket away, gone back to Conyers and got me a job teaching high school again.

"I'll call you as soon as I get in the hotel."

"I'll be waiting."

Joyce was teaching high school in Covington, and she was off for the summer. She was going to have lots of time to wait. It was the end of June, and I wasn't scheduled to get through and back home till mid-September. It was to be a long summer, especially for her.

△ △ △ △ △ △ △ △ △ △

THE FLIGHT WAS smooth, and we landed on time at the Baltimore Friendship Airport. Why I had been given a ticket to Baltimore to get to Washington was beyond me. I still had a lot to learn about government travel regulations.

"Can you take me to the Hotel Sonesta on DuPont Circle in Washington?"

"Sure, Mon. Crawl on in, and I'll get your bags."

In an earlier job as a personnel manager, I had been taken for a ride by a taxi driver in Chicago. I had been going to an office in Forest Park, but I was given the tour deluxe. After an hour cab ride, I had ended up just across the runway from O'Hare, where I had started. I didn't intend to make that mistake again.

"Let's take the short route, okay?"

"Sure, Mon. We go the straight way. I ain't no tief."

Thief had no *h* in his vocabulary. My very first Jamaican.

I was a little sheltered, coming from a rural home, going through the typically segregated southern high school, and through a virtually segregated university. By the time I graduated from the University of Georgia, there might have been enough black students to have filled one classroom, but I doubted it.

I relaxed, condemning myself as the racist most people outside the south considered us, and watched the ride into DC. We got to the Sonesta in quick time. I paid the fare, adding more tip than I should have. Guilt will do that.

△ △ △ △ △ △ △ △ △ △

THE BELL HOP wanted to help with my bags, but I was not having that. I could not afford another tip. I knew that I didn't have a lot to live on while I was at school, but had yet to learn how little.

I went to the front desk, where I had been told there would be someone from Headquarters to help me get squared away. There was, of course, no one but the desk clerk.

27

"Hi, I'm Wayne Smith. I'd like to check in."

"Do you have a reservation? We're full up."

"I'm here for the school. You know, the government."

Still in awe of my new affiliation, I was reluctant to even say the name of the agency. I wasn't all that sure how secret this stuff was and just what the hell I was supposed to say or do.

The clerk looked at me like I was from Mars. I could tell we weren't getting anywhere fast.

"BNDD?"

Again the Martian glare.

"Bureau of Narcotics and Dangerous Drugs?"

"Oh, you're one of the new narcs. What did you say your name was again?"

I guess that made it official. I was now a narc. I must be, someone had called me one. I would go on for thirty years with that job title, and would be called a lot worse. As a matter of fact, I would go on to be called a thief, a liar, a fascist, and various shades of pig, but this was the first time I had been called a narc. It felt good.

"Wayne Smith."

"You're rooming with Blakeney, William R., in room 312. He hasn't arrived."

I got the key, and lugged my bags across the lobby to the elevators. I was just beginning to notice that he hadn't said anything about paying for the room or how much it cost. I wasn't nearly as suspicious as I would become in my golden years.

The room didn't make me feel particularly welcome. Two twin beds. My 6'7," 245 pound body wasn't about to fit comfortably on one of them.

A roommate and twin beds. This was like back in college, but without a roommate I already knew and trusted. Starting over was not good.

I looked at the placard on the back of the door. All hotel rooms have them, and I've noticed over the years that they usually present a much higher price for the room than one actually paid. I guess it's supposed to make you feel like you're getting a bargain. This one was a bit of a shock.

The room was priced at just a shade under a hundred dollars a night. I began to figure in my head, and my $500.00 was beginning to look a little short.

I got unpacked, scrupulously taking only half of the available space. I hadn't actually brought much in the way of clothes, mostly because I didn't have much of what seemed appropriate for what I was about to do.

When I got my belongings settled into place, I sat down on the bed I had chosen, and picked up the phone. No dial tone. I tapped the buttons in the cradle several times, but still no dial tone. Great, the damned phone didn't work.

I got up, and walked out and back down to the lobby. The same desk clerk was standing, waiting on new business, and I walked over.

"The phone in 312 doesn't work."

The Martian look again.

"Oh, it works. It's been turned off. You narcs don't get phone service in your rooms. There are payphones at the back of the lobby."

A narc and a second class citizen. This was going well. I walked back to the bank of pay phones, and started to call Joyce.

Then I then had a troubling thought. Back to my new friend, the desk clerk.

"If someone wants to get in touch with me here, how can they?"

The Martian glare, followed by, "We'll take messages. They will be available here at the desk. Have them call the hotel and just ask to leave a message."

I was getting tired of this guy's attitude, as tired as he was probably getting of me popping up every five minutes with a different question.

Over the years, I've had a lot of trouble with desk clerk attitudes. Maybe it was my fault, and it started here. I don't know.

I walked back to the pay phones.

"Collect call to Conyers, Georgia. Station to station. 555-1212. My name is Wayne Smith. I'll speak to anyone."

"Just a second, sir."

Two rings and Joyce answered.

"Collect call from Washington, D.C., for anyone. Wayne Smith calling. Will you accept the charges?"

"Yes."

"Hey, babe, I'm here. You got a pencil handy?"

We talked for only the requisite three minutes automatically included in the price of any long-distance call, since collect calls were outrageously expensive. I gave her the hotel number and the procedure for contacting me. I didn't want her to feel any more alone than was necessary, and I hated her not being able to call me directly.

"I'll get a number for Headquarters tomorrow, and I'll call you with it. If there gets to be a problem, call Mr. Joseph in Atlanta, and I'm sure he'll be able to get in touch with me."

△ △ △ △ △ △ △ △ △ △

I WENT ON back up to my new living quarters. I was to be here for the next twelve weeks, and I guessed I had better start getting used to the room.

It was on the front of the hotel, looking out onto DuPont Circle. There was a People's Drug Store on the wedge shaped corner facing the hotel. It seemed strange that there would be so much foot traffic around a drug store on a hot summer Sunday afternoon, but the people walking around looked to be a non-ending stream.

Then I noticed that there were mostly women walking around the corner. Weird, I thought.

I went out and scouted the eating establishments around the hotel. The restaurant in the hotel had been immediately off my list. My prejudice against hotel food is long standing, and I'd much rather eat at McDonalds than most hotels I've visited.

This one was no exception. Besides, their prices immediately put them out of my range. Till I had some idea of how we were going to do this food and hotel thing, I was looking for cheap eats.

I found a sandwich shop on the left, just a block or so down the street from the hotel. Assembly line sandwiches, good selection, and priced where I felt comfortable. I got a hoagie, and went back to the hotel to eat.

Then I ran into another one of my nemeses, hotel soft drink machines. Cokes were a quarter a bottle in machines everywhere else in the world, but were fifty cents a bottle in the hotel.

I figured out pretty quick that since I could get all the free ice I wanted, I was just going to buy my drinks somewhere else.

△ △ △ △ △ △ △ △ △ △

I FINISHED MY sandwich and started to read a paperback I had brought along. The door opened, and the bellhop came into the room without so much as a hello. I didn't mind too much not having a phone, but this shit was just not going to happen. I rose off the bed, ready to jump on somebody, when I saw the short black man just behind the bellhop.

"This room is already taken." As blunt as I could be.

"Well, this is your new roommate, and he's moving in." Equally blunt.

The bellhop's comment left me a bit confused, and I was struggling to make sense of what I was seeing. The short, to me at least, black man stepped to me and raised his hand.

"Hi, I'm Randy."

Okay, I'm a white boy. Raised in the rural south in the fifties, I was way over being eligible to vote before I had spoken to any black man who wasn't scraping off my plate after lunch in grammar school. I knew very few black folks to speak of or to, not because I chose to avoid them, but because the South was so completely segregated.

My last years at the University of Georgia had put me into visual contact with a few black students, with even a couple as members of the Demosthenian Literary Society, but my contact with them had been limited to listening to their speeches occasionally.

Shortly after my tenure at Georgia, I had taken a one-year position as a teacher at the Franklin County High School. The school, unlike many in the Deep South, had just been fully and completely integrated the summer of 1967, when I was hired. Previously there had been two schools, one black and one white. The white school burned down, and because there wasn't enough money to build and run two separate institutions and integration loomed on the horizon anyway, they built just one school big enough for everybody.

That first and only year of teaching had been a little challenging, but I had thoroughly enjoyed being there. Although I considered myself a Republican, had voted for Nixon and Bo Calloway, on racial issues I was a raving moderate.

The next year when I had worked one year as Personnel Manager in a sewing plant in Conyers, the plant employed a fairly large number of blacks, but in largely menial job descriptions. One of the reasons I'd left that job was a rising criticism of my inability to find trained, skilled blacks to bring into better paying positions.

These criticisms came down from Chicago, and I initially wrote them off as Yankee blather. Where the hell was I supposed to find a skilled, experienced black sewing machine mechanic? There just weren't any qualified minorities standing around in Rockdale County, Georgia, asking for the job. I kept insisting that we would just have to raise our own, starting with some younger black men who had mechanical skills, and training them, but Chicago wanted them now.

By then I had tired of the job, and when BNDD became a possibility in my life, I was ready to go, even if it meant working part time at K-Mart for a while. And I was glad when I learned that this agency and one of its predecessor, FBN, had recruited black agents long before other, more high profile, federal agencies.

△ △ △ △ △ △ △ △ △ △

"I'M WAYNE SMITH," I said as I extended my hand. Randy's handshake was firm and dry, and I looked forward to getting to know my new roomie. He seemed okay, and he was cool enough to have had the bellhop bring up his stuff.

Impressed already, I sat out of the way while Randy started to put away the stuff from his bags. He had about the same amount of clothes as me, but his seemed a much better quality. He finished in a few minutes, and then looked at me.

"I'm from Philadelphia."

"I'm from a little town just outside Atlanta, Georgia."

I felt compelled to add the Georgia, as if no one else would know where Atlanta was located, while everyone on the planet knew where Philadelphia was sited.

We sat and talked for an hour or so. I learned little about Randy, except that he had gone to Temple University, and was as interested as I in becoming an agent for BNDD. I was impressed with his accent. The only blacks I had experienced were Southerners, who had the patois of the region.

Randy sounded like a Yankee. As the regional accent overpowered whatever image I had of a Northern black, I began to relax while talking to him. We were going to get along, and I had a good feeling about our relationship.

"Well, what are we going to do in the morning?"

I had silently been wondering the same thing.

"I assumed that, since you got here earlier, you were met by the people I was assured would be here to get us settled in."

"Randy, there wasn't a soul from BNDD when I got here. I ain't heard a word about what we're supposed to do in the morning, except go to the school. Hell, I don't even know where Headquarters is."

"This is ridiculous. They were supposed to have someone here to help us. How are we supposed to be where we need to be if we don't know where that is?"

"There's no point worrying about it now. It's late, and I'm sure there ain't anybody here now. One of the guys from Atlanta is supposed to be a counselor in this school, but I was told he wouldn't be here till later in the week. Looks like we're on our own."

△ △ △ △ △ △ △ △ △ △

MORNING CAME EARLY, and I jumped up and hit the shower first. By the time Randy was dressed, I had already made a trip to the lobby where I had run into three other prospective narcs who also didn't have a clue of what or where they were to be.

Randy and I went down together and met up with the others. It was decided that someone should make a phone call to see just what the hell was going on. When no one else volunteered, I grabbed the pay phone and the DC phone book and went to work.

The only listing I could find turned out to be for the District Office, the enforcement unit in the city. I got a secretary, who very promptly told me I had the wrong number. When I tried to explain, I got cut off.

"The bitch hung up on me. I have had this shit up to here. Somebody else try!"

No one jumped to grab the phone, so I shoved in another dime, and started over.

"Bureau of Narcotics."

"Yes, ma'am. I'm a new agent here for training, and nobody has told us a damned thing, and we don't know where to go, or what we're supposed to do. Can you please help me?"

"Well, let's see. First, where are you?"

"We're at the Sonesta on DuPont Circle, and we don't know where Headquarters is. How do we get to you?"

"Well, you don't need to come here. This is the enforcement office, not Headquarters. These damned Food and Drug phonies don't know how to treat people. You need to go down about three blocks to the corner of 14th Street and I Street. The so called Headquarters is upstairs over a Savings and Loan at 1405 I Street."

This was my very first taste of the hostility between the people from the old Federal Bureau of Narcotics and the folks from the Bureau of Drug Abuse Control. When FBN from Treasury had been merged with BDAC from the Food and Drug Administration to form BNDD, a lot of bad blood had resulted from this Lyndon Johnson tinkering with federal law enforcement. The story was that BNDD was a sop to Bobby Kennedy, who had visions of bringing all Federal law enforcement into the Department of Justice, where the new organization had ended up.

"Thank you, ma'am. We ought to be able to find it on our own now."

△ △ △ △ △ △ △ △ △ △

ARMED WITH ALL this information, the five of us marched down to the corner of 14th and I, where we found the savings and loan, nestled right next door to the Golden Eagle Tavern. There was an entrance into the lobby, where a small sign on a board indicated that the Bureau of Narcotics and Dangerous Drugs was in this building and that one had only to get into the elevator and go up three floors to enter that world.

We went up.

The world soon got bigger as we all began to realize how little we knew. We got lectured on the law, on pharmacology, on the evils of drug trafficking, and in between we heard war stories from the agents acting as class counselors.

We went to the Walter Jenkins Memorial YMCA for PT. That was not actually the name of that branch of the YMCA, but it had sprung from the Lyndon Johnson aide, Walter Jenkins, who had made newspaper headline for groping someone in the dressing room there. Now little windows were cut into all the walls, so not a square foot of private space could be found in the whole place.

We went to Ft. Belvoir, Virginia, for firearms practice under the tutelage of Jesse Sweat.

We got seemingly mindless assignments to do book reports and to write papers about topics we didn't really understand.

△ △ △ △ △ △ △ △ △ △

THEREIN CAME A problem. Those stupid, simple written assignments to do back in the hotel room. I had a degree from the University of Georgia, and I had taught high school for a year. My wife, who had a degree in English, had seen to my abilities to put words on paper. These assignments were beneath me.

They weren't beneath Randy, however. The night of the first book report, I knocked mine out in thirty minutes while Randy struggled for what seemed to be hours. When he appeared to have finished, I started getting ready for bed.

"Wayne, you mind taking a look at this? I'm no good at this sort of thing, and it might need a little help."

37

I picked up the limp sheets and started to read. I was immediately taken back to Franklin County High. His writing seemed worse than a lot of the ninth grade history students I had dealt with. Their industry and dedication was never in doubt, but their writing was sometimes horrible.

So was Randy's. I read over the piece, took a look at the book Randy was supposed to have read. He seemed to have captured the idea, but his verbs didn't match, and his spelling was bad. Really bad.

From what I know now, and I'm obviously no expert, I'd guess that Randy had a disorder like dyslexia, which would have been easily overcome if he had been in elementary school thirty years later and had received the proper help. What I couldn't figure was how he had gotten through college. Maybe some other roommate had been helpful.

I began to make corrections, and in a few minutes, I had the report in shape that would pass muster. Randy re-copied it, and we went to bed.

The matter wasn't spoken of again.

△ △ △ △ △ △ △ △ △ △

TURNED OUT THAT Randy had another skill even less developed than writing. At the pistol range he couldn't hit a bull in the ass with a bass fiddle. We were learning to shoot the old fashioned way, one handed, bull's eye targets, duelist style.

Randy consistently scored at the very bottom of the list.

One of the guys, Loy Weaver, who had been an FBI agent before coming over to BNDD, was so good the rest of us hated to shoot in the same relay with him. Loy took the two inch barreled model 10, and made it a target pistol. He shot tight groups, beautiful bull's eyes, and made it look so damned easy.

Although no one wanted to be compared to Loy, everybody wanted to shoot in the relay with Randy, since no matter how badly you shot, there was always at least one worse than you.

Jesse Sweat, chief firearms instructor, was a double dipper. He had retired from the Army and was now the *only* firearms instructor for BNDD. His teaching technique was savage. He cursed and screamed at us, telling us we were all failures and would never get a badge or a gun or be put on the street.

He then took us to lunch at the Ft. Belvoir NCO club, where he held court like a king. Everybody there knew him, and while we struggled down the meat and three from the chow line, he sat at a table in the bar and consumed a lunch of hops, barley and malt.

We were allowed to come in and watch the topless dancers after we had eaten, but we watched dry. What was good for Jesse was apparently not good for us.

△ △ △ △ △ △ △ △ △ △

AFTER LUNCH, WE shifted to silhouette targets, and were working down at the seven yard line. It was hot, we were tired and sweaty, and we weren't doing all that well with the Model 10's.

"Goddamn it, Blakeney! You can't hit shit with that pistol! Just what the hell is wrong with you?"

The "boy" at the end of the sentence was at least left unspoken.

"If you can't shoot it, at least throw the goddamned gun at it!"

He shouldn't have said it, and I think he realized it almost immediately. Randy leaned forward, and then threw the blued Smith &

Wesson with all his might. It cleared the berm in front of the targets, missed the silhouette, and stuck, barrel first, into the mud at the foot of the target.

Jesse's face got redder. He looked at Randy, then looked at the nearest class counselor.

"You take these pussies. I gotta have a beer."

We didn't see Mr. Sweat again that day.

△ △ △ △ △ △ △ △ △ △

NOT SO MANY days later I ran head on into one of those situations that you inevitably face in life. The ones that don't have a solution that makes anybody happy. The ones that try your soul and leave you not knowing what the hell to do.

I was sitting in class minding my own business, listening to a lady try to teach us about pharmacology. She could have made sex boring. I didn't have a clue what she was talking about.

Rudy Ramirez, with his classic Tex-Mex accent, had made a comment on her lecture during the last break.

"I still don't know shit from Shinola about this stuff."

Suddenly one of the Headquarters staff guys came into the class and spoke with the lady. If we were lucky they were firing her and replacing her with someone who spoke only Chinese. No such luck.

"Mr. Smith, they want you upstairs."

This was not good. I knew from experience that getting called out from class was a bad thing. No good could ever come from this. I looked up, and the staffer stood at the door waiting.

This was one of those scenes where the student leaves the class and is never seen again. Saw this in a movie, and I don't think the guy was promoted and sent on a secret assignment.

I walked to the door, as if on my way to the gallows. We silently walked down the hall, up the elevator to a small office where the class counselors were assembled with the class coordinator. I began to wonder if they would hire me back in the cotton mill where I had worked my way through college. I was a fair hand with a wrench. Maybe they would take me back.

△ △ △ △ △ △ △ △ △ △

"WAYNE, SIT DOWN."

Good. Now at least I wouldn't fall down.

"Wayne, you know why you are here?"

I wasn't about to start guessing. Not now.

"No, sir."

"Wayne, you are Randy Blakeney's roommate, right?"

This was bullshit. They knew damned well we were roommates. There had been a few bad jokes about us being the only interracial couple in the school. Two classes running, and all the white guys had white roommates, and all the black guys had black roommates. All but me and Randy.

At the beginning, I assumed it was just an odd number of black agents. Then I had dark thoughts about them trying to run the white redneck off by putting him in with a black guy.

"Yes, sir."

"We'll get right to it. Are you helping him with his writing assignments back at the hotel?"

41

Not what I had expected.

"Well, yeah, a little bit. You know I was a teacher, and Randy kinda asked for a little help, and I helped him some. Not on the ideas or anything, just on a little of his writing."

"Well, it stops now. Don't help him anymore, not even a little bit. You want this job, that's an order from upstairs. No help. None at all. You understand?"

I understood. They didn't want Randy to make it, and this was all about making sure he wasn't going to.

"I understand. No help, at all."

"You know he's got a criminal record?"

The eyes of the guys that didn't say that immediately went wide. Full alert. This wasn't in the script. The staff guy was winging it.

△ △ △ △ △ △ △ △ △ △

"YEAH, HE WAS arrested in a riot or something in Philadelphia. We had to hire him anyway. They said it was just a demonstration, but I heard it was a riot."

If all the kids I knew that had been arrested for sitting in at a lunch counter had actually been put in jail, they'd have to build a bunch of prisons. I didn't like this. This was ugly, and I wanted no part of it.

I had been, however, ordered to stop helping Randy. If I didn't do what I was told, I could lose this job. Besides, on paper he was as qualified as I was, and he shouldn't need any help. When he was out on the street, there wouldn't be anyone to write his reports for him. He had to be able to write and shoot to keep the job.

My decision was made, and now I was justifying it.

I went back to class, and during the break I got grilled about my trip upstairs. I made up some bullshit about my background investigation, and it passed.

△ △ △ △ △ △ △ △ △ △

THE SCHOOL PASSED as well. We struggled through surveillances in downtown D.C., in the heat of summer, on foot, in the rain.

Almost never would I later do a foot surveillance, but I got the practice here.

We shifted to Super-Vel high velocity ammunition and shot silhouettes over and over. We even had a disastrous night firing exercise in which all were lucky we hadn't killed someone.

Week ten. Home stretch. No one had ever failed one of these academies, at least not at the last minute, and we were all looking forward to getting our field assignments so we could begin to plan our lives. I don't remember the lecture, but I clearly remember the same staffer walking into the class and speaking quietly to the lecturer.

"Mr. Blakeney, they need to see you upstairs."

When I got back to the Sonesta that afternoon, there was no trace of William Randolph Blakeney III. Not a sock or a t-shirt.

Randy was gone, and I never saw him again.

The Game
Atlanta, 1969

I DIDN'T DRINK coffee when I was hired. I had never developed a taste for the stuff. While I was in college, the little coils for heating water were banned from the dormitories, although everybody except me seemed to have one. That and a jar of instant coffee. Late night studying had never been my thing, and coffee seemed unnecessary.

Now I was a real federal agent, sworn to enforce the law and required to carry a handgun. I was a real, grown up adult, but I still didn't drink coffee. Then I encountered the game, and learned a lot about people and coffee.

Every morning at 1831 Peachtree Road, N.E., someone made a huge pot of coffee. The office was in a single floor building with a glass front facing onto Peachtree Road. The office of the boss, the Resident Agent in Charge, was in front at the south end where he sat with all of Atlanta traffic flowing past, with only a sheet of plate glass between him and the world. Those were the days.

The coffee urn was the old fashioned drip type, and it held a huge amount of the finished product. For the first few days after I was back from training, I sat at my desk while everyone gathered in the coffee room at the back of the building. We all came and went through the back door, right next to the break room.

"Wayne, you just going to sit there and stare at the ceiling? Come on back and have a cup with the rest of us."

Luther Cooke was a senior agent, from the old Bureau of Drug Abuse Control in the Food and Drug Administration. He and Joe had been partners when I got back from training and broke up that arrangement. Luther had been with the Border Patrol before going to BDAC, and he was the best pistol shot I had ever seen.

Luther carried an old square butt Smith & Wesson Chief's Special that had the front sight filed off at an odd angle. It looked like a piece of junk, but Luther could cut ten rings on the bull's eye targets with it all day long. He was less friendly than some of the others, but I figured it was just me being the FNG and moving in on his partner and their big case.

△ △ △ △ △ △ △ △ △

I WALKED TO the back, where I sat while some sort of ritual was taking place. Carlos Harrison was holding a folded napkin. Everyone else at the table had a napkin, and they were writing on theirs. Then Carlos turned out his napkin, revealing a number.

There were hoots from the group, and everyone put money into a coffee can labeled "Honor System." As I sat by Joe, listening while the crew talked about their weekend, the RAC, Dick Bly, tried to steer the talk to the day's work. He had little luck, and after a cup or two each, the guys started to file out into the office bay, most to start their daily reports for the previous weekend.

△ △ △ △ △ △ △ △ △ △

THE DAMNED DAILY had already gotten me into trouble. We were required to fill one out each day, listing the day's activities, cases worked, hours to be applied, mileage on the G-car, and any expenses encumbered. About Tuesday of my first week back from training, the secretary approached me with a scowl. She was young, working part time at the office. One of her functions was to transcribe the individual daily reports into an office report summing up all the hours, cases, and miles.

"I'm missing two daily reports from you."

It was Tuesday, and I had the partially finished Monday form on the corner of my desk. I picked it up, made a notation about the totals, and handed it to her.

"Here's this one, and I don't think I have to turn in today's till after close of business."

"No, I'm talking about the ones for Saturday and Sunday."

"I have to do a daily for days when I don't work?"

"You have to do one for every day in the year, whether you work or not. If you didn't work on the weekend, you can do one report for the two days."

"So, I got to do a report saying I didn't do anything?"

"Yes, and it's late."

Welcome to the federal government. I got up, and walked over to Joe's desk. He had a grin a mile wide and was just sitting back watching me approach.

"Brenda gotcha, huh?"

"Why the hell do I got to do a report on days I didn't do anything? Is she shitting me?"

"Every day, period. Just wait, it'll get a whole lot worse. This monster lives on paper."

Joe was right.

△ △ △ △ △ △ △ △ △ △

THE COFFEE RITUAL intrigued me. Even though I still didn't drink the stuff, I sat in the break room every morning and watched. Some days I would drink a Coke, much to the disapproval of the older guys.

The game, it appeared, was based on guessing a random number between zero and fifty. One agent, the loser of the previous day usually, would take a napkin and write down a number. Each agent in the coffee room would then take a napkin and write down his guess.

If you hit the number, your coffee was free, but if you were the closest to the number, then you bought a round for everyone. The free coffee was rare, but every morning, somebody bought a round for the house. The odds were lopsidedly on the house's side, and I didn't see the need to play.

It was a rigged game, and the losers griped and moaned, but they always kicked in the nickel a cup for everybody in the room. I sat outside the circle. Since I didn't drink the stuff, I didn't play the game.

As time passed, I began to see the point. It was a great way to start the day in a job where every day brought surprises, confusion, and hazard. I began to take a napkin and write down a number. I paid for several rounds of coffee but still didn't drink the stuff. I had become sort of one of the guys, sitting, listening to the stories about their kids, the soccer games, the problems with lawns and air conditioners and leaks.

△ △ △ △ △ △ △ △ △ △

THAT DAY WOLFGANG Preissler was the designated number guy.

"Thirty nine."

He unfolded the napkin, laying it on the stained Formica table top. Wolf was a young agent, much like me. In the last class BDAC had trained, he had come to that agency directly from Florida State. He was now a BNDD agent.

He had been hired as a GS-5, and was promised his GS-7 at the end of his first year. I had been hired as a GS-7. Wolf still had a month or so to go for his promotion, and he let me know in many not so subtle ways that he was not happy with my higher rank.

I turned my napkin over, exposing the three and the nine in blue ink. Wolf stood, picked up one of the communal cups for visitors, filled it from the urn, and set it in front of me. The swirl of conversation had resumed, and I sat looking at the coffee. How bad could it be?

I had tried to drink the nasty stuff on other occasions, away from the office, and genuinely disliked the taste. I looked to my left and saw Wolf watching me. This wasn't going to be easy. I feared a sudden bringing of attention to my coffeelessness, and stood, walking to the counter where the coffee accessories lay.

I dumped two heaping teaspoons of sugar and a large glob of artificial creamer into the cup, running it over on the counter. My "lucky" napkin finally came in handy, as I wiped up the excess. I came back over and sat next to Joe.

"Well, looks like you've grown up," so low and quiet that no one else heard it over the din. "Next time you come over to pick me up in the morning, I'll give you a cup of Bonnie's coffee. It'll make you glad to drink anything else."

The smile was sincere, as Joe was. I learned to drink the foul potion, loaded with sweetener and creamer, covering the bitter taste with a mask of blandness. I played the game every morning. The ritual became as important to me as it was to the others.

The days we started early, directly from home, without the office procedure, I felt a hole in my day. I learned that it wasn't the damned coffee. It was the crew, the relaxation before the day's storms that was important.

The ritual faded out as new management showed up. We moved into an office downtown, high up, with a view of I-75 and little else. There was no break room, no coffee pot, no morning ritual.

I missed those mornings the rest of my career.

Berkeley

San Francisco, 1970

I WAS STILL as green as grass. When the Acting RAC called me in to his office, late on a Friday, I was nervous. I was still on probation, and could be fired at the drop of a hat.

We had recently lost one of the agents in the bull pen just like that. J. D. had done the ultimate evil, and then had just disappeared one day. Same kind of deal, called to Dick's office, cleaned out his desk, and went home.

Never mess with the dope, the money or the women, and J. D. had been turned for sleeping with a CI. Messed with a woman, and not just any woman, but a documented Confidential Informant. Would have been worse, I guess, if she had been a defendant.

I walked in and sat erect in the GSA chair, sited squarely in front of the ARAC's desk. Dick was a tall guy from the mountains of North Carolina, and had the drawl that went with the region. He had a degree in chemistry, and had started with the Food and Drug Administration as an Inspector in the division that regulated the pharmaceutical industry. He always seemed somewhat amazed to be carrying a gun and arresting long haired drug dealers in dark alleys.

I was expecting another chewing out, like the one I had gotten after my first wreck in a government car. The other guy had run a red light, turned left in front of me, and I couldn't stop. Hit him square-on, broadside. Dick had officially notified me that the wreck was preventable and that had I only been practicing defensive driving, I would not have hit the El Camino.

All these buzzards circled in my head as I sat. Dick had a sheet of yellow paper in front of him, and I immediately recognized it as a sheet torn from the teletype machine. Now he had my full attention. Teletypes came from the seat of government and foretold ominous events.

"Have you ever been to California?"

I had expected anything but that.

Headquarters was asking for a levy of manpower from the regions for a special operation in San Francisco, and it soon began to look like I was the chosen one.

△ △ △ △ △ △ △ △ △ △

I FLOATED BACK to the squad bay, where my grizzled old cowboy partner sat, filling out his daily time and attendance report and drinking the latest of his innumerable cups of coffee during the day. Joe liked especially to drink the stuff from the bottom of the big old coffee maker in the break room, after it was four or five hours old. His dining habits had freaked me out early on, and the coffee was only one of his endless culinary peculiarities.

I sat at my desk, and Joe said, "Well, did the blue bird shit on you again?" That came from a long story, but the gist is that the notes we got for minor reprimands always came on blue paper.

I was sufficiently excited about being selected for the special assignment that I could hardly restrain myself. I launched into the details of the duty, tracking down labs making lysergic acid diethylamide in San Francisco, the LSD capital of the world at the time. A select group, special operation, handpicked, major national importance and other such phrases flowed off my tongue like water off a rock in an Appalachian creek.

Joe grinned, and I got the real story.

"You are the FNG, the fucking new guy, and you just got handed a shit detail. Don't get so puffed up. Give it a couple of months, living out of a suitcase in a cheap hotel, and you may not be so cheerful."

Well the balloon didn't burst so easily, and I drifted home in my cloud.

Joe was, as usual, about half right.

In San Francisco, I lived in a dumpy hotel just across from the federal building for a couple of days, and then partnered up with an agent from New York, also assigned to Operation Beacon.

We found a small apartment in Sausalito, one big room with a kitchen and bathroom on a hall. No furniture, no heat, no nothing. We managed to get a phone put in, used the place for doing undercover calls, and slept on the floor.

It wasn't heaven, but here I was living on the San Francisco Bay, playing out some part in a movie. I missed home.

Because of the time difference and the hours we worked, I couldn't to talk to Joyce very often, maybe once a week. We had begun planning for her to fly out and spend a week later, if the Operation continued.

△ △ △ △ △ △ △ △ △ △

SO, THE ROUTINE began. We had a series of CI's flown in from all over the country, each with the sure promise of "taking you straight to the lab."

The straight path never seemed to get there, and we kept busting LSD dealers, but not getting to the kitchens where the goodies were cooked. We were processing mountains of evidence, and the LSD was coming in every form known to man. The usual was a powder, in one of many pastel colors, with a small amount of LSD mixed therein.

Mixing this concoction was a formidable task. Since there was so little actual LSD involved in a dose, the drug could get lost in an ounce of vegetable starch, and the customer could end up with individual doses that didn't actually contain any LSD. Sort of like throwing ten red ping pong balls into a garbage can with a thousand white ones. It was not always possible to get a red one in each handful.

The best method of production came from a group making what was called clear-light, day-light, or windowpane acid. They were sophisticated, mixing the LSD into a liquid gelatin solution to insure even distribution, and then drying the gelatin in a device apparently designed to make scientific film. The water evaporated from the solution, leaving a sheet of dried gelatin thinner than typing paper. The sheet was then cut into squares so small that over a hundred dosage units could be put inside a No. 10 gelatin capsule.

The Task Force was very interested in anyone that capable. Besides, the daylight acid was gaining popularity with the users, showing up all over the country. There had even been a find inside a federal prison, where the drug had been concealed behind the stamp on a letter to an inmate.

Our leader was putting pressure on us to get at these people, and we were working the phones, calling all over the country trying to find that snitch who could really take us straight to the lab.

An agent who had been my classmate in the BNDD academy turned up a CI from Kansas City. The CI swore that his guy was the source of supply for LSD for the entire Midwest. The group groaned when I told them the tale, and I got the chorus of "straight to the lab" again.

The CI showed up in a few days, much neater and a little more of a business man than we had expected. LSD in the Midwest must be different than the long-haired California version. My partner and roomie, Jerry Hochman, was going with the CI to meet with the bad guy. Jerry was a whiz in the role. The ultimate negotiator, he could wheedle anything out of anyone. After getting their stories down, the two of them made a call to, of all places, Berkeley.

"Here we go again, over to Berkeley, to meet the one true source," chortled Charlie Bullock.

A Salt Lake City agent, Charlie bore the distinction of being the only Fed in SLC who was not a member of the Church of Jesus Christ of the Latter Day Saints, and he was already as skeptical as I was to become.

Charlie had an early start, and his acerbity eventually landed him in the U. S. Marshal's lock-up, charged with contempt, after he verbalized his discontent about a District Court Judge's sentencing in a heroin case. These contempt charges, coming in the midst of a company touting their canned seafood on television, prompted a rash of "*FREE CHARLIE THE TUNA*" bumper stickers on G-cars across the country.

But back to our important California case. The phone call was made, with arrangements to meet the bad guy, Cecil, in a coffee shop on Telegraph Avenue, near the campus of UC Berkeley.

"Great!" bellowed Charlie. "Oh, we not only got to go to Berkeley again, but we got to go to Telegraph, home of ninety percent of the assholes in the western hemisphere."

We all trooped to the parking lot and chose up sides for the surveillance. If I heard "straight to the lab" one more time, I was going to scream, so I decided to ride with Charlie, because when we worked he was all business. No showboating and always on task. We paired up and took the Bay Bridge over to Berkeley, Charlie driving. We all set up on the coffee shop about a half hour before the scheduled meet.

Jerry was supposed to be a friend of the CI, in from New York to score some major windowpane. With his accent, Jerry couldn't pretend to be from anywhere else. My Georgia drawl typed me immediately, but Jerry's New Yorkisms almost gave you a street address.

Because this was a preliminary meet, nothing was to be transacted but a little conversation. We didn't have Cecil identified, and we weren't spending buy money on strangers. The game was to do the initial meet, get a look at Cecil, maybe get his tag number, and, if lucky, follow him to the place where he laid his head.

Jerry showed up in the rental car, parked and went into the coffee shop with the CI. As was our custom, on this first meet Jerry was not wearing a wire or transmitter. We had already experienced several pat-downs by prospective sellers, and one idiot brought a Radio Shack signal strength meter to an initial meet. Somehow after the first get-together, the dealers always seemed to get over their shyness.

Since we had no idea what was going on in the shop, we took turns parking nearby and walking in to get a cup to go, hoping to sneak an early look at the bad guy.

△ △ △ △ △ △ △ △ △ △

ONE OF THESE forays struck gold, and over the radio we got, "Five Zero Nine to the units. He's meeting a white male, long brown hair, red plaid shirt, jeans. He's a big guy, over six feet."

That was a lot of help. Five Zero Nine had just described about a third of the population of Berkeley.

"Five Hundred to Five Zero Nine. I see about six of him on the corner now. Anything else?"

The answer came back in the negative, so we sat and waited. An hour dragged by, but it seemed like a week. Not knowing made it longer, and everyone grew impatient.

"Is he going to get engaged to this guy? What's taking so long?"

The usual radio traffic.

"Hold it down. We got movement!"

Now something was happening. The CI, Jerry, and our new friend Cecil walked out onto the sidewalk. He looked just as described, like about a third of the population. Jerry did his touch the top of the head pose, letting us know this was the guy and that he was a player. Jerry and the CI stood for a moment, then walked off to their car.

We saw Cecil crane his neck to get a look at the tag numbers as they drove off. Since they were using a rental car, listed to the CI, we weren't at all concerned about the tag, but the bad guy's interest seemed significant. Cecil stood, like a cigar store figure, looking around the area as our guys drove off.

Jerry headed back toward the Bay Bridge, and soon his voice came up on the air. He had a small radio concealed under the front seat, and had broken it out to call.

"Five Zero Two to the units. This may be the real thing. The guy talks chemistry like a professor, and he is talking weight way over what we had figured. Stay on him, and see where he goes."

Charlie snorted, "Well, what the hell do you think we're sitting out here for? Jesus Christ on the cross!"

After Jerry was clear of the area, we waited for Cecil to make his move. Cecil stood, not moving, staring at the cars parked near the coffee shop.

"Five Hundred to the units. Stay off the radio till this mope gets in his short. Let's not burn this one before it starts."

"Who died and left you in charge, Georgia boy?"

I got a lot of heat about my accent. Seems these California people never heard anyone talk like me that was not on *Hee Haw*. Of course, I had never heard the term "short" used for a car before either.

Cecil began to walk south on Telegraph. He crossed the street, walked a block back north, and then went into one of the bookstores that dotted the area. He came out after a few minutes, carrying a copy of the *Berkeley Barb*, still walking north. He crossed back over, and started south. This time he stopped in the middle of the next block and started talking to a young girl who was panhandling for spare change on the Avenue. He put something in her hand and then turned and got into a new Mercury Cougar parked on the street. Since he had just walked by this car a few minutes ago, it appeared he was just doing his counter surveillance thing.

"Five Hundred to the units. This guy is hinky big time. Let's give him plenty of room when he rolls. Who's facing southbound? He's getting into a white Mercury Cougar on the Avenue, facing south. I'll call him out when he moves. Who's gonna get him?"

Two units spoke at the same time, and then after a second or two, Five Zero Six and Five Zero Nine both called separately, stating they would take him when he moved.

"Five Hundred to Five Zero Six and Nine. He's rolling out, south on the Avenue. Got him?"

A long moment dragged by.

"Five Zero Nine. Got him."

Charlie turned our car around, and then got stuck in traffic pulling back out onto Telegraph.

"Five Hundred to the units. We're way back. Keep us advised."

△ △ △ △ △ △ △ △ △ △

THE SURVEILLANCE CREPT on. It was about five in the afternoon on a Friday, and everybody seemed to be going somewhere at the same time we were.

"Five Zero Nine. He's turning west on Dwight Way."

"Which way is west, left or right?"

I have no sense of direction, and I hate it when people tell me to turn west. I understand right and left, but nothing ever seems to actually turn west, and I wouldn't know which way it was anyway.

"Right, Georgia boy."

Charlie was starting to get frustrated because we didn't seem to be able to catch up with the team. We hit Dwight and took a right, only to see a line of cars stopped by someone trying to back into a driveway.

"Five Hundred to Five Zero Nine. You still got the eyeball?"

A very long moment of non-prayerful silence.

"He just jumped a light on us, and he's a block ahead. Still see him, but we need to close up."

Damn, this wasn't good.

"Five Zero Nine to the units. He's crossing Sacramento, still headed west."

Charlie was pushing the G-car as hard as he could in the traffic, but we were not gaining on the surveillance at all.

I switched to the main channel.

"San Francisco, Five Hundred."

When the duty agent answered, I asked for a tag check on the Mercury. In a very few minutes, San Francisco said that the Mercury was registered to a Cecil Bryant at an address in Oakland. That made things easier.

Back to the surveillance channel.

"Five Hundred to Surveillance. The tag goes to an address in East Oakland."

"Five Zero Six. He'll probably take San Pablo to Oakland, since he already crossed Sacramento."

Five Zero Six, or Bob Voorhees, was a local agent on the task force, and he knew the streets better than any of us imports.

Almost instantly, we heard, "Five Zero Nine. He's taking a left onto San Pablo"

San Pablo was crowded, and as we turned left, Charlie immediately began a stream of curses that would have mortified any Mormon within blocks. I wondered how long he could make Salt Lake his duty station.

"I'm going to jump over one, go parallel, and try to get ahead of this mope."

A good plan, but I was from Atlanta, where there is no such thing as two streets that actually run parallel. Charlie, on the other hand, was from Salt Lake where all streets are parallel, clean and straight. He pushed the G-car harder, and we began to make some headway. Without having to worry about the bad guy seeing us, Charlie was passing everything in sight. Hell, we were on the wrong side of the street more than on our side.

△ △ △ △ △ △ △ △ △ △

I BEGAN TO have visions of the car chase scene in the movie *Bullitt*.

As we approached a traffic signal, things suddenly got very clear and seemed to go in slow motion. A small, tan compact car came out of the intersection to our right, against the light. I could see the driver, a huge Afro mashed down under the low top. Charlie jerked the wheel to the left, and we began to move that way, trying to go around the tan car's front end.

As Charlie just got around, we were facing a Ford LTD station wagon, headed straight at us. Charlie cranked the wheel back to the right, and we broke traction. I could feel the car skidding, and looked ahead to see a line of cars parked on the street. If we could just straighten up, we could make this.

We were going to be all right, and then I saw us hit the rear of the first parked car after the corner.

Jeez, it was just like the movies.

We went up, over the trunk of the car we had hit, and were, for a very brief moment, airborne. The impact with the side of the red brick apartment building was not that severe. We had just totaled four cars, and our ride was ready for the junk yard before we hit. Brick dust flew, and the screeching, crashing noise died down.

It was suddenly very quiet in the car.

61

My head hurt. It hurt a lot.

I felt my face. When I drew my hand back, I saw blood sparkling with bits of glass. I looked at the windshield, spider-webbed with cracks, also red with blood.

Shit, that was my blood. This was not good. I was going to get in trouble for not having my seat belt fastened.

I looked at Charlie, just sitting, staring out at the brick wall we had hit.

"Jesus fucking Christ!"

I guessed that that was an appropriate response to the situation. We both crawled out of the car, and I got the Motorola lunchbox-shaped portable radio from the floor between my feet. I switched channels.

"San Francisco, Five Hundred. San Francisco, Five Hundred."

Here on the west coast they did radio backward. We always used Georgia State Patrol radio procedure at home, and you said your call sign first, then the sign of the unit you were calling. Here on the left coast it was reversed.

"San Francisco, Five Hundred. Please answer!"

"Five Hundred, San Francisco. What's your problem?"

Very informal here in the City by the Bay.

"San Francisco, Five Hundred. We had a wreck, car is totaled. Can you get the Berkeley PD to respond?"

"Five Hundred, San Francisco. Ten-twenty?"

I suddenly realized I didn't even know what street we were on. I handed Charlie the handset, so that he could give directions, and I sat down on the sidewalk. A very nice young lady came out of the apartment building and looked us over.

"Are you all right?"

I had just run headlong into her building, totaling four or five cars, and I was most certainly not all right. The macho cop took over.

"Naw, it's just a scratch."

She went inside, came out with some wet cloths, and was wiping the blood off my face, when I noticed blood all over the radio. I looked, and Charlie's left arm was dripping a pretty steady stream of blood onto the radio set and the sidewalk.

"Charlie, what the fuck did you do to your arm?"

Charlie looked at me as if I were speaking Farsi, then looked at his arm. His elbow was shredded. He had taken out the side window in the car when we hit the building. I took the cloth from the girl and wrapped Charlie's arm, trying to stop the bleeding.

△ △ △ △ △ △ △ △ △ △

THE BERKELEY COPS arrived and took charge in a very brisk manner. The senior guy bundled us into the back of his cruiser and asked us if we wanted to go to the hospital here or in San Francisco.

"Your dispatcher told us who you are, and I think we ought to get you out of this area now!"

I was about to tell him how much I appreciated the service, when I got a horror story about some of the local long hairs throwing garbage at an injured Berkeley officer after a wreck in the city.

Oh, great. I thought I was one of the good guys, and now I have to be hidden from view.

"If you want me to take you to the emergency room here, I will, but they're not all that friendly."

Since we didn't have a clue about any health care facilities in San Francisco, we opted for the Emergency Room at the hospital in Berkeley.

The sergeant drove us to the entrance and dropped us off. I grabbed the Motorola out of the back seat, and we went in.

After a bit of the universal bureaucratic BS, we got started doing the paperwork, and then were told to sit on a bench in the hall.

We sat.

The towel wrapped around Charlie's arm was starting to leak blood onto the floor. My face had stopped dripping, but I could feel the bits of glass in my forehead each time I put my hand up there. I knew better than to keep touching it, but I didn't seem to be able to stop.

I looked at the new Seiko my wife had given me for Christmas and realized that we had been sitting for almost an hour. I walked back to the glassed-in station where we had started the procedure and asked the nice lady what was taking so long.

She looked up, smiled, and pointed at two men standing behind her, both wearing the hospital green scrubs. One was holding a couple of sheets of paper, staring at them.

The other man looked up at me, then down at the floor.

"Fuck the pigs! I ain't treating them, and you're not going to either."

After his statement stopped ringing in my ears, I saw him throw the paper onto the floor and walk away.

"San Francisco, Five Hundred. San Francisco, Five Hundred."

"Five Hundred, San Francisco. Go ahead."

"San Francisco, Five Hundred. Can you get a unit to pick us up at the hospital in Berkeley? We're finished here."

Guess it wasn't like the movies after all.

Trial and Error
Atlanta, 1970

I T WAS MIAMI'S case at first, and we just got asked to help. It then turned into our baby. To keep the confidential informant cool, and to keep the undercover agents out of court for a while, we got asked to do the take down and arrests.

The deal was a load of marijuana, being flown out of Jamaica, and the decision had been made to let it come to Atlanta. Then we'd down the bad guys with the dope, while letting the airplane, pilot, and load crew slip away. Sounded simple.

"Wayne, you're on this one. Let me know what you need, and keep me up on what you're doing."

Marion Joseph was the Acting RAC since Dick Bly had been sent to Headquarters. Dick had only been the ARAC as well. The office hadn't had a real boss in more than a year when Dick had been transferred to Washington.

"Joe, I'll cover it. I've already talked to the Supervisor in Miami, and I'll get anything they think I need to know. This ought to be fun."

"Glad *you're* having fun. I gotta go shovel more paper."

Joe wasn't real happy about being in charge. He couldn't go out and play with the troops as much anymore. Over the years I would learn just how hard it is to sit in the office and hear somebody else on the radio doing what I want to do.

△ △ △ △ △ △ △ △ △ △

I HAD GOTTEN a lead from Miami about one of the players on the deal. Turned out they were all from the Atlanta area, and one name sounded familiar to me. I was just starting to get a mental file of names of bad guys, but this one sounded like one I had heard before.

I headed out to the Atlanta Police Department Records Office to talk with a clerk there. Slight of build and wearing thick glasses, Baron could find any record that existed. I spoke with him on the phone on a regular basis, but I needed to see him occasionally, lest he forget me, and shuffle me off to become one of the "NO RECORD" people.

The windows at Records weren't designed for my 6'7" frame, and I ended up bent double to speak with the guy.

"Officer Baron, I'm Wayne Smith with Federal Narcotics."

Two things. He probably wasn't an officer. I wasn't sure exactly what his title was, but I wasn't about to call him a clerk. The other was the Federal Narcotics. No one knew what BNDD was. When I used the real name, I ended up giving a ten minute explanation that really solved nothing.

"Yeah, Smith. Good to see you again."

"Like always, I need your help. All I got is a male, white, last name REGISTER, possibly a Larry or a Lawrence."

"Let me see what I can do."

66

He walked off, and I knew what he was about to do. He would look into file drawers holding thousands of three by five cards, some in order, some not. Some by nickname, some by first name, most by last name. No keyboard, no computer, no Boolean search algorithm. Just pulling cards, looking, guessing, then pulling the whole paper files to verify the guesses.

"Here you go, Smith. This has to be your boy. A couple of drug arrests, and from the looks of the picture, he deserved them."

It had taken Baron about five minutes to come up with what I could never have gotten on my own. Now I had the rap sheet and two glowing pictures of Lawrence Alan Register.

This was great. Miami had said the guy was in Negril and would be flying out to Atlanta from Kingston in a day or two to set up the offload crew here for the load plane. I was already getting somewhere on this case.

"Thanks much. You've saved my ass again. I really needed that picture."

"Smith, you don't need to come over here to get me to do this stuff. Just call and I'll have it ready when you get here."

"Yeah, Baron, but it's good to get to see the voice on the phone. You do good work. I feel like I always owe you. Lunch is on me, just name a day."

"I eat at my desk, don't have time to go out and eat. Thanks anyway."

"Could you have the techs make me a couple of extra pictures? I need to send one to Miami."

"I'd give you an extra now, but those were the last two in his envelope. I'll have them make a couple of blow ups if you want, and have them for you tomorrow.

"Thanks again."

I drove back to the office after a stop at Georgia State Patrol on Confederate Avenue to get a copy of Register's driver's history. They would also make me a copy of his picture, but it would take at least three days.

"Joe, I wish there was some way to send this picture down to Gillis in Miami. They'd like to get a look at Register's picture, but if I mail it now, it'll be next week."

"Maybe one of these days."

△ △ △ △ △ △ △ △ △ △

I PUT IN a call to Miami, but Gillis wasn't in. I left a message, and went on to do some other stuff that I was already late with. It was Thursday, and I hadn't done my daily report for Monday yet.

Each week I didn't have to turn in my dailies till Monday morning, and I usually put something together on Friday evening. I had a travel voucher to do as well. I had spent the money, and wouldn't get it back till I did the SF-1012. I was not timely in my paperwork, officially. My last fitness report had clearly stated so.

Alice Lee, the longest serving secretary in Federal Service, called me on the intercom.

"Gillis from Miami is on line two. How well do you know him?"

"Alice, I don't know him at all. I've only been talking to him for a day or so. Why?"

"He sounds cute, and I was just wondering."

He was also probably young enough to be her son. A spinster lady was our Alice Lee.

"Gillis, this is Smith. What can I do for you?"

68

"You get anything on the Register guy?"

"Yeah, that's why I called. He's got a sheet here, local stuff. Couple of 'DC: Occupying a Dive's' and one marijuana arrest."

"What the hell's a 'DC: Occupying a Dive' anyway?"

"Disorderly Conduct. There are half a dozen counts that can get added to a DC, but this one means he was in a place that got raided, there was dope, and he didn't get charged with the drugs."

"You got a picture?"

"Yeah, I got one, kinda small. Typical mug shot. I've got the PD doing a blow up. I can send it to you tomorrow."

"Be way too late. He's flying in tomorrow morning. The undercovers down in Jamaica are the only ones ever seen him. He's got to come through Miami to get to Atlanta, but since we ain't got a clue what he looks like, we'll let you take him on when he gets to Atlanta."

"What's the plan?"

"He's supposed to come up, get some money together, and come back down. We're making him pay for all the hotels, food, everything, and he's run out of cash. This should be a quick turnaround for him."

"I'll pick him up at the airport, get a look at him, maybe his car and his house."

"That'd be a stroke of luck. What kind of coverage you gonna do at the airport?"

"Probably just me. We're shorthanded, and I don't want to call in the locals on this one, not just yet."

"Good idea. Don't get the locals in on this at all. Too many leaks."

He didn't know *my* locals. GBI agents Phil Peters, the first of three Phils to work closely with me over my career, and Bill Padgett were already in on this. I had briefed them yesterday. I was going to need help on the takedown, and I wasn't about to spring this at the last minute.

Frankly, I trusted them more than I did the voice on the phone from Miami.

"Sure. I'll call you after the airport. Can you give me the flight numbers?"

△ △ △ △ △ △ △ △ △ △

I GOT ALL the information Gillis had, or at least all he was willing to share with me. This was beginning to look like a deal that had been set to come to Atlanta from the get-go. It was going to be interesting.

It was my second brush with smuggling cases, and the first had left a distinctly bad taste in my mouth. We had had a running battle with U. S. Customs. They had the idea that all dope was smuggled, so all dope cases were theirs. There was a Memorandum of Understanding that outlined just when a case shifted from USC jurisdiction to BNDD, but we were getting a lot of MOUs and damned little cooperation.

My first time with Customs had been a disaster. We were working a group smuggling bulk pharmaceutical grade amphetamine powder from Italy. We had the green light from HQ to let the load enter the country, follow it to the stash, and take all the players at once.

U.S. Customs in Buffalo, New York, had other ideas. When the bad guys from Canton, Georgia, brought the first load across the lake from Canada in their bass boats, Customs hit them. Instead of the amphetamine powder, they got a shipment of tetracycline and zoaline, destined to be added to chicken feed for the poultry industry in North Georgia. The FDA had banned this stuff, but the chicken farmers wanted it. If you smuggle people dope, why not chicken dope?

The main player in the bunch was a veterinarian who had the connections for both kinds of dope. Only problem was BNDD's *two-year* investigation on the vet was ruined, and Customs got headlines in the Buffalo paper for a day or two. They never bothered to tell the media about the lab analysis of the powder touted as amphetamine.

"Joe, I got that deal from Miami this afternoon. Anybody going to be able to give me a hand?"

"We're all sold out. Bennie and Ludlow are going to Savannah this morning. We got everybody else already down there. I got faith in you, you can handle it. Besides, this is simple, I could get one of my kids to do it."

I was never sure if Joe was telling me I was capable or that I was asking for help I didn't really need. After all, this was going to be pretty easy. All I had to do was eyeball Register getting off the plane and then give at least lip service to following him away. Nobody would be too upset if I just watched him walk through the terminal and disappear.

△ △ △ △ △ △ △ △ △ △

THE FLIGHT FROM Miami arrived on time, and I sat in the gate area, watching the passengers stream off. The Atlanta airport was small then, compared to the monster that now sits on the spot, and surveillance was easy. No security screeners, no sterile area, and a fairly small number of passengers.

This was the proverbial piece of cake. I watched Register walk off the plane and into the terminal, turn right and head for the lobby. I fell in behind, marveling at how easy it had been to recognize him from the picture. We walked on through the lobby and out the front doors into the sunlight. Register kept walking as if he had done this a million times. No luggage.

Realizing that he was headed to the parking lot, I kept behind, walking directly in front of the terminal. In these old days, it was possible to park right at the terminal and not have to take a shuttle to the outlying lot to collect a car.

Register's manner was purposeful, and he knew exactly where he was going. I began to hold back, toying with the idea of trying to follow him when and if he got to his car. He strode up to a new yellow Oldsmobile 442.

Nice car. I began to have visions of seizing it and making it my new G-car.

It was an easy car to spot, so I turned and started to the space where I had parked the 1965 Ford pickup that was my current G-ride. If I could get situated right, I could pick him up after he paid for parking and rolled out of the lot.

I must have been living right. The yellow Olds slid out of the lot and headed for Virginia Avenue still in my line of sight.

"Eight Zero to Base."

Silence.

"Eight Zero to Base."

"Eight Zero, this is Atlanta Base."

Alice Lee. Not my favorite person to speak with on the radio, always becoming fussy and very literal.

"Base, can you get me a 10-28 on Georgia one David three seven nine nine five, Fulton county?"

"Eight Zero. Yes, I can."

Now the question arose. Was Alice Lee jerking me around and merely indicating that she *could* do it, not that she was going to? One never knew.

"Eight Zero to Base. Can you also get Seven Three to the radio?"

72

"Base to Eight Zero. That is ten four."

A few moments of silence while we maneuvered around the Virginia Avenue area, eventually getting on I-85 northbound.

"Seventy Three to Eight Zero."

"Joe, I got him headed northbound into the city. Alice has the tag number. Let me know what she gets."

That ought to make damned sure that I got the information, and sooner rather than later.

△ △ △ △ △ △ △ △ △ △

WE MOVED ON into Atlanta proper, after merging with I-75. Light traffic and Register was driving with the flow. He was making this all too easy.

One thing for sure, he wasn't feeling any heat here and hadn't even hinted at trying to make or shake a tail. We rolled on, and he shifted to the right lane as we approached North Avenue.

He was off in a flash, and I almost didn't make the cut. I really needed that tag info, so I might have a hint of where we were going.

West Peachtree, and then onto North Ave, and immediately left into the Varsity parking lot. A grease fix. The Atlanta boy had been away from home too long.

Chili dogs and onion rings danced in my head as well. Register went into the building, so I parked and followed. Although curb service would have been better for surveillance, so far this had gone too well to complain.

Inside, I learned that it was not a grease fix, but the bank of pay phones, that interested him.

Register was shoving quarters into one as I walked by. Calling in to Jamaica?

I noted which phone in the group he used, so I could get records later if we needed them. In only a very few minutes, he walked back to the Olds, and I scrambled to get to the Ford and get ready.

I got the engine started, and the first sound I heard was Joe.

"Seventy three to Eight Zero. Where the hell are you?"

I hadn't cleared out of the car when I parked, and Joe must have been calling me for several minutes. His voice had a decidedly unpleasant edge to it.

"Eight Zero, I'm here. Go ahead."

"Wayne, the tag comes back to an apartment about three blocks north of the office and about two blocks west off Peachtree. Where were you?"

"Joe, he ducked into the Varsity and made a pay phone call. We're back on West Peachtree, headed north. I'm going to give him a lot of room, and if he makes that left off Peachtree, I'll drop him. I'll go back and verify the car later."

"Ten four."

△ △ △ △ △ △ △ △ △ △

DAYS ROLLED BY, and Register had gone back to Jamaica. The Miami guys kept me in the loop, and we were getting close to the day the load was to fly north. Our undercovers had agreed to fly north with the load. Their function was to do the offload and then return to Jamaica. The old C-47 flying the dope up belonged to a CI who was being well paid by the group to provide the transportation.

74

Since this was an all BNDD undercover operation, the decision had been made not to notify U. S. Customs at all. Tickled me to death. The local Customs guys wouldn't have wanted to go anyway. Might get their Brooks Brothers shirts dirty.

Joe briefed the Georgia Bureau of Investigation bosses, and we had a total commitment of manpower. Because the GBI were doing a lot of street level deals, the idea of a big load appealed to them all.

The shipment was estimated to be about a ton and a half. That was more dope than any of us had ever seen, and the prospect was exciting. The day of the deal arrived. The agreement was for the C-47 to land at Charlie Brown Airport and offload the marijuana into a truck to be provided by Register and the group.

Sure enough, it went just as planned. I think back now, and am more than a little amazed. We had a plane fly directly from Jamaica to Atlanta, land at a municipal airport at midday, unload over a ton of marijuana into a truck being driven by a bunch of long haired, bearded youths, and no one paid a damned bit of attention.

The dawn of air smuggling had not yet arrived in Georgia. It was coming, and it would bring more trouble than any of us could have imagined.

△ △ △ △ △ △ △ △ △ △

WE FOLLOWED THE truck and the yellow Olds out into rural Henry County, eventually becoming a circus parade on the country road. A truck load of dope, followed by Register in the yellow 442, in turn followed by every GBI narcotics agent in the state and the few of us from BNDD.

The take down went smoothly, with the crew having only two or three firearms. The marijuana weighed in at about thirty-two hundred pounds, a record seizure, and we all had our pictures made standing in front of the stack of burlap wrapped bundles. We didn't foresee the tidal wave of pot that was to follow in the next years or guess that it would get to the point that nobody was interested in a mere ton or so of the stinking weed.

We charged the crew with possession of marijuana not being in an original tax stamped container, because this arrest predated the Controlled Substances Act of 1970, and the case was to be prosecuted under the old Harrison Narcotics Act. This was a weird piece of law. It was not illegal to possess marijuana. It was illegal to possess it if it was not in an original container bearing a federal tax stamp.

The catch was that the Treasury Department had never issued a tax stamp for marijuana. You couldn't get a stamp without admitting that you had the marijuana, and if you had the marijuana, you were breaking the law. The old law eventually didn't pass muster with the Supremes, and was mercifully replaced in late 1970.

One interesting side effect in this case was the $100 an ounce tax on marijuana. IRS showed up a few days after the arrest and served the lads in Henry County jail with a tax lien of $100 times each of the sixteen ounces in each of the 3200 pounds. The interest alone kept them in jail, since the tax lien covered any collateral they could have posted for bond.

△ △ △ △ △ △ △ △ △ △

MORE DAYS PASSED. Since I was the case agent for the Atlanta end, I worked with Col. Robert Smith, the Assistant United States Attorney assigned to prosecute the matter. Although I knew Col. Smith was a wheel in the U. S. Attorney's office, I had not previously worked with him.

This was the first federal court case in which I was to testify. I was terrified that it would go badly, but was constantly assured by Joe and the Colonel that it was a simple case, and that the trial would take only one day.

I was about to learn a lesson that I would never forget. There are no simple trials. You cannot ever over prepare for court, and testifying is hard work. We went through Grand Jury, suppression hearings, and other smaller matters, and the day for trial finally arrived.

As usual, the government used a variety of agents, saving the main one for the trial itself. One agent testified at the Grand Jury hearing and Joe handled the suppression hearing. I was to learn that this strategy was well and often used.

△ △ △ △ △ △ △ △ △ △

IT WAS NOW my time to sit in the box, be sworn, and tell the simple truth.

"Now, Agent Smith, will you tell the court just how you are employed and what training you have had."

"Yes, sir. I am a Special Agent with the United States Department of Justice, Bureau of Narcotics and Dangerous Drugs."

Preliminary questions droned on, and it seemed no one in the room was listening. I looked straight ahead, locked on Col. Smith. The defense attorneys were huddled together, writing notes, and leaning over to speak to each other and their clients. This was going well.

"Now, Agent Smith, did there come a time when you went to the Atlanta Airport?"

"Yes, sir."

"What were you there to do?"

"Sir, I was there to observe the passengers get off a plane from Miami and to see if Mr. Register was among those passengers."

"Did Mr. Register, in fact, get off that airplane?"

"Yes, sir, he did."

"Agent Smith, how did you recognize Mr. Register?"

Hmmm, a question we had not gone over in trial prep.

"Sir, I had obtained a mug shot of Mr. Register from the Atlanta Police Department, and I had that mug shot with me."

Suddenly, all those people I was sure weren't paying attention drew in one deep breath, all at the same instant. It became absolutely quiet in the room.

Col. Smith stared at me as if I were a three-headed monster. Four defense attorneys rose as one, and their voices made a perfectly pitched quartet as all said, "Mistrial, your honor!"

The judge slammed down his gavel and said one word, "Granted."

△ △ △ △ △ △ △ △ △ △

THE NEXT BIT of time was warped. It might have been four minutes or four weeks. I heard the judge excuse the jury, thanking them kindly for their important service. I sat in the witness box and watched the scene blur around me.

The defense attorneys were huddled together with their clients, and Col. Robert Smith still stood where he had asked the last question, as if he had been transformed into one of the blocks of salt at Sodom and Gomorrah. His face was glowing as bright red as I have ever seen. I was as confused as I have ever been, before or since. My mind couldn't grasp what had just happened.

We had lost this easy case. My mind circled over and over what I had just said. That could not have possibly been the cause of this debacle, but what else could have caused it?

I had told the truth, as I had been cautioned so many times to do. I was drowning in the witness box. I couldn't breathe.

The judge finally noticed me, and looked over with a sad sympathy in his eyes. "Mr. Witness, you are excused. You may stand down."

Col. Smith walked away from me as I got down from the stand. He had all his papers and law books under his arm, and he was walking at a brisk clip away from me.

I followed, not knowing what else to do. Agent Terry Fernandez, one of the undercover agents, and the other witnesses were standing in the hall outside the courtroom, and we marched by them without a word.

Col. Smith wasn't able to speak, and I was afraid to. The United States Attorney's Office was on the same floor, and we blew past the receptionist, and into Smith's office.

"Well, goddamnit, you screwed this up. Didn't they teach you anything at that school in Washington?"

They actually hadn't. Not about this anyway. In the twelve weeks I was at 1405 I Street, learning to be an agent, we had not spent one minute talking about how to, or how not to, testify in court.

Joyce and I had been talking about maybe buying a house, starting a family. Now I was going to have to go out to Tucker and explain to her how I had lost the best job anyone ever had. I was going to have to start looking for something else. How could I possibly go back to work in an office after having been a narc?

My world had ended.

"Now, I got to go back, and strike another goddamn jury, and go through all that shit again. We're gonna have to do all this work over, just because you ain't got a goddamn clue of what the hell you are supposed to be doing. Don't you know a goddamn thing?"

Strike a new jury? Start over again?

"Sir, did we just lose the case?"

"Godamnit! You *are* stupid. We just got a mistrial. *You* just got us a mistrial. Now we got to pick another jury and start over. Don't you know anything about the law?"

Apparently not.

"Sir, all I did was tell the truth. What was it that I did that caused all this?"

"You referred to Mr. Register's criminal record. You can't do that. By saying that it was an APD mug shot, you inferred that he had a criminal record. You can't do that."

"But it was an APD mug shot, and he does have a criminal record."

"Boy, you are new at this, ain't you? The truth don't matter a damn. It's what you can say and what you can't. It's about the rules, it ain't about the truth!"

△ △ △ △ △ △ △ △ △ △

WE WENT ON, we tried the case, and we won. I was as scared of losing my job as it was possible to be. I was on probation for the first year, and I saw others lose theirs with a single slip of paper, and no appeal.

Nietzsche made some comment about anything that doesn't kill you makes you stronger. He had something there.

This disaster made me a better witness. It made me a damned good witness. I learned from my mistake and I learned a lot. I learned that attorneys will ask you questions that they ought not ask. I learned that being too quick, or even too thorough, in answering these lawyer questions can cause you a world of trouble. I learned to be slow in court, to think through my answer, and to not say one word above the absolute minimum required to answer the question.

My answer should have been "From a photograph."

Not *one* word more.

I learned that principle for life, and when I watched the O.J. Simpson trial on TV, I saw a whole police department that obviously had not learned it.

As a matter of fact, I think that bunch would have given Col. Robert Smith the stroke I first thought I had given him.

R. D.
Atlanta, 1970

I HADN'T BEEN on the job all that long when I got to meet a real criminal. I answered the phone on a Monday morning, and started a trip into the Twilight Zone of the Dixie Mafia.

The caller wanted to meet with an agent to pass on some information about drug smuggling. I went to my senior partner and asked if I could run with the deal. He asked if that wasn't what I was getting paid to do and then suggested that I ought to, by God, then just do it.

I got back on the phone, and learned that the caller was an Air Force pilot, stationed at Dobbins AFB, who wanted to meet me near that facility. I was out the back door of the office in a flash, into the 1965 Ford pickup, and headed toward I-75.

As usual, I had set the meeting at a Waffle House. I was stuck on them for meeting people, since it would not have been unusual to see the twelve disciples meeting with Gandhi in one. Nobody was ever out of place or time at the Waffle House.

The guy was a typical jet jockey. Short and wiry, he came up to about my armpit and weighed about as much as my boots. I settled across from him in the booth and looked at the name tag on his flight suit.

"Well, Lieutenant, what do you need to tell me?"

The story started slowly, with the lieutenant telling me about his life, his skill, and a lot of other stuff that I wasn't particularly interested in. Sometimes you have to wade through the swamp to get to the island. I wanted to get him to the point, but Joe had already drilled me repeatedly in not rushing people.

"Let 'em tell their own story their own way," in his west Texas drawl.

Chuck finally got to the point. He loved to shoot bumper pool. That wasn't the point, but it got us there. He had been shooting pool at a little beer joint on the back side of Dobbins in the evenings before going home to his efficiency apartment off Delk Road. We eventually got to the time he started shooting pool with a guy who was very interested in just what it was Chuck did for the Air Force. The man Chuck came to know as R. D. was a very good shooter, and seemed extremely interested in airplanes and flying.

"Yeah, he just flat out asked me what I could fly, was I any good, and did I ever do any off-duty flying."

"Well, what did you tell him?"

"Just the plain, unvarnished truth. I can fly anything with wings and a motor, even them sick things with wings that go round and round. I'm better than good. I'm pretty damned great, actually."

Like my partner and most of the other pilots I was to meet in my work, he was proud of his craft, and not at all hesitant to tell anyone and everyone just how damned good he was.

84

"I flew cargo all over Viet Nam, got shot at and shit on."

I knew where he was going before he even started.

"That man wanted me to fly dope for him. I knew it. I saw way too many grunts in Nam doped out of their minds with that shit, and I ain't about to be part of it here."

"Did he ever get around to asking about drugs, or are you just guessing?"

"He asked me if I would consider flying somewhere and picking up something and bringing it back to him. He maybe never said dope, but there is absolutely no question in my military mind that was what he was talking about."

"Well, now, there's a world of difference in somewhere and something and a shipment of dope. We can't just guess this old boy into the penitentiary. We got to have some evidence. You willing to play out the string and see what happens with this guy? It may mean testifying in court, and I'll have to get the Air Force OSI involved at some point. This could end up causing you more than a little trouble. I need to know now if you're committed to this, cause I don't want to start something I can't ever get to finish."

"Let me think about this a little. I didn't know it would be such a big deal. I thought I could just tell you about the guy, and you could handle it from there."

"That would be nice, but that's not how this stuff gets done. I can't just walk up to Mr. R. D., and tell him I'm his pilot, and I'm gonna fly his dope. He courted you for a while before he made his pitch, right? Kinda picked you out of the herd?"

"Yeah, he bought me a Heineken or two, and I think he might have played me just a little easy on the table for the last few games."

I explained to the Lieutenant just how we did things at the Bureau of Narcotics and Dangerous Drugs, how the paperwork had to be done, and how we could work this thing out so that there would be minimal impact on him. I was taught by Joe never to lie to a prospective snitch, that it would bite you in the end. I was as straight as I could be without scaring Chuck off completely. I wanted to find out if this pool shark was a player in the dope business, and I had a lot of homework to do before we could go any further with the game I had in mind.

"Let me do some of this investigating they pay me for, and I'll get back to you later this week. You don't think this guy has something on his mind for tomorrow or maybe Wednesday, do you?"

"Naw, he hasn't even asked me anything serious yet. I can just play dumb for the next few days."

"Better yet, stay out of that beer joint till I get back with you. I got the coffee."

I paid for the coffee, money that I would never get back, and walked out to my truck. I knew I was looking to find out about someone called R. D., a small white guy who liked to shoot bumper pool.

△ △ △ △ △ △ △ △ △ △

BACK AT THE office, I ran down the story to my senior partner. I was still on probation as a federal employee, and Joe was patiently trying to teach me all the things they were supposed to have taught me at 1405 I Street in DC.

"Air Force OSI is not about to let him go playing games for you. They will shut this down before you can say 'spit.'"

"What about interagency cooperation? We keep getting told we have to play nice with everybody else."

"Yeah, that's us. The military doesn't exactly see it that way. They won't want to have any kind of a piece of this. Who's the bad guy?"

I told Joe all I had learned about the infamous R. D. This narc stuff was getting more and more complicated. There were days when I wondered if I would not have been better off still teaching at Franklin County High.

"Call Hightower up in Cobb County. If this guy is shit, Hightower will know him."

Robert Hightower was the Vice, Narcotics, Intelligence, Whatever guy at the Cobb County PD. He was an acknowledged expert on hoodlums, particularly a bunch known as the Dixie Mafia. Hightower knew the criminal histories, family trees, and sexual habits of more criminals than the FBI had in their Washington files.

I spent the next three or four hours playing phone tag, looking for Bob Hightower. This was, thank God, before the day of the automated telephone answering systems, and I was at least allowed to talk with the secretary, who assured me Bob was "out in the field," and would call me back as soon as he got in.

The call came about time to go home.

I had put my stuff in my briefcase, and was getting squared away for leaving when one of the other agents in the squad bay fielded a call. After a moment, Carlos waved at me, and shouted that I had a call on line two.

"You Wayne Smith?"

"Yes, how can I help you?"

"This is Bob Hightower, and I understand you been bugging my girl all afternoon looking for me. What can I do for the feds today?"

87

When they call you "the feds" in the first breath, things usually don't go well. I had heard really good stuff about Hightower, so I tried to be as nice as possible.

"Yes, sir, I have been looking for you. My partner, Marion Joseph, told me to call you, that maybe you could help me in identifying a crook up in your county."

"Well, how is that sonofabitch? He never calls just to shoot the shit, just when he wants something."

"Joe's doing good, he's just been busy. The old boss got transferred to Washington, and Joe is Acting in Charge."

"I didn't know Dick had gone to the Seat of Government. He always acted like a headquarters kind of guy, though."

Mr. Hightower seemed awfully familiar with our office and people. There were folks in other BNDD offices who didn't know us that well.

"Well, Mr. Hightower, I needed to ask about a guy up in Cobb that might be in the dope business."

"Son, I'm just Bob. Who we looking at?"

I laid out what I could about the man I knew only as R. D. Before I even got started, I was interrupted by an impatient burst of gruff noise.

"Hell, yes, I know him. He's trouble, for sure. You sure who we're talking about here?"

I seemed to have hit a nerve.

"For starters, he *owns* that beer joint you're talking about. He don't own it on paper, cause he can't. Felony convictions. A bunch of them. He ain't been into dope very heavy, but if it's illegal and makes money, he'll do it. One more thing, you better tell your source to play this careful. R. D.'s killed before, and he'd do it again to keep out of prison. He's mean as a snake."

"Who is he?"

"David Ray Anderson. One of the charter members of the Dixie Mafia. Broke every law wrote on paper and some that ain't. He loves bumper pool, that's why he bought that beer joint. If he says he wants your man to fly somewhere and get something, I know whatever he has in mind is illegal, and he has the money to do it."

"So you think it's worth working on?"

"Worth working on! I'll get you every scrap of manpower and help there is if you need it. I have a desperate need to see R. D. back in the hole he belongs in. Anything you need, just call me. Call me anyway, and let me know what's going on. I'd just like to know he's going to a federal prison, sooner rather than later."

"Mr. Hightower, I mean Bob, I do have one more question. Why do they call him R. D. when his initials are D. R.?"

"Well, I was told that when he was a kid he wrote stuff backwards all the time. Wrote his initials as R. D. Sort of stuck, I guess, that's all I've ever heard him called. That's what I heard, but I don't know for sure."

△ △ △ △ △ △ △ △ △ △

IT WAS LATE by the time I got off the phone, so I dug through my pockets and came up with the scrap of paper with Chuck's telephone number. I called and got nothing but a lot of rings.

I looked around the office, hoping to tell someone about the really bad guy I was working, but everyone was gone. Joe was coaching soccer and was out in DeKalb County for a game. I was alone.

This was bad, because I had never locked up the office and set the alarm by myself before. It was a complicated process, and ADT was unforgiving. More than one agent had ended up dealing with red faced sweaty cops at the back door when they set off the alarm by accident.

Somehow I managed to get through the whole procedure correctly the first time and was soon off and away home.

Over the next day or two, I dug into the background of Mr. Anderson. Trouble was, there wasn't much. He didn't have a car registered to him, no telephone in his name, and as far as I could tell he didn't have an address I could tie to him. I warned my CI about his being a bad ass Dixie Mafia guy, but Chuck wasn't very impressed.

A lot of the guys back from Nam didn't seem to take stuff like this as seriously as some other folks did. I told Chuck to steer clear till we had our ducks in a row and that I needed him to come in and let us do some paperwork on his cooperation, just to cover his butt.

He agreed, but said he had a deer hunting, beer drinking trip set up for the weekend and asked could we do it when he got back. Hating paperwork like I already did, I was all too glad to put it off till next week.

Friday morning rolled around, and I took a call from Chuck early. He said he had taken a day's leave from the USAF and was driving over to South Carolina early for his deer hunt. I wished him well, and was relieved that there was nothing else to do on this case for the weekend.

About thirty minute later I thought it was strange when Alice Lee called me and said I had a phone call from Chuck on line three.

"Wayne, I got to do something on this thing before I leave."

"Chuck, I told you to stay away from this till we get set up. What is so damned important you got to do it today?"

"R. D. called me a few minutes ago, said he would like to have a word with me before I left town. He knew I was going over to South Carolina this weekend, and he called me on the off chance I might be at home. This is not a big deal, but I will get to see where this guy lives. He wants me to meet him at an apartment complex in Smyrna. Just for a minute."

△ △ △ △ △ △ △ △ △ △

THE ROOKIE IN me came out in full force. I took what he said at face value and didn't lift up the rock to see what was underneath.

"Sure, run by and see what he's got to say. I need that address to do some more checks, so how about you go ahead and tell me now, just in case you get shot deer hunting."

Chuck gave me the name of the complex and the apartment number. I wrote it on a scrap of paper and stuck it in my shirt pocket. I'd get around to running a utility check on it later.

About three o'clock, Alice Lee called me on the intercom.

"It's that Chuck guy, and he's all upset and shouting. Please inform him I don't like to be cursed at, thank you. Line one."

"Chuck, what is your major problem? You're upsetting the hired help."

"Goddamn it, I'm in jail. You got to come get me out. I'm in deep shit. You gotta help me!"

"Slow down. Where exactly are you in jail and what the hell have you done?"

"Cobb County and I have not done one damned thing. I got roughed up and arrested, and I have not done one damned thing. Wayne, you gotta get up here and help me. I'm in real trouble, and I don't have a clue what's going on."

"Okay, Chuck. Who arrested you?"

"The Cobb County Sheriff's arrested me!"

"No, Chuck. I mean *exactly* who arrested you. I need a name, so I can get you out of there."

"There was a bunch of detectives from the Sheriff's Office. The main one was named Burkhalter."

"Good, now I got something to go on. Just sit still, don't make any statements to anybody, and don't mention my name. I'll take care of this. You didn't tell them you were working for me, did you?"

"Not yet, but I'm about to, if I don't get some help!"

"Chuck, calm down, take it easy. You are the cool pilot type guy, just calm down. What have they got you charged with?"

"Making terroristic threats, and some kind of sexual assault thing. I don't understand it at all. I just went to see our friend, and the cops were waiting for me. He wasn't there, but there was a boatload of cops waiting on me at the apartment!"

"Chuck, whatever you do, don't talk about our business there. I'll get on the phone and fix this right now."

△ △ △ △ △ △ △ △ △ △

I LOOKED AROUND the office for help, but it was three in the afternoon on a Friday in the fall. The weather was good, and I was alone. I called Alice Lee and asked where the duty agent had gotten off to. She said he left an hour ago, and said he would be back to close up. He didn't have a radio in his car.

I called for Bob Hightower, but he was out of the office. I told his secretary that I needed him badly, that a CI had been arrested and was at the County jail. I needed help in getting him out. She said she would try to find him.

92

My next call was to the Sheriff's Department, and after a little mishandling, the call went through to the detective unit, and eventually Detective Burkhalter. I was more than a little shocked at the story I got.

"This guy you're interested in is a real piece of work. He's been calling this young girl all week, talking dirty, telling her just what he's gonna do to her and how he's gonna do it. Then the bastard has the balls to come right over to her apartment, just like he said he would, dressed just like he said he was. He's a real pervert, this guy is."

"Chuck has been calling her all week? He's in the Air Force, and he's been flying most of the week. Ain't no phone in those C-124's."

"We got all the calls today on tape. He's just lucky on the earlier ones, we didn't have them. She called us on Wednesday, and we got her phone wired on Thursday. Today was the first time he's called since we got hooked up. He was plain as day on the phone, about what he was going to do and all. Even told her how he was dressed."

△ △ △ △ △ △ △ △ △ △

THE LIGHT CAME on. I dug in the pocket of my corduroy jacket, and came up with the scrap of paper with the address Chuck had given me. I hadn't taken time to run the checks on the address yet.

"That apartment wouldn't happen to be in Smyrna, would it?"

"Yeah, it's . . . . "

I interrupted before he could give me the address. I read the apartment complex name and the apartment number from the slip.

"How the hell did you know the address, you some kind of partners with this pervert?"

"Look, you don't know me from Adam's off ox, but I'm with BNDD. This guy Chuck is working for me, and you gotta let him go."

"You are right about one thing, I don't know you. I ain't letting nobody go without some proof, and it ain't coming over no phone. And if you don't mind, just what the merry hell is a BNDD?"

"We're the Federal Narcotics agents."

△ △ △ △ △ △ △ △ △

THAT SAME LIGHT came on again. "I'm working on this big case with Bob Hightower, and we need this guy out, like now!"

"Why didn't you say you were working with Mr. Hightower? You get him to call me, and your guy is on the street."

"I can't find Bob right now, but I got his secretary working on it. Can you meet me at the jail in about twenty minutes? We can straighten this out."

Well, if you know anything about Atlanta, you know that you cannot get from downtown to the Cobb County Jail in twenty minutes, even in the early 70's. Maybe at three in the morning, but not at three in the afternoon.

I left the office in a hurry. I did stop to make one call on the way out. I told the young lady at Bob's office what I was up to and that I needed him to meet me at the jail, more than I needed air to breathe.

I then proceeded to drive to Marietta. I drove like I was possessed. Juan Manuel Fangio couldn't have stayed up with me. I drove over a mile up the wrong side of Highway 41, to get to a red light where traffic was stopped on my side. I blew through the intersection from the wrong side, crossed over, and actually made it to the jail on time.

I got to the booking area, looking for a friendly face. There was a crowd of people in the area, and I knew none of them. After a moment of standing, I was approached by a cherubic man, who asked loudly if I was, in fact, Special Agent Smith My affirmative reply caused him to identify himself as Detective Burkhalter.

"Haven't heard from Mr. Hightower. You got something to show me?"

I removed the shiny, squeaky new credentials from my inside jacket pocket, and proudly displayed them. Det. Burkhalter was suitably impressed and, without a word, disappeared into the holding area. He returned in a minute with Chuck, who was ashen.

Just then, a tall gray haired gentleman entered the booking area, and almost immediately turned and walked out. Det. Burkhalter had his back turned to the tall stranger, not seeing his appearance and departure. With as few words as possible, I got Chuck in tow, and asked about his pickup truck.

Det. Burkhalter told me it was in the lot where Chuck had been arrested, and then he handed over a manila sleeve with all Chuck's property from Booking. After Chuck shakily signed the proffered receipt, we walked out into the sun, away from the jail smell that was to become part of my life.

As we walked toward my G-car, that tall gray haired gentleman appeared in the lot as if he'd sprung from the asphalt. He approached, and before he spoke, I knew who he was.

"Wayne, did you see the short man in the green golf shirt and jeans in the booking area? Standing over on the left side?"

So much for formalities. I had now met Bob Hightower, it seems. Before I could answer, or even formulate an answer, he continued.

"That was R. D.!"

"How the hell did he get into the booking area? What's going on here. Your guys arrest my snitch and set me up with a major crook in your own jail! Whose side are you guys on up here?"

"Well, it was them, not us. That was the Sheriff's Department, not the PD. They ain't crooked, just not very sharp. Looks like we all got set up. I told you R. D. is dangerous, but this was much, even for him. I'll find out what happened here, and I'll get the truth out of everybody involved. There won't be no hiding from this. You need to get this boy on out of town, and it'll probably be best for him if he finds somewhere else to live after this."

△ △ △ △ △ △ △ △ △ △

OVER THE NEXT few days, I was busy with our own United States Air Force, attempting to convince them that Chuck needed to be transferred far away from Cobb County, Georgia, preferably Pakistan or Turkey or Korea. I got the call from Bob by midweek, and it was all as he had said. Seems R. D. had a card identifying him as an employee of a local bail bond company, and had just happened to be in the booking area looking to see if one of their clients was in the lockup. Just a coincidence. Sure.

As to the arrest, the young lady in question was beyond reproach and had in fact received the calls in question. Phone systems then were not like the ones of today, and it wasn't possible to determine from whence the calls came.

The taped calls were not clearly the voice of Chuck, but then the tape recorder came from K-Mart, and the quality left a bit to be desired. One of the neatest set ups I have ever encountered.

I learned a lot from this case, but the greatest lesson was never to underestimate the mind of one of our own home grown criminals. I ran across R. D. several times over the next few years, even got to pat him down once. He just grinned and said, "Don't I know you from somewhere?"

House Arrest
Atlanta, 1972

I WAS IN the BNDD office by myself. That is, no other agents were there. Most of the clerical staff were around, sort of. We had one part-timer, and she was gone for the day. Then Gloria Smith, the file clerk, had bailed out early to do some Christmas shopping, and that left the dragon lady, Alice Lee.

Between phone calls to others of her persuasion all over the country she was pounding away on the typewriter. She had a better intelligence network than the CIA.

She had briefed me earlier in the week about the Resident Agent in Charge of a Midwest city who had taken the office imprest fund and all the Government Travel Requests, forms as good as gold in any airport, and had run away from home. I hadn't heard a word from anyone else, but Alice Lee had all the juicy details.

Seems the young RAC had been selected to go to Washington to become part of the Inspection Division. Apparently there had been undiscovered financial irregularities in his office, and rather than show up at Headquarters, the lad started flying. He would take a GTR to the airline counter, inquire about the next flight going anywhere, issue the GTR in return for a ticket, and take off.

He circled the globe twice, according to Alice Lee, before he was apprehended in Cairo. It was an interesting story, but Alice Lee had a bad habit of telling the most negative things that could be imagined about other BNDD employees, especially agents. Because she had a particular dislike for those who had come from the old BDAC at Food and Drug, she showed them no mercy and gave them no help in the office.

Russ Jessup, an old hand from FBN, once said of her, "If you go to Sears and order a trainload of bitches, and go down to the railroad yards, and one rusty box car rolls up, and Alice Lee gets out, you will have just gotten your money's worth."

△ △ △ △ △ △ △ △ △

THE FRONT DOOR bell rang, and I looked up at Alice Lee. She must have been deaf, since she sat and held the phone like it was a religious object. I knew she wasn't going to move, so I dragged myself to the front.

A distinguished black gentleman stood at the door, dressed in a suit that probably cost more than my entire wardrobe and holding an over coat that cost even more.

"Yes, sir. How can I help you?"

"You can take me to the Agent in Charge's office, now."

"Sir, Mr. Perry is out of the office at present. You could come back later, leave a number, or if you'd like, you can wait here."

I indicated the limited seating area with three or four chairs just inside the front door.

"I'll wait in Mr. Perry's office."

"No, sir, you will not. You will not go into Mr. Perry's office until he gets back."

"Do you know who I am?"

"No, sir, I don't"

I didn't add that besides knowing he was being a smartass, I didn't know shit about the gentleman, and had reached the point very quickly where I didn't want to know any more.

He produced a slim leather case from inside his suit coat and held it open.

"Inspector Jack Peterson, Office of Inspections."

His credentials looked like mine, except for a much nicer case. Alligator, I think.

"Yes, sir. Come this way."

When I led him into the main office area, I got the surprise of my young life. As he walked in, he immediately approached Alice Lee and introduced himself. She underwent a transformation heretofore unseen by human eyes. She became absolutely giddy, giggling and preening before the rude son of a bitch.

I went to my desk and sat, watching the show. It was like driving by an automobile accident. No matter how repulsive it is, you can't not look.

I had never seen Alice Lee act this way, except maybe on an occasion when the name of John Evans had been mentioned. The lionized old FBN agent, now in charge of the Chicago District, had once served in Atlanta, and Alice Lee, from the way she revered him, might still be carrying a lock of his hair tucked into her bosom.

This was far worse.

"Agent Smith, come here."

Well, good old Alice had already taken care of the introductions.

"Smith, get me all your 1012s for the last year, and bring me your travel advance. I'm here to audit the imprest fund, and I'm starting with you."

Now if this guy was looking to scare me, he already had me when he flashed the Inspection credentials. I'd been on the job a few years, and though I already had a junior partner, I was still easily impressed by administrators, and this guy had big shot written all over him. I went back to my desk and began to search through the junk that filled the drawers.

I finally located the folder carrying the SF-1012s, or travel vouchers to civilians. I flipped through quickly, and did a little third grade math. Seemed the G owed me a touch more than the $500.00 I was given as a travel advance.

I had done the vouchers, but hadn't been reimbursed by Miami in months. They were slow, very slow when it came to paying you money they owed you. But you didn't ever want to get in the other situation, or the people in Administration would drive you nuts over a quarter you owed them. One of the ladies in the Admin group had been overheard to remark that BNDD would be a good place to work if it wasn't for all the damned agents.

"Sir, here are all my outstanding vouchers. I'm owed a good bit more than my advance, so I don't have any cash to show you."

"You just do these yesterday?"

"No, sir. The oldest one goes back about a month and a half. Miami doesn't think paying us is much of a priority, I guess."

"I'm sure you don't have any idea what Miami considers a priority. You probably never will, either." He then added, "Why are you dressed like that? Are you cleaning the office tonight?"

I had on hunting boots, jeans, and a flannel shirt. Pretty much how I usually dressed to go out and work on the redneck peckerwoods that had been my job for the last few months. What the hell did he expect? I was really getting to hate this guy, and we still hadn't been formally introduced.

"I had a surveillance planned for tonight."

It was a lie, but not a really big one.

"Lumberjacks?"

"No, sir, just rednecks."

He took my stack of vouchers, and sat back beside Alice Lee. She continued to giggle like a schoolgirl. Then she walked to my desk.

△ △ △ △ △ △ △ △ △ △

"WAYNE, MR. PETERSON would like some coffee. Why don't you make a pot?"

It was after four in the afternoon. The huge coffee urn made about fifty cups of coffee, and I had no idea if it could be rigged to make one cup for Mr. Peterson.

"Alice Lee, I think we're out of coffee. I'm supposed to bring some in on Monday. I'll go check."

Her face turned red in a flash. Apparently she had already promised Mr. Peterson a cup of coffee.

"You better find some. Mr. Peterson is not very happy with you anyway. If you can't come up with coffee, he may make things hard on you."

"Christ, Alice, what the hell is he here for anyway?"

She couldn't resist.

"He's here to audit the funds. You know, after that RAC ran off with all the money, they found him shorting the office. They're checking everybody. He already doesn't like you, so you better come up with something."

I knew that whether he liked me or not was irrelevant, but I was also sure that my good friend Alice Lee was doing her best to sink me on the spot.

I got up and went to the back, grabbing a walkie talkie as I left the room. I knew there was coffee, so I hid it under the counter below the urn. Damned if I was making the bastard coffee.

I stepped out the back door.

"Eight Zero to Seven One. Eight Zero to Seven One!"

I had no idea what Phil was doing, but I needed to talk to him in the worst way.

"Seven One. Go ahead, Eight Zero."

"Boss, I got a problem. Call me on the bat phone."

"It'll be about fifteen or so. Real problem?"

"Real problem."

I went back into the office and tried to come up with a way to kill the time till Phil could call.

△ △ △ △ △ △ △ △ △

"WE'RE OUT OF coffee, sorry."

The two glares I got would have melted steel. Superman would not have been a match for these two. I thought for a second, and then I screwed up.

104

"I'm going across the street to the bank. I'll get you a cup. How do you take it?"

"You are not going anywhere! Go to your desk and sit down! That is an order."

"Sir?"

"*You* are under house arrest. *You* are not going to any bank. *You* sit down."

Oh, shit. I had done it now. I guess bank was a bad choice of words. There was a C&S Bank across the side street from the office, and they had a coffee room, with fresh coffee all the time. I guess it was the bank part that set him off. I slunk back to my desk.

The next ten minutes dragged by like death. I heard the undercover phone ring, and I began to glimpse daylight again.

"Hello."

"Wayne, it's Phil. What's the problem?"

"Phil, there's an inspector here to audit the imprest. He's put me under house arrest. I need you to get back here, now!"

△ △ △ △ △ △ △ △ △ △

"HOUSE ARREST? WHAT the hell are you talking about? Who *is* this fuck?"

"I said something about going to the bank, and he ordered me to my desk, said I was under house arrest. His name is Peterson. I don't know what's going on. I ain't seen the ball since the kickoff."

"Big black guy? Scar on his head?"

"He's big and black. I haven't paid any attention to his head."

"It's Blackjack Peterson. He's got a metal plate in his head. He's certifiable. Don't worry. I'm on the way in."

105

The fifteen minutes of sitting there, scared to death, passed as slowly as you'd think.

The back door came open, and then slammed shut. Phil stormed into the office like a hurricane, and blew up to Alice Lee's desk where Peterson was camped.

"Don't you ever tell one of MY people they're under house arrest! Let's go to my office!"

Peterson followed Phil Perry into the front office, and the door slammed, even louder than the back door had.

The traffic on Peachtree was drowned out by the screaming. I sat in the back and didn't want to hear. Alice Lee, having done her bit for flag and country, got her coat and waltzed out the back door, bearing a blissful look I have seldom seen in the eyes of a clothed lady.

A little later, Phil came out and told me to go home.

He said, "This is going to be a long night, and you don't need to stay."

The Phoenix

Atlanta, 1972

THE *FLIGHT OF the Phoenix* was Joe's favorite movie. He talked about it all the time, and as flying was his life, the movie became his movie. Jimmy Stewart and Paul Mantz were the kind of Americans all of us fifties kids had as heroes, and with Stewart, a real pilot, starring and Mantz doing the stunt flying, the movie was a lock.

More than the movie, Joe loved the idea of having an air force for BNDD. He bootlegged Georgia National Guard airplanes to use for surveillance, since our agency had no budget for renting them. Joe wanted his own air force, and he worked like hell to get one.

"Hey, Wayne, we got a line on some birds for the Bureau!"

Joe's office was just down the hall from mine in our new building downtown. The RAC, Phil Perry, had cut a deal with HQ to let Joe go airplane hunting, and they had let him run with the project, not working cases or anything else.

"So what are you getting, P-51's or Phantoms?"

"Helio Couriers."

What the hell is a Helio Courier?

Joe lived and breathed airplanes. I had sat at his desk in the afternoons and watched him prowl through GSA surplus bulletins, looking for a Cessna or something similar that could be used for surveillance. He had even found a Schweitzer motor glider that some agency was putting out to pasture, but it just wasn't practical for what he had in mind.

"Hell, Wayne, this is the perfect airplane. It couldn't get any better. It's as good as a Pilatus Porter and this one is gonna be free. We're gonna get this airplane."

"Where is this perfect airplane, and just who is going to give it to us?"

"It's at Davis Monthan, and the good old USAF is looking to get rid of a couple of them. I just got off the phone with a colonel there, and he says nobody has asked about them, and they're just sitting in the desert getting dirty. He thinks the Air Force can work out some kind of lend-lease deal on it, and we can get our hands on one pretty quick."

"Joe, what the hell is a Helio Courier, and what kind of shape are they in?"

"It's a STOL tail dragger. Big engine, lots of power, high wing, flies real slow when you hang out all the boards, and it'll take off from a football field. This is the thing! They make a turbine powered one called a Stallion, but this one will be easy to maintain, and we won't need to start all over learning about the motor."

△ △ △ △ △ △ △ △ △ △

THIS STARTED A quest that took on a life of its own. I wasn't supposed to be involved, but Joe had infected me with the airplane fever long ago, and it wasn't going to go away now.

We started looking at what we could do to get the thing back to Atlanta, and then get an airworthiness certificate from the FAA. The people in HQ had no idea what Joe was doing, or how he was doing it. They did, however, lay down some rules, and the FAA certificate was one of them.

Ludlow Adams had an office between Joe's and mine, and Joe had been Ludlow's training agent just as he had been mine. People who worked with Joe bonded with him, and the relationships became permanent. Ludlow had taken some flying lessons while he was in college, and had always wanted to fly. Like me, he got the bug from Joe, but unlike me, he latched onto Joe's air force idea with a death grip. Lud immediately started taking more lessons at a strip south of town, and was working his ass off to get a private ticket before Joe got the air force off the ground. If Joe was to be the General, then Ludlow was to be the First Pilot.

We sat over a couple of cups of really bad coffee, while Joe spun out the saga, bringing Ludlow and me up to current level on the airplane story. Three weeks had passed since Joe had found the Helios, and he had made a ton of progress.

"Headquarters said yes. I think they said yes because they didn't think I could get the Air Force to give up the birds. I suckered them. I had the yes from the Air Force first. When I got the go ahead from HQ, all I had to do was call Davis Monthan and tell them it was a "go." We got airplanes! Now we got to get them here, get them overhauled, get them certified, get a budget to buy fuel and do maintenance, and we got us an air force."

"Joe, did you know that Fulton County Vocational school has an A and E program? Turns out certified mechanics."

"Hell, Lud, that might be the ticket to get the work done. Why don't you go over and talk to them, see if you can get them to agree to do the overhaul. We could work out some kind of payment deal, and it'll be a damned sight cheaper than paying some aviation shop to do it. It's going to cost us a lot get these things certified, and Washington ain't gonna let us fly them without the FAA tickets."

△ △ △ △ △ △ △ △ △ △

THE DEAL WAS starting to come together, but I was working a lot of Joe's old cases, and I couldn't do my street work and keep up with the air force. Joe was gone a lot, the light in his office hardly ever on. I missed talking to him, but I had gotten to be the liaison with the GBI, and that was turning into a full time job.

There was also Metro Atlanta Narcotics Squad that had started from a grant, and I tried to sit in with them as much as possible. The MANS was a joint operation, pulling together all the departments in the city. They worked out of a private office building, and had detectives assigned from each department, all working under the direction of Lt. Gene Woods of the APD.

It was an experiment, and it seemed to be working well. It was still a shock to see fifteen detectives assigned to work drug cases together. When I had arrived in Atlanta from school in 1969, the city had two detectives assigned to work narcotics and vice, and the GBI had one agent working drugs.

My assignment to work with the GBI turned out to be another advantage for the air force project. When I was talking with GBI Agent Kenny Copeland about the airplane situation, he volunteered to help.

"Wayne, you need to move that airplane, just give me the word. I'll get us a tractor trailer rig from the Department of Transportation, and we'll drive out to Arizona and haul it back here. Since I need some practice driving a rig for this undercover deal we're getting ready to do at the truck stops, I think they'll let me do it."

The idea of dragging the airplane back in a state truck from Arizona sounded like a great lark to me, but it didn't sound all that practical.

"Kenny, if we need that sucker hauled anywhere, you're the man. I'll let Joe know that you're available and can steal us a truck."

I didn't mention the truck idea to Joe, since I didn't see him for several weeks. When I had gotten back from my TDY assignment in San Francisco, I had been handed all Joe's open cases to close out. Joe was playing pilot full time, and the RAC had decided that I was just the guy to take them on.

One was proving to be a problem. Joe had gotten into a bunch of people dealing LSD. The main player was a young kid, even younger than me. Joe had been introduced to him, and it turned out the kid had an older sister living with him.

She had gotten way too chummy with Joe during the buys Joe had made, and now I was trying to cut Joe out and buy up the brother into a bigger deal. I was supposed to be the LSD expert after working the Operation Beacon Task Force in San Francisco, but this wasn't going well.

I didn't like the brother. He was a whiny, spineless puke. The sister, who was way older than me, constantly hung around, and made herself part of drug transactions that she could have just as easily stayed the hell out of. She bugged me about Joe every time I showed up at the East Point apartment.

I couldn't talk dope with the brother without having to explain to the sister about Joe being out of the country and why he wouldn't be back anytime soon. I finally tired of the whole thing and got permission from the boss to just shut it down and make the arrests.

That turned into another of the fine messes that Joe got me into over the years. I had not yet forgiven him for talking me into spending the night in the Hall county jail in an attempt to set up an undercover operation. This one looked worse.

When I eventually made the arrests, the sister went nuts. In the initial appearance before the U. S. Commissioner, she screamed that she was innocent, and that if she could just find "JOE," the true love of her life, he could explain it all.

When the trial came up, she had finally realized who and what Joe was, and her lawyer filed papers with the court, alleging entrapment on the part of the government. The words "seduced and sexually enslaved" were in the document.

I sat with the U. S. Attorney and mostly looked embarrassed during the hearing about the entrapment issue. It came to nothing, and Joe always swore to me that he never touched her, never played house, or even offered to.

"Sorry about putting you through all that. She's crazy as hell. The AUSA wasn't too pissed, was he?"

"Joe, you know damned well he was pissed. Assistant U. S. Attorneys think we're all one step from being criminals ourselves, and this little show didn't help at all. He still doesn't understand why I don't wear a suit when I come over to the courthouse to meet with him."

"He's queer for the FBI, and he ain't ever gonna get over it. They never arrest anyone without getting a warrant first, so he never gets surprised on Friday afternoon by them. He's just a touch lazy, that's all. I'll go over and talk to him, end of the week. He'll be cooled down by then."

"Let it rest, Joe. We won the motion on the entrapment defense, and it looks like we're going to get a plea from all of them. Like the man said, let sleeping dogs lie. You know the Judge won't send them off anyway. Now that all the minimum mandatories are gone, nobody goes to prison anymore."

"We shoulda took it to Fulton County. The state would've give 'em something to think about."

△ △ △ △ △ △ △ △ △ △

"SO WHERE ARE we with the airplane?"

"The Phoenix is rising. I got a buddy in the Guard that flies the C-124's out of Dobbins. I talked with his wing commander, and I got us a deal. They're flying cargo over the pond to Nam, doing a couple of flights a week. They bring back junk, and occasionally bodies, stop off in Oakland, then come home empty. They're trying to figure a reason to stop off at Davis Monthan on the way home on a flight. When they do, we're gonna stuff the Phoenix in one of the dollar twenty fours and fly it home."

"How the hell big is a C-124? Can you get a whole airplane inside one? You sure this'll work?"

"We'll have to take the wings off, roll the fuselage inside, and then stack the wings alongside. It'll work great, already got the specs. No problem at all. Well, there is one, actually. We can get the Phoenix to

113

Dobbins, but Ludlow hasn't been able to figure a way to get it down to Fulton County Tech."

"Joe, you know Ken Copeland over at GBI?"

"Yeah, he's the new guy Phil got to work dope. He seems like a good guy. Don't know what kind of narc he'll make, though."

"He's doing good working the truck stops. He's bought off a ton of drivers, and he's just getting started. I think he's gonna do real good. He brought up something a while back, though. It might just be the ticket to get the Phoenix down to the school. He's got to be a decent rig driver, and he says he can borrow a tractor and trailer from DOT. Let me talk to him, and maybe we can figure a way to haul the bird down to Fulton County."

"If he can do it, let Lud know. I'm flying out to Arizona in two days, and I'll be there till we get the Phoenix out of the boneyard and on its way here. Lud's handling all the stuff on this end."

"I'll get us a truck. Tell Ludlow that I got it taken care of, and I'll holler at him to get a time when you'll be back with the airplane."

"I'm probably not going to come back with the Phoenix. I've got some other stuff to do with the Air Force. This is just the beginning. We've got lots to do."

△ △ △ △ △ △ △ △ △ △

JOE WAS GETTING his air force. He was becoming a boss, and an administrator. Before, all we could talk about was the Phoenix, and now he saw beyond that. His flying days were not over, but he was on his way to becoming the first Chief Pilot of both BNDD and the later to be formed DEA. My old partner, my training officer, the man who hired

114

me, was going to be a big deal in our world. His star was rising like a comet.

I spoke with Kenny twice that day, and he began to make the arrangements to beg, borrow, or steal a truck from the state.

"What kind of truck are you going to get, Kenny? I'm not sure what the Phoenix will fit on, or in."

"I think a low boy for hauling earth moving equipment ought to do just fine. It's plenty wide, and it's got all sorts of places to tie the bird down. I don't think anyone will raise a stink if I get one on the road for a few hours. I'll get Phil to call somebody at Department of Transportation and grease the skids."

Phil was Phil Peters, Kenny's boss at GBI. Back when I came to Atlanta, Phil was the only GBI agent assigned to work drug cases. He was working with Joe and Luther Cooke on a case, and I got to know him well. He had been an APD officer, as well as a radio operator for the Highway Patrol. Phil's mom worked at the Confederate Avenue Headquarters of both the GBI and GSP. He had great contacts all through state government, and was able to get almost anything done. He eventually worked his way from GSP radio operator to Director of the GBI. One hell of a narc.

I passed on all the arrangements to Ludlow, and waited. I had to keep working cases, but with an ear to the ground, waiting to hear about the airplane. Late on a Tuesday, Lud called me on the office phone intercom.

"Joe's on the line from Davis Monthan. Come on over."

I walked the three doors to Joe's office, where Lud sat at Joe's desk, looking at home there.

Seeing Ludlow Adams with a phone to his ear was as natural as seeing the sun come up in the morning. My wife said it grew out of his head. She was always amazed when he would come by the house, to pick me up or for some other reason, and within minutes he had seized our telephone and begun to call people, carrying on conversations about things no one but he understood.

No junkie was as addicted to heroin as Lud was to the telephone. This was in the days before digital pagers and cell phones. God only knows what he would have been like had he had access to all the technology we now take for granted.

Lud waved me to a seat, continuing to talk to Joe. I wondered how he had taken time to put Joe on hold to call me. From Lud's end of the conversation, it was apparent that the Phoenix was about to move.

"Wayne's here now."

Lud handed me the phone.

"Hey, we're on the move. I got the bird prepped, and we'll take the wings off in the morning. The Air Force is doing a great job, and so far it ain't cost me a cent. You get Kenny ready with the truck?"

"Joe, I had no idea we were so close. I can call Kenny at home tonight, but he hasn't made any hard plans yet. Didn't know we were moving."

"Hell, I told Mudhole to keep you up on where we were. He's too damned busy trying to get that FAA license in his pocket to do anything else. Do me a favor and call Kenny now. I'll hang on with Lud till you get some word."

I handed the phone to Ludlow, and walked back to my office. I had the feeling the BNDD air force was about to pass me by. I wanted to stay in the game, but there was no room for anyone else, and Lud was making absolutely sure that he was first in line.

Hell, I was too big to be a pilot. Most of the little Cessnas wouldn't accommodate my big body, and I couldn't afford to take the time or money to learn to fly on my own. I saw the future of aviation in BNDD, and I wasn't in it.

"Ms. Copeland, is Kenny there?"

Sounded like "can Kenny come out and play?" The wives of narcs are always suspicious of phone calls at home after normal business hours. It usually means their husbands are about to go out into the night, to do something desperate and ill-planned that might or might not find that husband home before the sun came up.

"Who is this?"

Blunt question to my question.

"Wayne Smith with the feds. It ain't about working tonight."

"He's right here."

I walked back to Joe's office and slapped the desk top. Lud looked up, mumbled to Joe that I was back, and handed me the phone.

"Joe, Kenny says he can do it tomorrow, or Thursday, but he's going to Savannah on a deal Friday. Be there for the weekend."

"How about next week?"

"You know how dope deals go. If they bag the guy in Savannah over the weekend, he'll be back home by Monday afternoon. He says he's good for the rest of the week."

"The Guard is flying to Nam this weekend, be back to Oakland on Tuesday. They've gotten half-assed permission to drop by Davis Monthan on the return flight to look into some spare parts for the 124's. It's a smokescreen, but it gets them permission to land here, and we'll have a crew of Air Force guys ready to shove the Phoenix up in the 124. Won't take but a couple of hours, and no one will ever know. By the way, don't make a big deal at Dobbins about what y'all are there for."

117

Don't make a big deal about what I'm there for? Now I'm supposed to sneak a damned tractor trailer into an Air Force base and drive off with an airplane on the back without making a big deal of it. The damned airplane belongs to the Air Force. What the hell are they supposed to think about what we are about to do?

"Joe, that may be a problem. They're not going to just let us drive on the base, steal an airplane and drive off without at least asking what I'm doing. Can't the pilots get us some kind of clearance?"

"The pilots are stretching this thin just by hauling back an unmanifested airplane. I can't ask them to do much more. See what you can come up with."

I handed the phone back to Lud.

See what you can come up with. The hell you say. I was at a loss. I didn't have a clue as to what I was supposed to come up with.

I was getting to hold the bag on this one. If we got onto the base, got the Phoenix loaded, we wouldn't have anything to prove it was ours or how it got onto the base. Anything we did at that point was going to get the pilots in deep trouble. The whole deal looked grim, and it looked as if it was going to be my fault.

I turned and walked out, as Ludlow and Joe began to discuss this new problem. Somehow every time a new problem had come up, one of us had found a way to overcome the impasse.

△ △ △ △ △ △ △ △ △ △

THIS TIME IT was on me, and I was stuck. I walked back to my office and called Joyce. I needed to tell her I was about to leave for the house and explain why I was late again.

As I told her the story in twenty words or less, she listened, and then cut right to the answer.

"Your Uncle Bill works there, doesn't he? Maybe he knows what you can do."

Bill Garner, my mother's brother, was a Warrant Officer in the Georgia Air National Guard. He was a full time civilian employee during the week and pulled Guard duty for drills once a month. He was a true military man. From killing tanks at the Battle of the Bulge to testing the hydrogen bomb at Eniwetok, his life had been the military. He worked at Dobbins, knew everyone there, and if anyone could fix this, Bill could.

"Thanks, babe! You just saved the air force."

I sprinted back to Joe's office, where Lud was making goodbye noises.

"Tell him to hold on, I got it!"

I went home, had dinner, and then called Bill. I explained the whole deal to him, expecting that he would be shocked, or at least surprised. He wasn't. From the way the conversation went, it seems the military did stuff like this all the time. Equipment disappeared and reappeared, getting it to the people that really needed it without a lot of unnecessary paperwork. Bill had left me with simple instructions.

"Come to the front gate, show 'em your ID. Tell them that you are here to see me. I'll take care of everything else."

The weekend dragged by, and Kenny called Saturday night with good news. They had busted out on the undercover deal, and he was coming home on Sunday. He had talked with Phil about the truck, and we were set for either Wednesday or Thursday, depending on the C-124.

119

This was looking easy. All the serious bumps had been smoothed, and the air force was on its way to being born. I went to work on Monday, back to the cases, back to the snitches, and back to the job I was going to do forever.

Tuesday crept in, and I hung close to the office, waiting to hear if the 124 was on schedule. Nothing.

I went out to meet with a couple of cops from East Point. They had a line on a group that was supposed to be bringing in loads of powder containing LSD from San Francisco. The main player was supposed to be a Cuban kid, not even sixteen years old, who was using girls to mule loads of the stuff back on airline flights from San Francisco.

I was supposed to be the big expert on LSD and the west coast after my TDY there, so I was glad to hear about someone who was just selling the stuff, as opposed to the stories about going straight to the lab.

Back in the car, and heading uptown to the office, I got a call.

"Three Thousand Seventy-Four to Three Thousand Eighty."

"Eighty. Go ahead, Seventy-Four."

"Eighty, I got a call from Seventy-Three. It's on!"

"Eighty to Seventy-Four. I'm on the way in."

I drove back, in no hurry, since we had days to get this done. We had done all we could on our end, and now it was up to the Georgia Guard and good winds.

△ △ △ △ △ △ △ △ △ △

THURSDAY AFTERNOON, I met Kenny at the Waffle House on Highway 41, just south of the Dobbins main gate. Then I drove the American Motors Matador up to the gate house at the entrance to

120

Dobbins, followed right on my tail by Kenny in the big diesel tractor with the state emblems on the doors.

Kenny had on dark glasses, and looked the part of a bored state driver. I pulled my badge and ID out of my left hip pocket, showed it to the Air Policeman at the shack.

"Special Agent Wayne Smith to see Warrant Officer William Garner. The truck," I said, jerking my thumb back at the Peterbilt, "is with me."

I expected everything but what I got. A step back, a salute, and a wave in. We drove on in like we were expected. I had been told where to come, and as we drove toward the apron where the C-124 was sitting, I saw Bill standing on the concrete with a couple of other guys in fatigues.

Ludlow was with them, and they were waiting for us. We pulled up, stopped, and I got out.

"Hey, Lud. Bill, thanks for getting us in."

"Nothing to it."

"Lud, where you want the truck?"

Kenny walked over, and after a few minutes conversation, he backed the low boy trailer in front of the C-124, with its huge nose entrance now opening. The silver high winged airplane, minus its wings, sat in the huge cargo hold of the transport.

The air force crewmaster was already unhooking the straps that had held the Helio Courier in place during the flight from Arizona.

We all walked into the C-124, and looked at the bird. Plain aluminum finish, with no markings at all. No FAA "N" numbers, no air force numbers, nothing.

It was Christmas, and Ludlow was unwrapping his only present. He stood, almost in awe, and then reached out and touched the cold aluminum skin. I thought he was going to cry.

We had to get this show on the road, so I suggested that we push the little — by comparison with the huge monster that was holding it — airplane out onto the concrete. It was easy for the lot of us to move it, and Kenny already had the ramps down on the back of the trailer.

We swung the tail around, rolled the tail wheel to the trailer, lifted it up and brought it back onto the center of the trailer. The main gear wheels matched up with the ramp well, and we rolled the Phoenix onto the state low boy. Carrying the wings was a bit more exercise than I had planned on, but in due course, we had them strapped alongside the fuselage on the trailer.

"We've got to do something about the prop."

"What do you mean, Lud?"

"We have to secure the prop. It'll turn in the wind when we get this thing going down the interstate, and it can't. It has to stay still."

Prop turns, engine turns — there might be a problem. What if the airflow caused it to turn backward? This was not good.

"I got plenty of chain here, just let me get it on."

Kenny was dragging logging chain out of a locker on the trailer. In a matter of minutes, he had secured the big three-bladed prop to spots on the trailer, and we were as protected as we were going to get.

After a few million thank-yous, Ludlow jumped into his G-car, I got back into the Matador, and we headed out to the front gate of Dobbins Air Force Base. I put my Kojak red light on the dash, plugged it in, and we rolled out into the afternoon traffic, headed over to I-75 south and motored into Atlanta.

The drive south to University Avenue was simple. Then we exited and cut across to Fulton County Vocational Technical School, where the class of aviation mechanics were waiting. We drove up, and after a few minutes of talking to the head of the program, we turned the Phoenix over to their tender mercies.

Just before we left I looked inside the airplane, and the area back of the seats was littered with small pieces of paper, the size of a playing card. I picked one up, and in three languages, it proclaimed that the bearer would be guaranteed safe passage if he renounced the Viet Cong and surrendered himself to the appropriate authorities. CHU HOI.

I wish I had saved one of those.

△ △ △ △ △ △ △ △ △ △

THE AIR FORCE was born. Like most births, it was messy, involved, and a little ugly. Phoenix finished its course at Fulton County. It was a class project for the students, and the administration thanked us for the opportunity.

The wings came back off, Kenny borrowed the low boy again, and we trucked her out to Fulton County Airport, to the FAA hangar. The skillful mechanics at the FAA put the wings back on, and after a few days of inspection, the Phoenix was ready for a test flight

Joe and Ludlow had found a guy at Fulton County airport who was type rated in the Helio Courier. He had agreed to do the test flight.

We then hit another problem. Joe had no money to buy fuel for the beast. We all lined up, and each of us put fifty or sixty dollars of fuel on the cards that were supposed to be used to buy gas for the G-cars. We soon had enough av-gas to do the test flight.

The Phoenix flew.

Equal Justice for All
Atlanta, 1972

I HAD BEEN working in Savannah for a couple of months, on and off. It was a long drive from Atlanta, killing most of a day just to get there.

Stopping at Sweat's Barbecue near Metter was required, and it was almost worth the drive. The place wasn't fancy, wasn't particularly spotless, but had the best pulled pork in the southern half of the state.

I had assisted the Savannah Metro unit, making undercover buys from a few of their targets. They had money and pretty good intelligence about the traffickers, but no unknown faces to do the undercover work. Since we had provided them help on several occasions, they always reciprocated when we needed assistance.

The U.S. Attorney's Office in Savannah called and told me that one of my cases was going to plead on Tuesday, and that I would need to be there to provide the factual basis for the plea. Hearsay was admissible at such a hearing, so anyone could have testified, but the Assistant U. S. Attorney on the case insisted that I be there.

"Hey, Jack, I'm coming down for the plea on Armstrong tomorrow. You get me a place out at the beach?"

"Yeah, come on. I'll get you a rate, make you a deal."

Jack Levine was a solid hunk of muscle. He had worked for the PD for a while, and was well known all over Savannah. Nobody messed with Jack. I had seen him hit a guy once, and that was all I needed to convince me.

We had been at a bar just after closing, and a young PD officer was having a problem with a drunk who wanted to drive out of the lot. Jack and I had been riding together, looking for one of our bad guys when he saw the confrontation starting.

Jack slid out of the G-car and walked quietly over to the two men standing between two cars. As the drunk reached out and grabbed the young officer's shirt, Jack spun him around and hit him square on, one time. The drunk lifted over the hood and fell in a heap at the tire on the other side.

Jack never said a word, just turned and walked back to the car, and got in.

"What the hell was that all about?"

"That young cop just got a couple of days off for getting into a fight with a drunk. He's gotta learn to be more decisive. I was just giving him a lesson in how to successfully manage people."

People like Jack made doing the job a whole lot more interesting.

△ △ △ △ △ △ △ △ △ △

BACK IN THE real world, I knew I was about to start a minor battle. I went in to the boss's office and made my pitch for going to the

126

coast. He would be negative about it, because that's the way he approached everything.

"The Assistant U. S. Attorney in Savannah just called, and he needs me to come down tomorrow for a plea in that little meth case I made down there. I got a lot of other shit to do, and I tried to get out of it. Reckon you could call him and get me out of this one?"

"You're not going to get out of doing your job. You just get your ass on in to Admin, get a travel authorization, and get on your way. Don't you ever come in here and ask me to get you out of doing something like that. You know how important court is. What could you possibly have to do that is more important?"

"Okay, I'll go on. I just wanted to be around for that surveillance on Wednesday. I know it's gonna be a hard pull, and I didn't want to be unavailable."

"We can get by without you for one deal. You're not indispensable."

Actually, the case agent on that particular surveillance was an idiot, and the whole thing was just manufactured to make him look good in the boss's eyes. This fool had spent most of our operations funds for the quarter on a case that had no dope, no witnesses, and no conspiracy that anyone could see.

I was so glad to be out of town for this one that I almost leaned over the desk and kissed the RAC.

"Yes sir. I'm on the way."

Since I had already filled out a travel request, I walked down to the lady who handed out travel authorization numbers.

"The boss said for you to cut me orders to travel on this case number. Trial in Savannah."

"Well, it's going to take more than you saying it to make it so. I'll need him to personally authorize it. We're short of money this quarter."

"He said for you to cut the orders. You have a question, call him. He's making me go. I been trying to get out of it all day."

Her smile lighted up the room. She was tickled to write the orders if I didn't want to go. All these admin types seemed to think we went out and drank champagne and danced the nights away when we traveled. Warm beer and a Days Inn were far more likely to be in the picture.

I picked up the slip with the travel authorization numbers and waltzed back to my desk.

Chris looked up as I sat down. The big blonde former college baseball player had been my partner for about six months, and we were just beginning to get to know each other.

"How'd it go?"

I held up the sheet with the travel numbers and grinned.

"It's a dirty job, but somebody's got to do it."

My partner was not happy. He had been trying to get money to travel to Tampa to interview a witness for two weeks, with no success.

"I keep getting told to get an agent in Tampa to do that interview. It's gonna take me three hours to get him briefed up on what he's got to ask, and he's still gonna screw it up. How the hell did you get the boss to sign off on that?"

"He just likes me better than you, that's all."

"Bastard!"

△ △ △ △ △ △ △ △ △ △

I HUMPED DOWN to Savannah, with the necessary stop at Sweat's, and checked in at the hotel Jack had fixed up for me at the Beach.

Savannah Beach was dead in the winter, and I loved it. Almost nothing was open, but it was quiet, and there was no traffic. Even the Black Lace was down to only a customer or two at night, with their strippers lacking even minimal enthusiasm.

There were a couple of decent places to eat, including Desposito's, which you have to drive by to get to the beach. I love their boiled shrimp, served on a newspaper with a cold Blue Ribbon in a can. Hard to beat. Maybe later I'd stop by and try to make shrimp an endangered species.

Early the next morning I put on a suit and drove down to the Federal Court House. I had no idea where my case was slated in the batting order, and I wasn't about to be late.

Because it was plea day, the courtroom was filled with other federal agents, waiting their turn to sit by the AUSA and then go for a moment to the witness box to tick off the evil acts committed by the criminals who had seen the light and were pleading guilty to the offense charged. I looked for the Assistant handling my case, but he was not to be found.

"Excuse me sir, but do you know where Assistant U. S. Attorney White might be?"

The young Assistant sitting at the prosecution table looked up, with an expression of mild contempt.

"Who's your lawyer?"

It came on like thunder. I was wearing a suit, but I had a ratty beard and stringy shoulder length hair.

This happened a lot. Somehow the lawyers, and often the citizenry, looked at us narcs with disdain. They didn't seem to understand you couldn't run with the bad guys with a crew cut and wingtips.

"Mr. White is the Assistant assigned to prosecute my case."

"Well, you need to get your lawyer to talk to him. He won't talk to you."

"Look, I guess we got off on the wrong foot. I'm Wayne Smith, I'm an agent with Federal Narcotics, and I'm here to do a plea. I need to talk to White."

"Oh. Well, White is out of town, and I'm handling his pleas. What's the defendant's name?"

This was great. I have to drive across hell and half of Georgia to do a factual basis on a plea, and the AUSA is out of town. If that ass had told me he wasn't going to be here, I'd have stayed the hell in Atlanta, and spent the night at home with my family.

"Armstrong."

"He's up last on the docket. Probably be after lunch, at the earliest."

"It'll be today, though, right?"

"Yeah, today for sure."

Good news and bad news. The timing sucked, but at least I'd be free to eat lunch with the Metro guys. They always had lunch together, and it was always fun. No beer, though. Breathing hops and barley on the AUSA and the judge would not be good.

"Tommy, where y'all gonna go for lunch?"

T. C. Walton, or Top Cat, was one of my favorite people in the world. He was a really good narc, with a sense of humor beyond belief.

"Well, in your honor, we'll just go to Mrs. Wilkes' for lunch. Think you can handle it?"

Mrs. Wilkes' Boarding House was a legend in Savannah. It had started, according to the local lore, as a rooming house for railroad employees. The help-yourself lunch was at first attended by few, but now the line at noon went out the door and down the block. The food was truly homemade good, and there was always more of it than anyone could eat.

"Yeah, I can handle it."

△ △ △ △ △ △ △ △ △ △

BACK IN COURT after lunch, I was drowsy. Although it was cool outside, the courtroom was warm, and as the afternoon calendar droned on, I had to keep jerking myself awake.

The Assistant had assured me there were only three more cases, and that I was up just after the FBI case. I was fighting sleep and staring off into the distance, when the FBI case was called.

The young black defendant waddled to the defense table with his skinny white appointed attorney. The defendant was an overweight kid, who appeared to be a little less than bright. The case was called, and the kid was charged with aiding and abetting an Army deserter.

I had never heard of anyone being charged with that particular offense, so I perked up and began to pay attention.

The clerk read the indictment, and the young man just sat, staring at the judge with a blank look on his face. The defense attorney played his part in the drama, saying the right things at the right moments but apparently agreeing to everything the government had charged in the indictment.

It was, after all, Savannah, and it was near the end of our involvement in Viet Nam. There was a huge training facility just outside Savannah, where bright young men were being taught to fly helicopters, getting them ready to go to Nam and do what their country needed done. In the South there was a lot of public sentiment in favor of the war, particularly in towns that were highly impacted by the military.

131

The Assistant finished his preparations, then called the FBI agent to the stand to lay out the factual basis of the guilty plea. I expected to hear that the young man was a dastardly yellow dog who was subverting the efforts of the United States. What I heard banished my drowsiness.

"Now, Agent Terhune, please tell the court just how you came to arrest Mr. Brown."

"Agent Strothers and myself were in the Courts, looking for a deserter from the U. S. Army. We had been told that he was frequenting an apartment in the Courts where a particular young lady lived. We had reason to believe that we might find him there."

"What happened then?"

"We exited our vehicle and proceeded to approach a group of young men standing on the housing project basketball court. I displayed my official FBI credentials and advised them that I was a Special Agent looking for a U. S. Army deserter named Roderick Holmes. I asked if any of the individuals there present knew Mr. Holmes. I received replies in the negative."

"Agent Terhune, was Mr. Brown in that group of young men you approached?"

"Yes, he was."

"What happened then?"

"Agent Strothers and I then returned to the government vehicle and conducted surveillance on that area of the Courts."

"Go ahead, Agent. Tell us what happened then."

"As we sat conducting surveillance, we observed an individual who appeared to match the photograph of the deserter that we had received from the United States Army. That individual was walking across the parking lot, going in the general direction of the basketball court."

"Go ahead."

The Assistant was getting a little frustrated at having to prod the answers out of the blue suited, appropriately handkerchiefed Special Agent.

"Well, sir, the individual walked across the parking lot, and was then observed to approach the individuals on the basketball court."

A few moments passed as the Assistant just stared at the Agent.

"Yes, sir. The individual in question, the one who appeared to be the deserter for whom we were looking, then approached the young men. We observed Mr. Brown speak to the individual, and then point at the official government vehicle. We exited the vehicle and approached the individual, who began to run. I loudly stated that I was a Special Agent with the Federal Bureau of Investigation, but the individual continued to run. My partner and I gave chase, but could not apprehend the subject."

Another lengthy pause.

"My partner, Agent Strothers, and I then returned to the area of the basketball court. We observed that all the young men with the exception of Mr. Brown had left the area. We approached Mr. Brown, and asked him if the individual who had run was, in fact, Mr. Holmes, the deserter.

"Mr. Brown stated that he thought the individual was Mr. Holmes. I then asked Mr. Brown what he had said to Mr. Holmes when he had approached him. Mr. Brown stated that he had told Mr. Holmes that the FBI was in the green Matador, and they were looking for Mr. Holmes. I then placed Mr. Brown under arrest for aiding and abetting a deserter and transported him to the FBI office for processing."

Whew! In other words, when the FBI agents could not catch the fast, long legged soldier, they opted for what they could catch, a slow witted fat boy.

Did they advise him of his rights? Was his lawyer conscious? Was the judge going to allow this travesty? Was the fleeing "individual" really the long sought Mr. Holmes?

This kid had tried to do the FBI a favor by telling the deserter where the FBI might be found so that the deserter could turn himself in and take whatever punishment he deserved, and for that the young man was now pleading guilty to a federal felony. Surely the judge would not go along with this. Surely.

Back in those bad old days, there was no pre-sentence investigation, no probation officer to make recommendations on sentencing to the court. His honor, the judge, made all those decisions on his own. He not only made them, but he made them then and there, on the spot.

Having accepted the guilty plea, because Mr. Brown, represented by counsel, stood and pleaded guilty, his honor proceeded to sentence the young man.

Surely, surely, he would now give the lad a stiff jolt of probation. Maybe two or three years of reporting monthly to a probation officer in the federal building would teach young Mr. Brown a lesson.

"I hereby sentence you to serve a term of five years in the custody of the Attorney General, at an institution so designated for that service."

The U. S. Marshal escorted the harmless young man out of the courtroom. The FBI agents walked out, the room got quiet, and my case was called.

△ △ △ △ △ △ △ △ △ △

I WAS BAFFLED. My hopes were up for my case, though. If this mean son of a bitch judge would give that kid five years, the meth dealer I was doing here was going away for a while.

We walked through the drill, and I mounted the witness stand and told my story. On six different occasions I had made six different buys of methamphetamine from the skanky maggot sitting at the defense table.

The doper had not even had the good grace to clean up for court. He was still the skinny, ugly, pockmarked puke I had drunk wine with, and listened to, and paid good official United States currency to. He still looked like he needed a bath and a beating.

I methodically laid out each buy, what I had paid, what the lab report said, and how much dope was involved.

My testimony seemed to be going well. The doper sat and stared emotionlessly at me while I testified. I was hoping he would get upset, call me a liar, do something to show some spirit or life. No, he just sat.

I finished and returned to the prosecution table. The Assistant had asked me only one question, and I just told the whole story without further prompts. I knew that was what he wanted, so I gave it to him.

"Great job."

This guy just didn't know me. I prided myself on always doing a great job in court.

△ △ △ △ △ △ △ △ △ △

"I HEREBY SENTENCE you to serve one year of probation, and I will recommend minimal supervision. I feel that if you apply yourself, you can beat this drug problem and go on to amount to something."

All of a sudden I was ashamed of being a Southerner.

My mind flashed on the beer joint on the road between Atlanta and Savannah that had two doors, one marked *White* and one marked *Colored*.

It flashed on the Christmas I spent working in Charleston, where we were not allowed to enter bars because we had Ellis Dean, a black federal agent with us.

It flashed on the *Whites Only* water fountains I had seen all my childhood.

Apparently it was better to be a white maggot drug dealer than a black kid who was a little slow on the uptake and a lot slower on his feet.

I was raised in the segregated South. I had never spoken to a black person as an equal till I was in college. As far as racial understanding I had all the disadvantages a white redneck can have.

I suddenly wondered if I might be a little better person than I had thought.

"This is bullshit. This guy ain't got a drug problem. He *is* a drug problem! He deals. He sells the shit. What the hell does the judge think I was doing, wasting my time hanging around with that trash?"

"Let it go! He's made his decision, and he's not likely to change it. You say anything about it, and you'll find yourself in contempt. You want to spend a week in the Chatham County jail while we try to get you out on bond?"

Coward that I was, I walked out into the evening sunset. I called Tommy and Jack from a payphone.

"Let's go out to the Beach and get shitfaced."

We did.

The Joke

Atlanta, 1973

A SENSE OF humor is one of the most valuable tools in the cop's box. If you can't laugh at the misery you face every day, it'll drive you to drink, go nuts or worse. We were serious about practical jokes. They became an art form, each one trying to best the last. If you couldn't just laugh at the world, we'd make you laugh at yourself. The jokes defused, de-stressed, and gave idle hands a workshop.

"Hey, George, you done the paperwork on that Toyota yet?"

Bernie Coulter was the boss at the Task Force in Atlanta. A blunt fellow was Bernie. He had once been a Kansas City cop, got shot at and stabbed on that job. A Federal Narcotics agent of the old school, Bernie had come to Atlanta from San Juan, Puerto Rico, where he had opened a new BNDD office.

The George in question was George Faz, my new junior partner. George was fresh out of the academy, in his first post.

"Boss, I'm working on it, have it for you in a day."

Now I knew George was, in fact, not working on it. I, unfortunately, must have passed on my hatred for paperwork to George, as he was slower than me in getting the yellow sheets typed out and ready for review and signature.

I pulled George into my cubbyhole.

"Damnit, George, you got to stop doing that. Tell the old man anything, but don't lie to him. You know damn well you ain't even started on that paper, and he's gonna have your ass for this kind of stuff. Now you told him tomorrow, and it ain't gonna happen. He's old, but he ain't stupid. You keep that up, and he's going to send you down the hall to the District Office. You know what that means. In at zero eight hundred, coat and tie, and kissing up to the cowboy in charge."

"Partner, I'm going to do it. I'll get it done today."

"Now you're lying to *me*. We got two buy-busts to do today. We are not going to have time to sit in here and fill out all the stupid forms. Why did you seize that piece of shit, anyway? It ain't worth the paper we'll waste on it."

"I needed to do a car seizure. I've never done one before, and Bernie told me I needed to do one. I'm supposed to learn how to do all this stuff."

"Bernie's the boss, but you need to listen to *me*. I'm your partner, and I'm supposed to teach you all the shit they didn't tell you in Washington. If and when I think you need to learn car seizure, I'll find a decent car, so we don't just have a total waste of time. See if you can get one of the APD guys to seize the thing under state law. That worthless defendant that was living in it ain't getting out of jail for a couple of years, and he ain't gonna need it when he does."

"Okay, I'll talk to Don about the car."

△ △ △ △ △ △ △ △ △ △

THE TASK FORCE was what had been the ODALE program in Atlanta.

The Office of Drug Abuse Law Enforcement was another of Washington's half baked ideas about solving the drug problem. It had also been a total waste, except for the tons of money they threw at their idea. The concept involved bringing local cops into the BNDD office, setting them up with BNDD managers, along with Assistant United States Attorneys, all working together, in peace and harmony. Oh, there were guys from IRS and U. S. Customs assigned to the detail as well.

In Atlanta, the ODALE program had been located down the hall from the BNDD office, almost but not quite sharing space. But ODALE had newer, leased cars, more clerical staff than the Pentagon, and informant and buy money flowing out the doors.

They had had a grant administrator who was a cop buff, constantly inserting his views into the enforcement philosophy of the unit. That and the lawyers meant that nothing meaningful was being done, and as usual, Customs had been stealing us blind. Every shred of information that came into the office went straight to U. S. Customs, and also as usual, we had never gotten a word in return. A wonderful strategy for failure.

When a totally new organization, the Drug Enforcement Administration, or DEA, was formed in 1973 from BNDD and agents drafted from other organizations, supposedly to be more effective in the war on drugs and to eliminate interagency rivalry, the ODALE program morphed into the DEA Task Force. No IRS guys, no Customs agents, no useless lawyers, just a few DEA agents and the local cops. The result was a thing of beauty.

The newly formed DEA kept coming up with new concepts about winning the drug war, and it usually meant doing more paperwork than making arrests. The Task Force, however, was left alone. All we had to do was go out, buy dope, and then arrest the mopes. We didn't have to justify anything, we didn't have to get permission to do anything, we just put asses in jail. It was the best of times.

△ △ △ △ △ △ △ △ △ △

"HEY, DON, DID George say anything to you about that Toyota?"

"Hell, no. What has that little wetback done now?"

Don Wally Sanford was not about being subtle. He was as politically incorrect as humanly possible, and he worked hard to stay that way. George, a Hispanic with a Portuguese father and a mother of Mexican ancestry, would always be known affectionately as a wetback, or worse, to Don.

"Remember that bum that you bought the pot off of—well, George decided to kiss up to Bernie, told him he was seizing the car federally."

"Why, that idiot! That car is a stone piece of shit. After driving it back to the lot, I don't even know if it'll run again. I could hear bearings rattling way before I got it here."

"Don, do me a favor, see if you can do state paper on it. We need to get it out of the lot before Bernie sees it again and goes after George for not doing the paperwork."

"I'm not about to do all that paper for George. I'll show him the forms, let him do it."

"I don't think a fed can do a state seizure. I think it's like a state search warrant—no feds allowed."

Years before, we had lost a case when my old buddy Ludlow Adams had done a state search warrant. Georgia law didn't allow Federal agents to be affiants on state search warrants, but nobody realized it till Ludlow went to court.

"Okay, I'll do something with the car."

△ △ △ △ △ △ △ △ △ △

A FEW WEEKS rolled by. The task force was going great. We took all our cases to state court. The Fulton County DAs loved us because we actually wrote reports and gave them copies before the trial. We were winning all the cases and having fun doing it.

Then we hit a bad streak. We lost a hand-to-hand sale set up by Pee Wee, our star informant. We had sat through a simple trial, like all the rest. Yes, we searched the informant before he went into the apartment. Yes, we searched him when he came out. Yes, we had a written statement from him. Yes, we had the defendant identified, with pictures, before the buy. Yes, the defendant had a previous conviction for dealing heroin. Yes, a real police officer had handed the defendant the money and had received the heroin.

The jury went out and stayed out. Hours went by. These cases usually took an hour, hour and a half, tops. Not this one. The jury was out for five hours, then sent a message that they wanted to come back the next day. This was unheard of.

Thursday, a couple of us sat in the courthouse with the DA, waiting on the dawdling jury. The defendant was guilty as hell, and he needed to go. This would be his third drug conviction, and in Georgia that meant some real prison time. Not probation like all the defendants got in federal court in that era, but real prison time, maybe down at Reidsville where they kept the electric chair.

We finally got called to go into courtroom – the jury was returning. I sat in the front row and watched them file in. I looked straight at them, but most of them did not look at me. That was a bad sign. One older man, however, glared at me like I was Satan himself.

The jury had reached a verdict, all right. Not guilty! The judge slammed down his gavel, his face turning the color of tomato juice.

"Ladies and gentlemen of the jury. This is where I usually thank the jury for their service. I will not thank you, however. You have released into society a drug dealer who is as guilty as any man who has ever sat at that table. You are a disgrace to this state, and I plan to see that each of your names is permanently removed from the jury rolls of Fulton County. You are excused, with all the contempt that I am able to show."

You could have heard a mouse fart in the courtroom. The faces of the jurors now matched that of the judge, all but the older white gentleman, who it turned out was the foreman of this illustrious group. He was beaming.

Two days later, I had a phone call.

"Wayne, this is Paul from the DA's office. I thought you might like to know what happened on that heroin case the other day."

"Damn straight I'd like to know. What did you find out?"

"I interviewed that moron foreman. He swung that whole bunch."

"What is he, some kind of legalization nut, or what?"

"Looks like the *or what*. He convinced that whole jury that y'all had lied on the stand, that there was never any drug buy at all. His argument, and it's a doozy, was that if y'all had really bought drugs

142

from the guy, you would have had satellite pictures and video recordings of the whole deal. Said the Feds had all that stuff, and since you didn't show it, then you must have been lying."

"Shit, we can't even get batteries for our flashlights, and he wants pictures from inside the bad guy's apartment. I hope some junkie sticks a shiv in him for his last seventy five cents some night. Maybe then he'll understand."

"Don't be bitter!"

"Why not? It keeps me working these eighteen hour days, hanging out with scum. Some nights that's all that keeps me going."

△ △ △ △ △ △ △ △ △ △

LIFE WENT ON. I got to work one morning and noticed that the Toyota was gone. That was a good sign, maybe, depending on where it went.

"Don, what'd you do with the Toyota?" I knew better than to ask George.

"I took care of it. Don't you worry your big old Fed head."

"Seriously, Don, what did you do?"

"You really want to know. You really might not want to know, you know."

"Yeah, I really, really want to know."

"I parked it in a Tow Away zone late last night. It went to impound this morning, and I didn't have to do one single sheet of paper."

"Won't that come back and bite somebody in the ass?"

"The fool pleaded guilty last week, got five years to serve, and he's gone to Jackson Diagnostic. He ain't gonna need a car there or wherever else they send him. He won't be driving nothing but a state tractor for

143

the next five, and when he gets out, he won't even remember he had a Toyota. Anyway, I parked it pretty close to where we arrested him, and if we need us a story, I'll just say that's where he left it. We ain't done a piece of paper on it, and I know the Taco ain't gonna do one."

That took care of that. I didn't have my fingerprints on the deal, so it wasn't my worry. Anything to reduce the burden of paperwork on the government was a good thing.

Then we got to the joke.

"Hey, Wayne, you want to screw with the Taco a little?"

"Don, you know I'm always up for a little fun. What you got in mind?"

"I thought I might just ask the little greaser where his Toyota is."

"Could wait and ask him in the all hands meeting next week. That'd be a little slice of hell."

"Yeah, I could do that. Let me think about it."

We went on about our business. Pee Wee, a tall gangly black male who looked like a junkie, had gotten hot again, and we were buying dope every day. Truth was, Pee Wee wouldn't touch the shit, and he made a decent living selling us the dealers. His methodology was simple. He found a dealer, then lined him up as many customers as he could handle. Somewhere in the middle of the bunch was always a cop.

When the bust went down, the dealer would go looking for the snitch that set him up. Not often but occasionally, he would come to Pee Wee, and Pee Wee always had his story.

"Man, I brought you a dozen customers. I don't know who the cop was, do you?"

This act had served the CI well, and on more than one occasion, he took a cop back to buy off the same dealer who was out on bond waiting for his first trial.

But fate eventually caught up with Pee Wee. He was found shot to death in a garbage dump on the South Side. He deserved better.

We all mourned Pee Wee in our own ways, and then got back to business.

"Wayne, I got a better idea."

"Don, just what have you got a better idea about? We going to start selling dope instead of buying it?"

Don pulled the door to my office closed and started talking in a low voice.

"Instead of just busting George in the meeting, what if we make out like the doper has taken a warrant for George for car theft."

Now that had class. That was a championship idea.

"Don, maybe we could dummy up a warrant and show it to him. Maybe a copy of a warrant with his name spelled wrong or something."

"How can you misspell Faz?"

Time rolled on. We did stuff to other folk, and we had stuff done to us. As always, we hid from the bosses and did what we thought we were paid to do.

The new saying of the year arose.

"What does DEA stand for?"

"Don't Ever Ask. Forgiveness is easier to get than permission."

One night we were sitting in my little cubicle—Don, David Guy from Fulton County PD, Bob Taylor from APD—just going over the plans for the next week. We had a lot to do, and we were getting a little shorthanded. We were buying a lot of heroin, which usually meant black defendants because it wasn't popular with our white clientele, therefore the need for black undercover officers. We had used up the last two APD officers, who now were badly burnt on the street.

They, in the words of Don Sanford, "couldn't buy aspirin in a drug store."

Too many cups of coffee, I guess, and the conversation turned to George Faz and the Toyota.

"Wayne, what are you going to do about that Toyota? We got to get George on that. We can't just let him slide. He needs initiating."

Bob Taylor was stirring the pot. He had a wicked sense of humor and lived to pull pranks.

"Well, Don had the idea about doing a warrant, then showing it to him, but I don't know if that'll work."

"He's your little baby, you got to do something."

"I got an idea. We'll do Don's thing, but we can take it up a bit. Make it stronger."

"So, Bob, what you gonna do, have him arrested?"

That idea got out of control fast. Bob had worked at PD headquarters a long time and knew everybody there. He suggested, and those of us who should have known better went along, that we get a couple of auto theft detectives to come over with the warrant and serve it on George.

Poor George, sitting at home with his wife and kids, not having a clue of what was to befall him. We should have known better, we should have been more worried about the drug problem, about the safety of the citizenry, but it just seemed so easy and such a thing of beauty.

"Bernie, can I talk to you a minute?"

"Yeah, come on in."

My office was next to Bernie's. He had objected to my loud laugh, my taste in music, and my office mess. We weren't great pals. He was from a whole other era, and I sort of thought of him as one of the pre-Ice Age people.

I'm not sure what he thought of me, but today we came together.

"Bernie, remember that Toyota that Faz was supposed to seize?" I had to make my point, sell my story quick, or he'd be out hunting George's head.

"Yeah, goddamnit, what the fuck did he do with that? I'm gonna have his ass for this. Where's the car?"

"Boss, the car's taken care of. The city handled it."

The less said about that the better.

"I think we need to teach George a little lesson."

Well, Bernie agreed, and we began to make the late night plan into reality. I typed up a city arrest warrant, making the homeless bum the complainant and alleging that one George Faz had taken and converted to his own use a certain Toyota station wagon, valued in excess of $500.00. I even went so far as to sign the finished product for the judge. I think it is the only Atlanta City warrant ever signed by Earl Warren.

△ △ △ △ △ △ △ △ △ △

THE DAY ARRIVED for the big show. Working drugs is as close to theater as law enforcement gets, and this was, in fact, high drama. The two crew cut, blue suited, white handkerchiefed detectives arrived, parked the obvious Plymouth at the elevator in the basement, and took the elevator up to Bernie's office. Bernie paged Faz to come to his office, and everyone who was in on the story hid and tried to stifle the gut wrenching laughs that were unstoppable.

"George, these two men are from the Police Department. They need to talk to you."

As straight faced as Marine drill instructors, they looked at George like he was a grilled steak.

"We don't actually need to talk to you. What we need to do is read you your rights and place you under arrest."

It got real quiet, real fast.

"Sir, what do you mean? What would you arrest me for?"

"Automobile theft. We've had a complaint that you've stolen a Toyota station wagon, and a warrant was issued for your arrest."

"But, but—I didn't steal a car. We seized it."

Bernie the actor then came into his own.

"Well, actually, George, I haven't seen any paperwork on a seized Toyota. You'll have to go with these officers till I can get this straightened out. I'll have to call Chief Counsel to see if they will represent you. You'll need to leave your gun and credentials here."

An Academy Award performance if ever there was one. The two detectives told George they wouldn't handcuff him in the office, and all three walked out to the elevator.

Don, feeling guilty about starting this farce, walked with them. All rode down to the basement and then moved to the Plymouth. One detective opened the driver's door and got in, while the other stood with George at the rear passenger door. The standing detective got out his handcuffs and asked George to put his hands on the roof.

"Can I ride to the jail with him?"

"Sanford, you know better. Prisoners ride in the back, alone."

At this point, the driver started the Plymouth, the other detective slid into the passenger's seat, and the car rolled out of the basement, leaving George standing with his hands outstretched over where the car top had been.

George turned around to the elevator, stabbing the button like he wanted to kill it. A very small tear rolled down his cheek. He got into the arriving car and left the basement.

I was upstairs when he came off the elevator, and he flew past me like a jet.

He stormed into his office, slammed the door and stayed there the remainder of the day.

△ △ △ △ △ △ △ △ △ △

A LIFETIME LATER, George was a wheel in DEA, in charge of the entire polygraph program. He had risen to that point by his stellar performance doing native Spanish language polygraphs in the investigation of the torture and murder of Special Agent Enrique Camarena.

We met up with some other agents in a bar in Washington, all there for a Tech conference. George was drinking club soda with a twist, silent testimony to the devils he had fought for years.

George loudly called for attention and proclaimed to any and all that I was the best senior partner any agent ever had, that I was the one person that had chewed his ass and made him walk a chalk line when he was starting.

149

"All my other bosses let me get away with shit because I spoke Spanish and bought dope. Wayne made me work and do the right thing."

I remembered the Toyota and wondered if George did.

Bugs
Atlanta, 1974

WE WERE ALL sitting in the office, doing paperwork. We had just done a good thing, working a great CI who had turned us over twenty thousand pounds of marijuana, or *marihuana* as the Controlled Substance Act had spelled it and as we continued to spell it on all documents, and almost a quarter million dollars in cash. This was in the days just after DEA was formed, and we were all still carrying BNDD badges and credentials.

It was also before anyone had a glimmer of asset forfeiture, and we had turned the quarter million over to a confused IRS Tax Agent in Gainesville, Florida. He had no more idea of what to do with money than we did.

Bob Ginley was the RAC in Jacksonville, and the Operation Panhandle team was working for him. An old New York FBN agent, Ginley was a pure delight to work for. He backed his troops unquestioningly, and that support was always returned by guys who put out their best for him.

Bob walked into the squad bay and gave us a little sunshine — we could stop doing paper and get out on the street.

"The Alachua County guys and the Gainesville PD are following some mutt up the interstate this way. They're screaming for help, since they're about two counties outside their jurisdiction. Grab a couple of walkie talkies and go meet up with them."

Anything to get out of doing paperwork. Terry Fernandez, who was as anxious to get out as I was, beat me to the door. Tom Sprague was not far behind. The other guys working Panhandle would join up en route.

We took three cars, and headed south down I-95. Bob had given us a description of the Gainesville cars and their target, and he told us where they were the last time they were able to talk to their dispatcher.

We streamed onto the interstate and hurried south, trying to figure a point to meet them.

"Terry, you got a place in mind?"

"Hell, I don't have a clue. Let's go down about ten miles or so, then hunt an on-ramp northbound where we can sit and look for them."

We had worked closely with the drug squads of both the city and county in the marijuana case we had just completed, and we knew all of them by sight. One in particular stood out in my mind, since his name was also Wayne Smith, the only cop I had ever run into with the same name.

We got off, turned around, and put one car on the down ramp on the northbound side. Everybody else waited at the top of the ramp, well hidden from the highway.

"Hey, Terry, did Bob give you a clue of where these guys are going?"

"No, Wayne, that's why they're following them. If we knew where they're going we'd just go there and wait."

"Smartass."

"No. Bob said the Alachua guys knew this bandit, but had no idea about a destination. They said he might be coming to Jacksonville, though."

"I'm already packed to go home, so I'm ready for anything."

"Don't start that, I ain't even got a clean pair of drawers. This better be a short deal, right here in Duvall County."

We sat for almost an hour, waiting, watching every car that came by, looking for the Gainesville crew. Radio communications with local cops had always been a nightmare. I had worked deals where we had to use as many as four different sets of radios to communicate with all the troops involved. It can get people hurt.

We had a description of the target car, which we spotted first. The long bed Ford F-250 towing a Boston Whaler was hard to miss. Terry dropped in off the ramp, then slowed to match up with the Gainesville units.

I waited about thirty seconds and slid down the ramp in the big old Caprice I was driving. It was not fast, and it got really horrible gas mileage.

"T, you got the Gainesville units?"

"Yeah, I'm with one now."

"I'll go up and take the truck, and you can get them a radio."

"Gotcha."

I tucked in about six cars behind the big Ford. The driver was staying just below the speed limit, which was in itself suspicious. We cruised back north into Jacksonville. The Ford was camped in the center lane, hanging at the same speed, not sticking out, except for everyone northbound passing him.

"Terry, you got them a radio yet?"

"Yeah, I threw your brother one through his window. I wonder if I woulda had to pay for that sucker if I had missed."

"They'd take it out of your retirement."

"I ain't gonna live long enough to retire."

"Hey, A.W., you on the radio?"

Although his name was Wayne Smith, my brother, as Terry called him, preferred to be called by his initials. I hoped Terry had put the damned thing on the right channel before he tossed it through the window. Terry had been a professional football player before joining up with BNDD, and if anyone could have tossed the radio across a traffic lane and through the window, my money would have been on Big T.

"Hey, little brother, I'm here."

"So where the hell are we going?"

"Wayne, I thought this asshole was just driving over to the coast. We got no idea where he's going."

"So why are we following him?"

"He's a big time player in the pot business. Since we hit that last load with y'all, the market's been kinda slow. Maybe he's gonna meet up with a load crew."

"You got any more than that?"

"Yeah, he's been calling Jamaica about three times a day for the last two weeks."

"That's a clue."

△ △ △ △ △ △ △ △ △

WE ROLLED ON, past the I-10 interchange, still heading north. It was way past lunchtime, and none of us had eaten. I looked at my gas gauge, was surprised to see that I had over a half tank. We were right in

154

the middle of the 1974 gasoline crisis, and there had been days when we had to badge a filling station operator to get the tank filled. The long lines were subsiding a bit, but a lot of stations were still not allowing over ten gallons to a customer.

Soon the metro Jax area gave way to rural farm country, and we were headed straight to the Georgia line.

"Hey, A.W. This sumbitch going to New York?"

"You got me. We're gonna have to call home if he crosses that line. We ain't got much authority in Duvall County, and we damned sure ain't got none in Georgia."

"Don't sweat it, A.W. We got you covered. I'll deputize you when we cross the line."

"Terry, don't bullshit me, you ain't deputizing nobody."

The boat followed the Ford on north, across the state line into Georgia. Now we were on our own. There was soon to be a DEA office in Savannah, but as far as I knew, it wasn't operational yet.

"Hey, Sprague. You awake."

"Go ahead, Whalebody."

"You heard if the Savannah office is open yet?"

"You're the Georgia expert, you're supposed to know."

Tom Sprague was from the Tampa office, had been with us on Operation Panhandle from the beginning. An ex-customs Agent, Tom had come over to BNDD before the merger that had created DEA. Some of the folks he had hoped to get away from in Customs followed him at the merger, not making him very happy. At least once he had talked about trying to go back to Customs. The Treasury Department had the reputation of treating their agents a hell of a lot better than did Justice.

"I heard there was a guy coming up from South America to take the RAC job."

"Looks like we may be about to find out."

We drove on through Glynn county, then through what had once been three of the most corrupt counties in the state before former Governor Lester Maddox had sent the State Patrol in to break up a speed trap operation victimizing Yankees coming to Florida on vacation. Now I-95 allows them to bypass the whole area. Liberty, Long and McIntosh slid by, mostly rivers and swamps.

Our boy passed the first exits to Savannah, waiting till he hit the I-16 exit into town, then slid that big Ford eastbound. He drove like a stranger, haltingly, like he was looking for something. Once he got into the city, he went straight to a real estate office, moored the boat and truck, and went inside.

"Hey, A.W. Your boy gonna buy a house up here?"

"Hell, he owns a nice house in Gainesville."

"Yeah, but it's in Florida. I could see why a decent citizen might want to get out of that nest of Gators."

After about an hour in the real estate office, our lad came out, crawled into the cab of the Ford, and turned around. He headed out of town, toward Skidaway Island.

While he had been doing whatever he was doing inside the real estate office, I had hit a pay phone and called Atlanta. I learned that Gordon Raynor, the new Savannah RAC, had arrived and set up shop. He was alone, with no worker bees having yet been assigned to the office. I got a phone number for him, and I already had the phone numbers of the local narcs in Savannah from previously working this area out of Atlanta.

Of course, I was never asked to consider a job here. That would have made too much sense to send an agent who already knew the town and all the cops. Far better to bring someone from Paraguay or some other godforsaken hole.

Through Thunderbolt and on out to Savannah Beach our boy drove. We had gotten a good look at him in traffic, and he appeared to be following a brightly colored map that I guess he had gotten from the real estate agent.

This was not making a lot of sense. Till we could sit down and talk to the guys from Gainesville and get the rest of the story, we were in the dark completely.

"Okay, he's circling the block. He just came down this street in the other direction. Everybody back way off. I got the eyeball."

Sprague was watching the doper as he drove down the same block for the second time.

"He looking for a tail?"

"Naw, I think he's trying to find an address."

"Okay, he's got it. He's pulling into the drive of the third house from the corner. Big white house with a porch all around."

"Okay, I'm out of here. Let him sit a minute, Terry. Then you take a drive by."

Sprague gave orders like he was in charge. Truth was none of us was in charge. Ginley was in Jax, and we were on our own.

We worked like that. Whoever had the eye, whoever had a little extra knowledge took over. I never once heard an agent gripe about taking orders from a non-boss. We all just did what had to be done, and the guy with the hot hand did his best to keep the rest of us following a game plan. No prima donnas in this crowd.

I drove down the street in front of the house. The long haired driver of the Ford was standing at the edge of the street, pulling up a "FOR RENT" sign. We had just learned something.

"Our boy is pulling up a rental sign in the yard. Looks like he's here to stay a while."

△ △ △ △ △ △ △ △ △ △

OVER THE NEXT month, we introduced the cops from Florida to my friends from the Savannah Metro Squad. All the Gainesville cops rotated back home, grabbing up clothes and making explanations to families. They also spent a bit of time selling the idea to their bosses that they really needed to be back in Chatham County, Georgia.

The quarter million we had seized in Gainesville the month before was not the issue it became years later when the DEA asset sharing program put the bulk of seized money back into the treasuries of the locals. The issue now was that someone was doing something illegal, and that these guys had started the case, and that they had to see it through to the end. No good narc would ever do the work they had done, turn the case over to another bunch of cops, and walk off without a screaming match.

Terry, Wayne Henderson, Tom Sprague and the other Operation Panhandle agents also rotated back, to get clothes, gear, and make their goodbyes. I had all my stuff with me, since I was supposed to have been going home anyway.

I just checked into another motel room and settled in. We set up surveillance schedules and began to follow the suspect everywhere he went. He was a whiz at phone calls. This was pre-cellular phone, and we learned the house he had rented, at a princely sum, had no telephone.

He began to work a regular route of pay phones in the area. Gordon Raynor had fixed us up with administrative subpoenas, and with the cooperation of the local phone company, we knew about his calls almost as quick as he made them. He was calling dopers all over the southeast, and he was calling Jamaica, the same number over and over.

I phoned Marion Joseph, currently Acting Chief Pilot, and tried to get us an airplane for surveillance. Our cars could stay on this guy's bumper for only a limited time before he started waving at us when he left his driveway.

The airplane was not forthcoming. There just wasn't anything to be had. Joe was snowed under. Customs had dumped a bunch of military surplus helicopters on us at the time of the merger, but we didn't have any money to operate them. The whole air wing was bogged down from trying to deal with the budget problem.

On the other hand, the task force was currently working with funds assigned to Operation Panhandle. Bob Ginley had assured us that we had more money than we could spend and that, if we needed an airplane, we could rent one.

This was interesting. I had never been in such a situation before and wasn't sure it was exactly legal. Ginley was never one for following rules too closely, and when he gave the word, we found us a bird. Joe sent us a pilot and we were up and flying. The little Cessna 150 was not much of an air force, but it was getting us the relief we needed on surveillance.

Since I had had a lot of success with the small radio transmitters used to track cars, we decided to attach one to the Ford truck. Tommy Walton crawled up into the yard in the middle of the night and hung the "birddog" with its magnet mount way up under the truck.

The Ford was a three quarter ton, four wheel drive, which sat high off the ground. Tommy assured me that he had put the transmitter where it wouldn't be found. I hoped so, since I had already had one mailed back to me by a doper when his oil change garage had presented him with the unit.

159

△ △ △ △ △ △ △ △ △

THIS WAS THE job at its very best. We had cops from two totally different jurisdictions working together with a team of us pulled from all over the country. We were a good machine, doing so much that nobody had the time to bitch. We did what needed to be done, with what we had.

The "birddog" tracking receiver was working well from the cars, but our pilot, Wayne Henderson, kept insisting we try it in the airplane. We had the aircraft rented on an as needed basis, and we could usually get it when we had a need. Wayne, a former Navy flier, was soon to join the air wing as a full time pilot.

With a little duct tape and a lot of redneck engineering, we put the twin antennae for the unit on the struts of the Cessna. The plane's altitude gave us a tremendous boost in range. When we needed to find the Ford, we could put up the Cessna and locate it within a matter of minutes.

One afternoon at the Savannah airport, our pilot was approached by an employee of the Grumman Corporation. Their factory, where the G-5's were built, shared the runways of the Savannah Metro airport. The employee asked a lot of questions about the antennae hanging off the bottom of the Cessna.

He turned out to be an ex-Navy pilot also, and he and Henderson hit it off immediately. Within an hour, the engineers from Grumman had come over and taken the appropriate measurements from the struts of the Cessna.

Later that evening, they showed up with an aluminum spar complete with u-bolts. With holes drilled to space the two antennae the exact distance apart required, it fit neatly between the two struts. In an hour it was bolted on the Cessna, and we were in business for sure. We learned that they had shut down part of the production line to have the spar fabricated for us. Great folks.

On a Thursday morning our suspect got fired up early. He rolled out in the truck, without the boat following him. Within an hour, he had bought a second Boston Whaler, with trailer and motor, and dragged it back to the house at the beach.

When Tommy had sauntered into the boat dealer, he saw enough of the transaction to advise that our friend had paid in pure cash. The question of the day became just how one guy was going to operate two boats. This surely was going to be an offload from an ocean going vessel. Why here?

After we put him back in the house, the intermittent surveillance continued. We had tried to rent a house where we could watch him, but nothing was available, and the Savannah cops couldn't find a neighbor they trusted enough to approach.

We relied on the Cessna to track him down, even though one of the pilots declared the plane to be a flying deathtrap. Apparently the spar holding the antennae had brought the stall speed down to about sixty miles an hour.

△ △ △ △ △ △ △ △ △ △

ALL OUR WORK and time looked like it was about to pay off. Tommy had done a drive by and found the truck gone. When we put Air One up, the birddog led him to the truck in minutes. The guy was parked at the Mall on Abercorn Extension, actually near the new DEA office. The team was up and on him in a matter of ten or fifteen minutes, and a strange report followed.

"Wayne, you hear me."

"Go ahead, Terry."

"The guy's in the barber shop, getting his hair cut. All of it."

Our boy had shoulder length hair, and he had seemed to be very proud of it.

"Terry, say again."

"He's in the barber shop at the entrance to the mall. He's getting a crew cut. Maybe he's been drafted."

Terry, having gone into the mall with a handi-talkie in a paper bag, had a good eye on the suspect.

"Terry, stay with him. See what he's up to."

A little later, I saw Terry walking back to his car in the mall lot.

"T, what do you know?"

"He's gone into a health spa. I heard him asking if they had a sauna."

A haircut and a sauna. Maybe makeup at the department store counter next?

We pulled off the airplane and sat on the diesel truck. We hadn't had a clue the entire time we had been working on this guy, and now we were more confused than ever. Working a case like this from the outside, with no snitch, is a tough row to hoe. All this could be for nothing, in which case somebody was going to get screamed at for wasting the G's money.

An hour later, our lad, all trimmed, pink and healthy, came out of the mall, started up the big truck, and drove directly home. This was not a good sign. He went into the house, but them came straight back out. He had a folder under one arm and a cardboard box under the other. He stashed the stuff in the cab of the truck, backed around and hitched to the trailer of the Whaler at his house. The recently purchased one was still at the boat dealer.

Tommy peeled off, went to a pay phone, and called the pilot at the airfield, getting the Cessna back in the air.

The surveillance was short. From the house at the beach, back through Thunderbolt, back out Abercorn past the same mall, and on to a motel on the south edge of town. Our boy went into the lobby, came back out, and then drove around to the rear. He backed the boat trailer into a spot and unhitched and was off again.

I stayed behind and went into the motel, while the rest of the team went on with the truck.

"Hey, you the manager?"

"No, he's in the back room, doing the books. Why?"

"I need to talk to him."

"Just a minute."

The bald little mousey man from the back room showed up in a few minutes.

"Can I help you? Is there a problem with your room?"

"I don't have a room, but there is a problem. Can we talk in your office?"

After I explained the situation, the manager walked back to the front, returning with a card and a key. The card identified his newest guest, and the key was for a room directly over that of the guest in question. The identification on the card was not that of our boy from Gainesville, but that was no surprise.

I went out to my car, got a handi-talkie, and went to the room in the back. I had a great view of the trailered boat. I sat in a comfortably cool environment and waited for word from the surveillance. Since there was no repeater in Savannah and all radio communication was line of sight, I was no longer able to talk with the surveillance team, but I figured I'd be able to talk to the airplane once it got in the game.

In half an hour, I began to hear the airplane directing the surveillance. It sounded like the suspect had gone to the boat dealer and had hooked up the new boat. From the street names, I immediately realized that he was back en route to the motel.

"Air One, you copy?"

"Air One. Wayne, go ahead."

"Advise the units I have a room over the bad guy's room. I got the eye here."

"Wayne's got a room at the motel. He'll have the eye when the suspect arrives. Drop back, give him some room."

The truck slid into the back lot, backed the new boat into the slot next to the first one, unhitched, and then backed the truck into the next slot.

I watched with binoculars as he got out of the truck carrying the folder and the box. I could see into the box, which had three or four big old CB walkie talkies, binoculars, and some folded navigation charts. Damn, we were on — this deal was going to go, for sure.

"Terry, you copy?"

"Go, Wayne."

"He's got walkie talkies, maps, binoculars in the box. He's getting ready. I'm calling Gordon to get the Coast Guard and the Fish Police on standby."

△ △ △ △ △ △ △ △ △ △

IT WAS ALREADY late in the afternoon, and I thought the smuggler might sack out and get some sleep for a night time operation. I sat back from the window in a position where I could just barely see the top of the truck cab. Within a half hour, I had been joined in the room by a couple of the surveillance team, and we were expecting Gordon to show up any minute.

I knew that our boy would not be making phone calls from the room, and if the incoming load boat was as close as it seemed, he probably wouldn't be making any more pay phone calls either. One hot question in the room was why the need for two boats.

There had to be somebody else to drive the second boat, but we had never seen our boy meet with any locals. Maybe he had a friend on the load boat? It was a question that would never be answered.

A tap on the door, and I opened to let Gordon in.

"I got everybody and their brother on standby. Customs down in Brunswick is getting both their boats ready, and the Game and Fish people are at the dock, waiting. What do you think?"

"Looks good. He's been in the room for over an hour. The desk will call if he makes a call, but nothing yet. We'll just have to wait and see."

Like all dope deals, this one involved more waiting.

"He's coming out."

One of the Savannah Metro cops was at the window. He watched the suspect walk to the truck, carrying the same box and folder he had brought in.

"Don't get too close to the window. Let me know if he does anything else."

I moved over nearer to the window, unable to just sit and not watch. The driver's door was standing open, and the young man stood, sorting through the stuff in the cardboard box he had placed on the seat. I picked up my binoculars, hoping to get a better look at what he was doing.

What I saw him do made my heart stop. He stood up from the cab, holding a small black box in his hand. He extended an antenna from the box, and started twiddling the control on its face.

"What the hell is that?"

"It looks like a Radio Shack field strength meter. If it is, we got a problem."

"Why? What does it do?"

"It picks up radio signals. It'll find that damned birddog bug in about one minute if he knows what he's doing."

"How would he know what frequency? Ain't that some kind of big secret?"

"That gizmo doesn't need the frequency. It sees the whole spectrum, and the needle swings when you get close to the emitter. It's idiot simple. We're screwed."

The young man adjusted the meter to his liking and started to move around the truck, holding the antenna low and moving it under the truck. When he got to the driver's side door, he leaned down and swept the antenna under the area below the floorboard of the cab.

Tommy had put the bug up above the transmission and had dangled the antenna down between the transmission case and the floorboard on that side of the truck.

The young man suddenly stood erect, and started looking around the parking lot. He was rooted in place, looking like Custer watching for the Lakota. He walked to the rear of the truck and started back toward the front, holding the antenna of the device well under the truck frame.

This time when he got to the cab, he stopped, collapsed the antenna, and walked back to the passenger side. He tossed the device into the box, closed and locked the door, and walked back to the driver's side door.

"Wayne to surveillance. The guy's made the beeper on the truck. We're burned! Hold on."

Smoke clouded from the exhaust of the diesel, and the truck backed up, swinging around so that it approached the first boat. The young man jumped out, connected the trailer hitch, and drove slowly out of the back lot.

"All units, he's coming out. He made the beeper, and he's coming out. Give him plenty of room. Air One, you up?"

△ △ △ △ △ △ △ △ △ △

ALL THIS WORK down the drain because of ten dollars worth of transistors from Radio Shack.

"Air One, you got him?"

"Air One. Got the bird dog, and I'll have an eyeball in two."

"Ground units, hold and let Air One take him away."

The airplane did what it does best, and the truck was watched as it made its way back to I-95. A quick conference on the radio had resulted in the Gainesville units leading the ground surveillance as the truck took the southbound on-ramp.

I sat in the room and listened as the team moved onto the highway and began to take their positions behind the truck.

The rest was simple. The young man drove straight back the 220 miles to his house in Gainesville. He pulled the truck inside his fenced lot, disconnected the trailer, and backed out. He locked the gate, drove non-stop back to Savannah, picked up the second boat, and repeated the procedure. When he arrived at home the second time, he went in, after locking the gate, and locked himself in the house.

A week or so later, we got a court order from a federal magistrate allowing us to enter onto the property and remove the birddog. The young man never came out of the house, but I think I saw him looking through the curtains.

In the words of one of the veterans of the Miami coke wars, "Sometimes you eat the bear, sometimes the bear eats you."

Bear Creek

Atlanta, 1975

HE WAS A hell of a snitch. One of the kind they make the rule for, the rule that you don't have a personal relationship with a confidential informant, period. That period at the end was always emphasized. Zeke Black was that kind of guy. He had walked into our office, and offered his services unasked. No pending case on him, no money requested, just wanted to be of some help to us.

Hell, he had never even been arrested. He had done a couple of tours in Nam, flying A-6's, right in the dirt, doing close ground support. He now flew for fun and built houses for a living.

Big and gruff guy, like you might have pictured a real war hero. Zeke had met up with some fellows who were interested in having him do a little flying, and at first he was tempted.

"Yeah, they wanted me to make a trip to Mexico, pick up a little something, and make us all rich."

Zeke tugged at the Rolex GMT on his beefy wrist. The watch looked small on the man, and it's not a small watch.

Zeke didn't look like a pilot, many of whom are short and wiry. He was blond, with hairy forearms, calluses, and a sunburn. He worked for a living, and you could see it. The thinning hair displayed the reddened skin of his head, and for some reason he looked Irish to me.

"I was having a beer, actually a few beers, at a place called the Stone Pony on the south side, down below the airport, and we got to talking about one thing and another, and somebody got to talking about the guy flying under the arch in St. Louis. Set me off, real bad."

Ron looked at him with a gleam in his eye, and said, "How'd that set you off?"

"Hell, that ain't no big deal. I've flown through shit that would make that look like pushing a stroller through the Grant Park Zoo. I got my hackles up and started bragging about my airplane driving. It was the beer talking. I just shot my mouth off way too much. Next thing I know, one of the long haired hippie sumbitches was buying me beers and listening to my bellowing like I was the second coming."

An interesting description that fit the majority of the patrons of both genders at the Pony.

"Zeke, you didn't get a name on any of the maggots, did you?"

"Not to start with. I ain't got no use for these long-haired sumbitches at all, and I didn't particularly give a rat's ass what their names are. I still remember how we got treated after Nam, and I ain't the forgiving type. Hated the bums then, still do. Anyhow, I got a moment of clarity, seen a hole in the clouds, and got the hell out of there. Went home drunk, and the ol' lady just about wore me out. One of the reasons I'm here, to square it with her. I figure if I do some of this secret agent stuff, she'll ease up about my drinking and cut me a little slack."

I had been on the job a little over ten years, and I thought I had heard every reason to become a CI, but this was a new one. Joe, my old

170

first partner, had always said that no matter what they tell you, it's never the real reason they want to snitch. You may get to know them, work with them, but you will almost never know why they do what they do.

One of the forms we fill out always has the blank space for "CI's Motivation." I've always wanted to quote Joe, or just put "Beats the shit out of me" in the blank.

△ △ △ △ △ △ △ △ △ △

RON METCALF WAS senior to me by a mile. He had been an agent with the old Federal Bureau of Narcotics in Detroit and Chicago. He was as smooth as a baby's butt, having a degree in English Literature and known to quote Kipling in times of distress as well as in times of beer induced euphoria. He had been a trip to work with, and I had learned a lot from him, not all good.

He, like me, hated the book, and was always looking for ways to shortcut the paperwork and the system. He was new to the South, and the marijuana smugglers of the area presented a new experience for him. He seemed to be drinking the informant's story in, and I always assumed he was writing a novel in his head while we worked.

I knew way too much about smugglers, had spent way too many nights lying in mosquito-infested swamps by runways at deserted airstrips all over South Georgia. I had lost a lot of the desire necessary to get up for one of the long expeditions into the dark. GI bug repellent eating up the strap of a watch, chiggers invading my whole body, and me wandering lost in a boggy pine forest for hours were not fond remembrances.

"Zeke, we have to get a set of prints, a nice Polaroid photo, suitable for framing, and a personal history so that we can get you documented as working for us. I'll get you on down to the ID room, and we'll take care of that right now."

In talking to him I was careful not to say snitch, informant, CI or any of the other buzz words we used. I got the feeling he would be insulted at the terminology, and I didn't want to piss him off so early in the game.

"By the way, it's probably better you don't go home telling your old lady about this till we get a little further along. Beauty Shop gossip, you know."

"I've had the clearances and the briefings. I know a little about operational security. I also know this one guy at the Pony was serious. He was buying me beers as fast as I could drink them, and he wasn't drinking at all. I was worried at first that he was one of y'all, and was trying to set me up."

Ron was standing, leaned against the wall as I rolled the prints. I always rolled the prints. I was too good at it, and it always seemed to fall my lot.

Ron smiled and said, "How do you know he isn't one of us?"

I felt the muscles in Zeke's arm tighten and heard a sharp intake of breath. It probably did look a little strange, after all. He had walked in, and was now having a mug shot and fingerprints taken. He relaxed slightly and breathed deeply.

"Well, if this is a game, it's a hell of a good one. I just can't see you guys wasting all this time on me. If I was a target in this thing, I figure I'd be handcuffed, and sitting in an interview room with bright lights shining in my face, stead of drinking your sorry coffee, and acting like we're all bosom buddies. If you want me for this, you got me. If I done wrong, then go ahead and take me away."

Ron started to laugh. The twinkle in Zeke's eye had given him away, and he began to laugh as well. At least he had a good sense of humor. I hate working with people who can't take a joke.

Over the next few weeks, we started to narrow down the possibilities for Zeke's smugglers. We identified a couple of patrons of the Stone Pony who were involved in some heavy-duty pot dealing, but we still hadn't found the guy who had approached Zeke.

He, of course, went back to the pub and had a few beers every day after work. I began to wonder if this was all just a front to keep his wife off his ass for spending so much time drinking. He had told her a little about what we were doing, and it had eventually fallen to me to go out to the subdivision in Fayette County, identify myself to his wife, and cover his absences.

I had about lost hope in the venture, when the call came on an early Wednesday morning.

"I finally found the bastard!"

"So, you want a medal or what. Who is he? You got anything at all?"

"Got his phone number, got his tag number, got it all! This show is on the road now, for sure."

"Okay. We got to meet, like now. Name a place."

"Waffle House on Old National Highway in thirty minutes."

"I'm on the way."

Apparently I wasn't the only devotee of Waffle Houses for meetings. I had always preferred them for the anonymity, but now my snitches were picking them as well. Maybe Zeke liked the coffee.

We met, and I got a name, a phone number and a tag number. The name was totally unknown to me, but I could do the basic checks that would tell me if this was a real player, or just some wannabe with a big mouth, living out scenes from *Miami Vice* in his head.

He turned out to be Johnny Turnbull, a small timer with aspirations. The mope had a couple of marijuana arrests, a fine and some probation, but no jail time and no serious history.

But one small nugget, tucked away in the files, washed to the surface. One of his arrests had been in the company of a young lady with a fascinating past. Married to a Southern Bell telephone installer, Angela King had started as a Bunny at the Atlanta Playboy Club.

Angela and hubby later showed up operating a hotel in Jamaica, and both were reputed to be the connection for most of the pot coming into the area from the island. Word on the street had been that you could go, check in, drink a few of those cute drinks with the umbrellas, get a tan, and arrange delivery of a ton or so of really high quality, mountain grown sinsemilla, all on a long weekend.

Angela now lived north of Atlanta, and street word was that she was again brokering multi-ton marijuana deals from her half million dollar home up on Lake Lanier.

△ △ △ △ △ △ △ △ △ △

GIVEN THE POSSIBILITIES, we began the long march to permission for our CI to fly into Mexico, the current source of preference for Turnbell, and fly back with a ton and a half of pot.

This was not as simple as one might imagine. In the old days, we just did things like this—no harm, no foul. We never told the Mexican government, since the possibility our snitches were getting the dope directly from the army or the police was very high.

Now, in a newer and more cooperative era, we were required to notify our Mexico City office, who in turn notified the Mexican government, and we would all then wait for permission to proceed.

I assumed it was also to give the Mexicans time to make sure the government wasn't selling the load. If we got a "go," then we would have to send all the details in teletype to Headquarters and Mexico City, prior to takeoff. It also assured that if the CI got caught up in some unusual enforcement activity by the Mexicans, we would have some hope of getting him back in one piece. That had not always been the case.

We struggled on till we actually had the green light, and Zeke was ready to go flying for his government again. He had Turnbull front the money to rent a pretty nice old C-47 for the trip.

Zeke had not been able to get beyond the guy himself. We had tried every stall in the book to meet the people Turnbull represented, but we had had no luck. I had told Zeke to ask for an unreasonable amount of money up front, for the airplane and personal expenses, not to be deducted from his price for flying the load.

Although I had felt sure the demand would bring the principals out of the woodwork, Turnbull himself showed up with the cash in hand, and hadn't tried to negotiate Zeke down even a dollar.

It now looked like this was going to go all the way, and we geared up for the eventual take down and arrests.

I asked Zeke which airport he thought was best for the return to CONUS, or the Continental United States to nonmilitary types. He had suggested a couple of places, and we drove out and looked them over, but none seemed to fit the bill.

We needed a place with a runway long enough to handle the C-47, one with good cover for the bad guys to hide the unload crew and vehicles during the wait and one that allowed for us to have a vantage point to watch these goings on.

"Zeke, how about Bear Creek, down by the Atlanta International Raceway in Spalding County? Ever flown out of there?"

"That would work. It's long enough, and there ain't nobody around at night. We ought to be able to unload there without stirring up a hornet's nest of security guards and local police. I've flown in there late at night, and there wasn't a soul on the property. It sounds like a fine place for this."

"I'll run down tonight late, check it out. If it looks okay, I'll give you a call in the morning, and you can tell this turd Turnbull that you got a place, and let him have his people come take a look. I sure would like to get a peek at some of the other players in this episode. My paper would look better if it had some other names."

"I've tried everything you told me to get past him, but there don't seem to be a way around him. He just ain't talking about who else might be in this besides him."

"We'll just have to play this out and see who shows up for the party."

△ △ △ △ △ △ △ △ △

WE PLAYED. ZEKE had the airplane ready. Turnbull had given him the aeronautical charts with the Mexican strip marked. There was also a typed list of radio frequencies, times for contact, and call signs. Seemed pretty professional.

Turnbull must have been making all his calls from a pay phone, as his home phone records had shown nothing to link him with anyone else in the operation. We had a go date, and everyone in the office was starting to ask about surveillance schedules and assignments.

The entire task force was going to be used for the surveillance and arrests, but scheduling was going to be tricky. Although everybody wanted to be there for the take down, this was not possible, as we were not sure which night Zeke might be returning to us from Mexico.

We were sure that he would at least overnight in Mexico, but we never knew what might happen down there, and a stay of several nights was not out of the question. We would have no method of communicating with him after he left US airspace, but we had a radio network scheduled for his return.

If the Mexicans decided to send someone back with him, our problem would mushroom. It would not be the first time, and we all dreaded the possibility.

On Tuesday evening, Zeke lifted off in the C-47, with Turnbull parked beside the runway at Bear Creek. We followed Turnbull back to his apartment and left a team on him. The rest of us went home to get our last good night's sleep for what would turn out to be a mostly sleepless week.

On Wednesday, we set up surveillance at Bear Creek. One team was still sitting on Turnbull, and the remainder of the cars and agents were hiding inside the grounds of Atlanta International Raceway. We had approached the management earlier and had gotten access to a space for the cars, completely out of sight.

177

The team on Turnbull was to fold in with the rest of us when he came to the strip with the off load crew. We sat and waited. No one wanted to go home, and as a result, many slept in their cars, not wanting to miss out on the deal.

By Friday morning, we were a smelly, cold, scruffy looking lot, with red eyes and beard stubble.

Friday evening the team on Turnbull reported that he had gone to a motel on I-75 South, just north of I-285, and appeared to be meeting with a group of males in one of the rooms. There were two vehicles parked in front of the room, a Ford pickup with a camper shell, and a very large motor home, both with Virginia plates.

This threw us into a quandary. If the players were from Virginia, we were not prepared to convoy the load all the way. We didn't have enough reserves, and we had made no contact with offices that would be en route.

We still hoped the load was going up to Angela's place on Lake Lanier. Maybe the Virginia people were here to buy the entire load, but we were all convinced that Angela was involved.

As always, we never had enough intelligence information, or at least information we could depend on, to make really good plans or decisions. Trouble was, we had to go ahead and make the plans based on what we knew, or hoped we knew. We had no other choice.

About dark, our base radio operator, a truly green rookie, called. FAA had contacted the office, and passed on a radio communication they had received on the frequency and call sign we had arranged with Zeke.

The cryptic message indicated that he was loaded, alone, and on his way. We hunkered down. The December night was clear, good weather for flying, but bitingly cold. A lot of guys were searching trunks for extra clothing to bundle in for the night.

"One Twenty-One to One Ten"

"One Ten. Go ahead"

"One Ten, bad guys out of the room, loading into three vehicles."

It was about one in the morning, and it looked like we were on for tonight. I got everybody back into their cars and buttoned down.

"One Ten to the Eyeball."

"Eyeball. Go."

"Looks like the trucks are moving."

One unfortunate agent at a time had been rotating into the woods at the edge of the runway, serving as our eyeball to watch for any activity on the airstrip. In the current weather, about two hours was the maximum. The low powered radio the eyeball carried couldn't pick up the other surveillance team set up on the load crew at the hotel, so it was my duty to maintain communications.

"One Ten to Eyeball. You okay for the duration?"

"I had a hunch we were about ready. I got on three pair of long johns. I'm as ready as I can get."

△ △ △ △ △ △ △ △ △ △

WE WAITED.

"One Twenty-One to One Ten. We're headed toward I-85, coming your way."

"One Ten. Clear."

The team doing surveillance on the offload crew was operating on a separate channel, with just the lead switching over to keep us advised.

They should be arriving in forty-five minutes or so. Not much traffic on the roads this late.

"One Ten to base."

"Base. One Ten, go ahead."

"Base, tell Air One to fire up and stand by."

"Base. Will relay to Air One."

I always called him Air One. He had a radio number like the rest of us, but we went way back together. We had worked on a lot of stuff, including the great Phoenix project, wherein BNDD got its first aircraft. Ludlow went on to become one of our best surveillance pilots, and I went on to be just another agent, but that's another story.

△ △ △ △ △ △ △ △ △ △

TIME PASSED EVER so slowly.

"One Twenty-One to One Ten."

"One Ten. Go."

"We're approaching the turnoff to the airport. Got three. Motor home, pickup, and the Mustang that Turnbull's been driving."

"One Ten. Gotcha."

"One Ten to Eyeball."

"Eyeball. Go."

"Entering the property as we speak."

"Got the headlights."

"Keep me advised."

"Eyeball. Ten four."

Sitting in a dark car away from the scene, imagining what is going on, can drive you nuts. I knew Gary would let me know what he saw as soon as I needed to know. But I still got twitchy when I didn't hear anything.

More time passed.

"Base to One Ten."

"One Ten. Go base."

"One Ten, the bird is in the pattern."

"One Ten copies."

"One Ten to Air One."

"Flint Three Fifty Seven. Go ahead, One Ten."

"Mudhole, the bird is in the pattern."

"Flint Three Fifty Seven copies. I'm orbiting about ten miles south of your location. Got to stay out of Hartsfield's hair for now. Got clearance to go through if I need to."

"One Ten. Clear."

Now the surveillance team from the motel joined us at the racetrack, and we all sat together. Gary George had the eye, and we waited on the word.

"Eyeball to One Ten. They have a radio out, calling for our boy."

We were always equipment poor. I would liked to have had an aircraft band receiver to monitor this traffic, but times were hard, and we just didn't have the money to buy all the neat toys we needed.

The deep rumble of a pair of Curtiss Wright radials cut through the cold air, and I knew the C-47 was on the way down. Radial engines always remind me of a Harley Davidson engine. Old-fashioned, twenties technology that just won't die.

"One Ten to the units. He's on the way in."

The landing lights of the C-47 cut through the dark, and the old bird lumbered down onto the runway. Slowly, slickly, Zeke put the bird onto the asphalt, with nary a chirp.

"Wayne, they're taking the pickup over to the plane. All five guys with the truck."

"One Ten to eyeball. Got you."

"One Ten to surveillance. Looks like they're loading the pickup first. He may roll out when he has his load. One Twenty-Three, One Thirty-One, One Thirty-Four, One Twenty-Eight, all go with the truck if he leaves alone."

"One Ten. Air One."

"Flint Three Fifty-Seven. Go ahead, One Ten."

Old Ludlow was really proud of that Flint call sign. It let him talk on military radio frequencies and land at military installations. Well, he'd always just be Mudhole to me, and I'll call him Air One as long I got a radio.

"Air One, if the first load vehicle leaves before they get the second loaded, you go with the first team. I'll need comms with them, and you will be the only way we got to relay."

"Air One. Gotcha."

The red Ford with the camper shell loaded quickly and left almost immediately. The selected units strung out behind him as he started north toward the city.

Ludlow in the Helio Courier loitered overhead, slowed down to the speed of mere cars, and followed, keeping us advised of landmarks as they passed.

"Eyeball to One Ten. They're loading the motor home. Looks like most of the load is going into it."

"One Ten to eyeball. Gary, start trying to crawl out of there if you can. We're split now, and we're gonna need all the help we can get."

"Wayne, I'm coming out now."

Gary had done two tours in Nam and was as good in the brush as anyone I had seen. He would be a lot of help. He was a cool head in a problem and fast on his feet.

"One Ten to the units, move out and take up positions on the road out. We'll pick up the motor home as it leaves. The bird has gone north with the other team, and we'll have to do this the hard way."

△ △ △ △ △ △ △ △ △ △

THE SURVEILLANCE WAS uneventful as we passed through the southern suburbs and into the Atlanta area. The motor home was slow, and our biggest problem was holding our speed down to match it without bunching up and becoming obvious.

With an aircraft overhead, it would have been much easier. If the airplane could have taken the eyeball slot, all the cars could hang back a mile or two totally out of sight, and then catch up as needed.

We had one problem. We had only one aircraft, and it was working the pickup truck.

We had one other minor problem. The law. We were working what was, in fact, a smuggling case. We didn't exactly have jurisdiction over smuggling violations, but that was not the major problem.

We also didn't have what is known as border search authority, which allows warrantless search of any items brought into the country that have not been processed by Customs at the border, no matter where they are located. It's a long story, but back in the days of the Bureau of Narcotics and Dangerous Drugs, we were involved in what the media chose to call a turf war with U. S. Customs.

BNDD had had primary jurisdiction over drug cases, but Customs had jurisdiction over smuggling cases. The problem arose when the smugglers were smuggling drugs, which they usually were. To end the "turf war," the Drug Enforcement Administration was created out of the entire BNDD plus about 500 U.S. Customs agents.

The deal was to have been that the new DEA agents would have the old Customs border search authority. After the merger and the creation of DEA, Customs backed out on the agreement to give border search authority to the DEA agents, and we were back in the same old loop.

To solve that problem I had borrowed four U. S. Customs Patrol Officers to work this case with us so that the border search authority would be available. These guys were great officers, two from the local office in Atlanta and two from the office in Savannah. We had all worked together on other deals, and they fit in well with the cops from the Task Force.

It was strange, but I was the only DEA agent on the ground surveillance. All my guys were local cops, deputized to work in the Task Force. George Faz was manning the Base radio.

"Base to One Ten."

"One Ten. Go, Base."

"One Ten, I got word from One Twenty Three. They are north bound on I-85, approaching I-285 on the north side."

"One Ten to Base. Ask Flint to go to channel three."

"Base copies."

It was a crystal clear December night. Well below freezing outside. Inside the car I was sweating. To get the chill off, I had the heat turned up way too high when we started moving and had been too distracted to turn it down.

I cracked the window and cranked the heat back, letting in a little fresh air. It wasn't very pleasant in the Buick after three days of eating and sleeping in the ride.

"Flint Three Fifty-Seven to One Ten."

Even though he was thirty miles ahead, I could hear the aircraft as if he were next to me on the highway. That line of sight thing.

"One Ten to Flint. Let me know on this channel when y'all turn off the expressway. We're expecting a turn up toward Lake Lanier, and I'd like to know if they take it."

"Flint Three Fifty-Seven copies. I'll let you know."

△ △ △ △ △ △ △ △ △ △

WE ROLLED ON through downtown Atlanta, plodding behind the motor home. We swapped out point position a couple of times to give them a different set of headlights in their rearview, just in case they were looking. Some of the guys had gone to the trouble of rigging switches to turn off a headlight or a parking light, just to make their cars less identifiable on surveillance. Most hadn't.

"Flint Three Fifty-Seven to One Ten."

"One Ten. Go ahead, Air One."

"Wayne, we're passing up the cutoff to Gainesville. This guy is hammering on, doesn't look like he's gonna turn off."

"Mudhole, let me know if he makes another ten miles without turning off. We're not gonna let them drag us out into another state with this deal."

"One Ten to Base."

"Base. Go One Ten."

"George, see if you can get State Patrol headquarters on the phone, and get the Officer in charge to talk to you. We may have to get this turkey in the truck stopped on the interstate."

"Base copies. I'll let you know what I get."

185

Time slowed down to a crawl. All our plans were based on the sliver of intelligence about Turnbull's connection with Angela. If that turned out to be smoke, we were going to have to take some unplanned action, with little time to put it together.

"Flint to One Ten."

"One Ten. Go, Air One."

"Wayne, they're way past any turnoff to get them to the area we discussed. What do I tell the surveillance crew?"

"Mud, tell them I'm working on a plan to stop the truck on the freeway. Tell One Twenty-Three that they are not to allow that truck to leave the state. We want them as close to home as we can get."

"Flint copies."

Well, now we go to Plan B, only we ain't got a Plan B. We'll just have to make one up as we go along.

"One Ten to Base."

"Base. Go."

"Any luck with the troopers?"

"I got a Sergeant from headquarters over on Confederate Avenue on the line. He says you got anything they can give us. He wants details."

"George, run the deal down to him. Don't hold back anything. Tell him we will not let this load leave the state, and we are going to need his help to get the lead truck stopped on I-85. I'm trying to come up with a location now. Ask him what he's got up just south of the line, around Franklin County. Call me as soon as you get a status from him."

"One Ten, stand by."

"Base, One Ten."

"One Ten, go."

"Wayne, he heard what you said, and he's moving all his north units toward I-85 right now. He says he'll have at least three patrol units on I-85, south of the line in fifteen minutes."

God, I love it when cops are allowed to just do what they do, without having to ask six layers of administration for permission. This would not have happened as quickly in the middle of the day, middle of the week.

"George, tell him I said thanks, and we'll be in touch with a projected location in a minute or two."

△ △ △ △ △ △ △ △ △ △

I KNEW THE area up there pretty well since I had taught high school in Franklin County years before. I grabbed the state map from the briefcase on the passenger seat and started looking for an exit to stage the arrests. It looked like the exit at State Highway 51 would do okay. seemed to be a good off ramp, and it was just south of Carnesville, the county seat.

That would make it easy for putting the bad guys in the county jail. We would try the case in state court, since the Task Force never took cases to federal court. In Georgia, state court meant real prison time, and that was what counted.

"One Ten to Base."

"Base. Go ahead, One Ten."

"George, tell that Sergeant that we would like to do this at the State 51 exit off I-85. See if he can get his units that way, and we'll have you relay between Flint and the Troopers."

"Base, One Ten. I gotcha. I'll advise the Sergeant."

"One Ten to the units. We're going to take the lead truck down on the highway before he can get out of the state. Looks like they don't have the Virginia plates just for show. We'll take this one up to where the first one gets stopped, have all our eggs in one basket."

We rolled on. I was in a car by myself, mostly because I like it like that. I had the Customs guys doubled up with my Task Force agents in two man cars. We had plenty of people to do this, but we didn't have fancy sirens and PA systems in our cars, so we would let the marked Troopers do the stop.

The last thing I wanted to happen was for the bad guys to think they were getting robbed instead of arrested.

"One Ten to Base."

"Base. Go ahead."

"Base, we're going to switch over to channel three. I'll be able to talk to Flint way after I lose comms with you. Let Flint pass anything on to me that you get from the Troopers."

"Base copies."

In a very few minutes, I heard from Flint. Ludlow radioed me that the Troopers were in position, just south of Highway 51, and the truck was only a few miles short of the trap. We drove on, poking along on the interstate.

"Flint Three Fifty-Seven to One Ten."

"Go ahead, Ludlow."

"Wayne, they got the truck stopped at 51. Two in custody and your guys on the ground report that the Customs Patrol Officer has done a border search, and the load is there. Says it looks like about eight or nine hundred pounds."

"Lud, you headed back this way?"

"I'm southbound now. Give me a landmark."

188

"I'm looking."

△ △ △ △ △ △ △ △ △ △

IN A MATTER of a few minutes, the aircraft was overhead, and now we could drop way back out of sight of the motor home, and let the airplane do its thing. I reached over and turned up the CB radio under my dash. I was monitoring Channel 19, the truckers' talk around channel.

It had suddenly dawned on me that the truckers would have seen the traffic stop and might be putting it on the CB. I was right, and it scared me. They were giving great details on the stop and arrest, which the great bulk of the motoring population could hear.

"One Ten to the units. Did anyone notice if there was a CB antenna on that motor home? We already got all the good buddies telling everybody in the world about the arrest up north."

I got several opinions, but no one knew for sure if there had been an antenna. I could not imagine anyone would have a rig like that without a CB, but I guess anything could be possible. We drove on, slowly heading toward South Carolina.

"One Ten to Flint Three Fifty-Seven."

"Flint. Go."

"Lud, call base and ask George to tell the Troopers to stand by to assist us with the stop on the motor home."

"Way ahead of you, Wayne. I spoke with One Twenty Three at the scene, and they have the truck off the highway, hidden behind a service station. The bad guys are in the back of a Sheriff's car, and the Troopers are ready for number two."

"I shoulda known. You done good. Thanks, Lud."

I was up front at point, where I always wanted to be on a surveillance. Traffic was zooming around us, and the traffic on the CB was getting more and more intense. Details of the arrest and seizure of drugs was now the number one topic.

The drivers couldn't talk about anything else, with the location of the stop now more widely known than where drivers could get speed or get laid in the cabs of their rigs. This was going to cause us a problem, but there seemed to be nothing we could do. With the aircraft overhead, we were totally out of sight of the motor home, and at least we wouldn't burn the tail.

"One Thirty-One to One Ten."

"Go ahead, One Thirty-One."

"One Ten, I got a TV news crew in a marked unit passing me now. They got a camera running on the road in front of them. Looks like we got burned bad."

"One Ten. I'll handle it."

I dropped speed immediately and let all the other cars slide by me. In a moment, the news car moved up on my bumper, then passed me. I immediately turned on my Kojak blue light that I had stuck on the dash, and the news car pulled over onto the shoulder. I knew we were only a few miles from the arrest site and felt that if I could just delay these guys for a couple of minutes, I could keep them out of the way.

As soon as we were stopped, I got out and walked to the driver's side front window of the car. The driver had his window down and was already shouting about needing to get moving.

"Folks, I got to ask y'all to stay back just a bit. I'm with federal narcotics, and we got something going on here that you'll spook if you keep on with the cameras."

I had my badge out in front, and expected a blast about the first amendment and journalistic rights. What I got surprised me.

"If you can give us some good shots, we'll back off. We just want to get as much film as we can. You know, pictures of the dope and the two guys."

They already knew about the pot and the two arrests. This was beginning to sound even worse than I had expected. I was debating just how to handle the situation when the talking head in the back seat rolled down his window. He was the evening news guy on the channel and smooth as glass.

"Officer, we've heard all about the arrests and seizure over the scanner, and we just wanted to get some film for tomorrow. You could help us, and maybe we can help you. I can guarantee you some primetime coverage. We know there's another load on the road, and we'd like to get some real action footage of the stop and arrest."

Now I was really worried. They knew about the first arrest *and* the second truck. This was definitely not a good thing.

"Look, I can't let you guys get into the arrest situation, but I'll give you all the access I can when it's over. Promise. Just hang back a bit, and I'll get you everything I can."

They seemed to be satisfied, and I didn't want to hang on there and wait to see if they were in total agreement. I went back to the Buick and blew the carbon out of the engine. Catching up with the surveillance would not be easy, so I was detailing everything I knew into the radio.

"One Ten to One Thirty-One."

"Go ahead, Wayne."

"Bill, see if you can pass the motor home, stay in his lane just ahead of him. You can slow down, make it easy to stop him. Just stay a car length or two in front of him."

"One Ten to One Twenty-Three."

"One Twenty-Three. Go ahead."

"One Twenty-Three, tell the Troopers to stop the motor home before it gets to the off ramp. Bill will be in front of it, and he'll slow them down a bit more. Should be an easy stop."

"One Ten, I'm advising the Troopers now. I'm with the dope, got one Trooper with me."

"One Twenty Three, we're approaching the exit. If I remember, there's a downhill run to the exit, steep drop-off on the left, and a high bank on the right. Nowhere to go."

"One Twenty Three. That's right, One Ten. Troopers in position to stop just over the top of the hill, on the down slope."

"Bill, you in front of the motor home?"

"That's correct, One Ten."

I was last in line in the surveillance, hustling to catch up. When I topped the hill, I saw the blue lights come on as the Troopers started to stop the motor home. It was in the left lane and Bill was in front, slowed down to a crawl. I then took in the whole scene, and I guess I turned noticeably pale.

There were dozens of police cars, all colors and descriptions, parked on both sides of the interstate for hundreds of feet. I don't remember ever seeing so many cop cars in one place in my life. All these cops, and we had no direct communication with any of them.

The motor home slowed to a stop, and so did I. I jumped out of the car and started running the distance to the stop. Lights were flashing on at least thirty patrol units, the night afire with blue.

As I ran, I heard the sound of a single gunshot. My blood ran cold, as what we all feared most was occurring before my eyes. I drew the Browning from my shoulder holster and continued to run. I saw Bill, his flaming red hair glowing in the strobing blue lights, lying on the ground at the cab of the motor home.

Gary was just in front of me, and he turned to look at me, the unspoken question prominent in his face.

△ △ △ △ △ △ △ △ △ △

THEN IT STARTED. Noise like I had never heard. Shooting from all directions into the motor home. I crouched, hesitant to fire without a confirmed target. I looked at the motor home, saw the curtains blow out, and heard a round hit the ground just to my side.

I stroked off an entire magazine from the Browning into the motor home, just below the window.

As suddenly as it had started, the firing stopped.

Gary looked at me, and without a word, ran straight at the front of the vehicle, bent and grabbed Bill, and dragged him to the shoulder of the road, down the embankment below the line of fire. Seconds had passed, and I had reloaded my handgun when the shooting started again.

A Trooper standing just to my right rear unloaded the entire magazine of a shotgun into the side of the vehicle.

Gunsmoke filled the air, and sprinkles of broken safety glass fell like snow. My brain was in a whirl.

I started screaming, "Stop! Stop! Cease Fire! Cease Fire!"

The shooting again stopped, and Gary ran up the embankment toward me. We ran around the vehicle together. I had somehow re-holstered the Browning, and we both reached the door of the motor home at the same time.

I jerked the door open, expecting to see blood and carnage inside. Instead I saw two long haired white males crying and begging to get out of the truck.

We dragged them out and placed them face down onto the pavement. As we were getting them handcuffed, one looked ahead and said something that I will never forget.

"Fucking pig's dead!"

△ △ △ △ △ △ △ △ △ △

I LOOKED IN the direction he had been facing, and directly in front of the motor home just at the door of Bill's car lay George Singleton, U.S. Customs Patrol Officer, in a pool of blood. The long-hair on the pavement struggled to raise himself up, and then he began to laugh.

"Fucking pig's dead."

I kicked him in the head, in what I believed was an effort to subdue with appropriate force a prisoner trying to escape. I ran to Bill's car and knelt beside George Singleton lying face down, shot in the back of the head. The worst night of my life had just gotten a lot worse.

Gary approached and knelt beside me.

"How's Bill?"

"Wayne, he got shot, but it ain't real bad. George don't look good."

We moved George away from the car, getting a sleeping bag from the motor home to put under him and to cover him against the frigid night air. He had at least two wounds in the back of his head and maybe two more in his upper body. He was not responding at all.

I screamed at one of the officers nearby to call an ambulance on his radio. I immediately told another to get Bill into his car and take him to the nearest emergency facility. I was afraid to try to move George any more. He was totally unresponsive, and I couldn't tell if he was even breathing.

The rest of the night is a blur. I remember speaking to Ludlow on the radio and listening to him arranging to have the downtown connector closed off where it passed Grady Hospital. Lud was planning to land the Helio Courier on I-85, transport George back to Atlanta and land on the expressway in front of the hospital.

We soon nixed the idea out of good common sense.

An ambulance finally arrived to transport George, and since there was no real trauma unit in the area, they went south toward Atlanta. I worried that Joyce would hear about all this on the news before I could call her, and I later learned that she had, but I had many hours left to deal with the aftermath of this situation.

I also later learned that George was pronounced dead on arrival at Northside Hospital. The attending physician said the head wounds were so serious that earlier treatment would have made no difference. So much brain tissue was destroyed by the two pellets of double-ought buckshot that nothing could have helped.

△ △ △ △ △ △ △ △ △

DAYS LATER, AFTER being interviewed by DEA, GBI, FBI, Customs and anyone else who wanted a chance at me, I finally pieced together what must have happened that dark cold night in Franklin County.

When the motor home stopped, Bill was directly in front of it. He got out, and went back to the driver's window, shouting for the driver to get out and put his hands up. The driver released the brake and, for whatever reason, ran into the back of Bill's government car.

Bill assumed the driver was trying to get away, drew his Colt Commander, and shot out the driver's side front tire. This sort of thing is now frowned on generally by law enforcement, and this case may be one reason.

The round went through the sidewall of the tire, hit the rim, and ricocheted back out, striking Bill in the leg. He immediately fell to the ground.

All the numerous officers surrounding the scene, not realizing what was going on, heard a shot, and saw Bill fall to the ground wounded. The simple and immediate assumption was that Bill had been shot from the motor home, and the firing began.

We later discovered that there was not, in fact, a firearm in the motor home at all.

George's story is a little darker. He was shot in the back with a shotgun as he faced the motor home. There is no doubt that it was an officer who fired the shot that killed him. In the early morning hours we accounted for all the officers who had been there, many from municipal departments miles outside their jurisdictions.

When we had made our plans, one factor had not been taken into account—that all the local departments monitored the Highway Patrol frequency in the area. As the radio traffic played out on the first arrest and the impending second, everybody with a police car for miles around had just come over to help.

We heard that one deputy sheriff who had been at the scene had left abruptly and gone home. The sheriff called him in, and when we checked his car, we found that his shotgun had just received a thorough cleaning. He steadfastly denied being at the scene, even though several other officers were willing to swear he was there.

I suspect that there was a tinge of racism, rather than poor shooting skills, involved in the incident. George William Singleton was an African American, and I will always believe that the deputy came up, saw a black man with a gun at the scene, pointed the shotgun and let George have a load of double ought in the back.

Three of us from DEA went down to Savannah to the small black Catholic church to attend George's funeral. The huge number of police officers in attendance was impressive.

I was tortured with guilt. The funeral, like my many restless hours of darkness, was filled with one question. Was I responsible for the horror of that night?

I will never have a good answer.

Inspected

Atlanta, 1978

THE G-CAR WOULD not start. I fiddled with the carburetor for half an hour and finally got it to begin chugging. The automatic choke was obviously the problem, but our agency was broke again, and there was no — not only no, but hell no — money for car repairs.

I struggled along for a mile or so, then got a little heat in the riser, and the Chevy ran like a champ. This made me late — sweaty, dirty, but mostly late — for the Monday morning meeting. We always had one whether we really needed it or not. Gave the boss something to do.

I walked into the conference room, took a seat in the back, and tried to stay out of sight. It didn't work.

"Wayne, you need to come to my office as soon as we break up."

What had I done now? I sure as hell wasn't getting invited in for late morning coffee. I sat and scrolled through all the stuff I had done recently, and all the stuff I hadn't done, and all the stuff I was doing but was late on. Damn, it was a big list.

"Jim, you know why the old man wants to see me? You talked with him?"

"Look, the meeting's finished. Just go on in and get it over. I'll buy you a beer at lunch to calm you down. He hasn't had a piece of me, so it's something you did without me."

I hated not knowing almost as much as I hated going.

I got to the door, looked in, and saw two other suits sitting in the office. After the boss waved me in, I sat, feeling like the guest of honor at a firing squad.

"Wayne, these folks are here from Inspections to talk to you."

That was not what I wanted to hear. Inspections was the Headquarters unit that included what everyone else calls Internal Affairs They did other stuff, but mostly they bagged bad agents.

This was getting to be a very unpleasant morning. I turned and looked at the two suits, and immediately recognized one. When the office in Miami had collapsed, killing half a dozen employees, I had gone down to dig out people and stuff from the rubble. This inspector was one of the people who supervised the digging teams. We had spent several long hot Miami nights sweating together. I didn't think the chumminess was going to last, however.

"Agent Smith, we've had an allegation that we have to clear up. The RAC here has assured us that you will cooperate fully, and we'd like to get this over with this morning. We're going to need to interview you and the agent you were working with at the time of this incident."

I heard a cough behind me, and Special Agent George Faz walked into the office.

"Boss, you wanted to see me?"

"Gentlemen, this is Agent Faz."

200

Nobody ever called us agents in the office. Assholes maybe, but never agent. We were definitely in trouble.

"Agent Faz, we were just explaining to Agent Smith that there has been an allegation involving the two of you, and we are here to get to the truth. We're going to need you to be available all day. Don't leave the office, either of you. It would also help if the two of you didn't talk to each other. I'll make that an order if it will be clearer."

The two No Sir's came in perfect unison.

"We'll speak with you first, Smith."

We all got up and walked out. The inspectors already knew where the interview rooms were, and they walked straight to the first one.

△ △ △ △ △ △ △ △ △ △

I had set this room up, put in the sound proof paneling, picked out the uncomfortable chair for the interviewee, set the lights just right. Now I was caught in my own trap.

"Agent Smith, sit down, and let's get this started. This is not a criminal investigation, but it could turn into one. We are now in an administrative phase, and as such, you have no rights to refuse to answer any of our questions. Here's a waiver form, just a formality. Sign and date it."

In Miami this guy had been a sweaty, beer drinking buddy. What would it have been like with someone who didn't know me? I signed.

"There has been an allegation that you forced a Confidential Informant to sign a DEA-103 for eight hundred dollars, and kept five hundred, only giving him three. Would you like to respond now?"

"That is absolutely not true."

"How can you say that when you do not even know who we are talking about?"

"That's easy. It never happened. I've never stolen a dime from this outfit, and I'll take a polygraph on it right now."

"We do not give polygraphs to agent personnel."

"Okay, the snitch is lying. Bring him in and let him tell me that to my face."

"That is not how we work, and you well know it. Now, let's get to the issues. Is this your signature on the 103?"

I looked at the form as quickly as I could, trying to see the CI number, and the basis for payment. None of it looked even vaguely familiar.

"Yes, sir, that is my signature."

"Then you admit that you signed this form."

"Yes."

"Look at it again, and tell me what you know about this payment."

I held the form in my hands, straining not to let the shaking show. I read the form twice and realized that I could not remember a single thing about the payment. The CI number was not one from the Atlanta office but was a Miami issued number. The payment was for subsistence during a period a couple of years earlier.

"I don't remember making this payment. This is my signature, and the witness signature is Faz. He was my partner at about that time. I signed it, but I don't remember anything about it at all. Nothing."

"That's all you have to say about this?"

"Yes, sir. I signed the form. If I signed the form, then I paid the snitch. If the form says eight hundred dollars, then I paid the snitch eight hundred dollars. I know that. I don't remember the payment, but I know if it says eight hundred dollars, then the son of a bitch got eight hundred dollars."

"Would it help jog your memory if I told you that you paid the CI in a motel on Ponce de Leon Avenue, here in Atlanta?"

"Doesn't help at all. Why would I be paying a Miami CI here in Atlanta, anyway?"

"He was to testify in court in Miami. He was here, hiding out prior to that trial. The Miami office sent a request to Atlanta that he be paid subsistence expenses while he waited."

"I do not remember this at all. I pay CIs all the time. I just cannot remember this payment from almost three years ago."

"Well, we're through here then."

We all got up, and the Inspector I didn't know walked me out into the hall. George was sitting in a straight chair down the hall from the interview room.

The inspector called to him to follow him to the interview room. As we passed, George looked at me, his big brown eyes like a doe facing a deer hunter. I wanted to speak, to give him a sign, but we passed without a word.

△ △ △ △ △ △ △ △ △ △

I WENT TO my cubicle and fumed. Some asshole was lying about me. About me and George. We might have done some shaky enforcement stuff, but holding back on paying a CI was crazy. The words of Marion Allen Joseph, my first partner, mentor, older brother and patron saint, came back to me, shrouded in mist like holy writ.

"If they snitch for you, they'll snitch on you."

He had told me that was all I really needed to know about informants, and so far it had stood me in good stead. Now I had a problem, and I couldn't figure it out. I had absolutely no recollection of paying the CI. My memory was not that bad, and I could usually dredge up something, but I was getting a solid blank.

Jim Sweat came in, and was being extremely cheerful. That sucked. He asked if I wanted to go to lunch and reminded me he had promised me a beer. I passed, as it was way too early, and because the Inspectors had told me to stick around.

"Drink one for me."

Jim evaporated, and in a very few minutes, George dragged into the cubicle. He looked at me, fear in his eyes. He wanted to talk, but we were both afraid to say anything. He shook his head, as if to say no, and then walked out.

I sat at my desk all afternoon. At about two, I went downstairs to the cafeteria, got a sandwich to go, and went back to my cubicle to await the verdict. As I thought about the whole thing, I remembered several friends who had been the subjects of investigations by Inspections. They hadn't learned their fate for months. This could go on the rest of the year. This would put a damper on Christmas, for sure.

At about quarter after five, I closed up my briefcase, and got my jacket. I was, by God, going home. They hadn't said I couldn't go home, had they? I was out of here.

I was halfway to the door when my friend the Inspector came around the corner from the Boss's office. He motioned to me to follow him, and we returned to the interview room. As we sat down, I realized the other Inspector wasn't there. It was unusual to do one-on-one interviews for something like this.

"Wayne, you had a bad day?"

204

First names. Trying to get me to roll on somebody?

"I've had better."

"If it'll help your feelings any, this is a bullshit deal. We had to do what we did. Policy. The snitch got jammed up, stealing dope out of a package on a deal. He squealed like a stuck hog. He's snitching on everybody who ever met with him. You and Faz were last on our list. You don't have anything to worry about. Some of what he's said turned out to be true, and we had to check it all out. Most of it was bullshit. When he ran out of good stuff, he started making up shit."

"Thanks for the heads up. I wasn't expecting to sleep tonight. This'll help."

"It'll help more when I tell you we gave the fucker a polygraph test last week, and he flunked on the questions about you. You and George are in the clear. I owe you one for all the work you did in Miami. You can tell George, but you got to swear him to secrecy. I'm not supposed to say anything to you till this is final, but when you said you didn't remember any of it, I knew you were shooting straight. If you'd stolen the money, you'd a had a better story than that."

Thirty years later, I remember the damndest things, but I still cannot remember anything about paying that snitch.

Fog
Atlanta, 1979

S INCE DEA NOW had an office in Savannah, this should have been Savannah's case, but I was assigned to the GBI smuggling unit, and they were going, so I was going. The state cops in Savannah had a snitch who had tipped them to a shrimper load of pot coming in from Colombia, and everybody wanted in on the act.

Since Phil Price was driving his GBI car, I hitched a ride to save gas for the G, and so that I couldn't get called back if things slowed down. Phil was a gadget freak, and his state car had more bells and whistles than the space shuttle.

The long drive to Brunswick was, at best, uneventful. Phil kept the GSP frequency on the radio, and all the way down we listened to tag checks, shift roll calls, and wrecks. We were supposed to meet up with everyone at the Customs facility in Brunswick, and there were to be quite a few law enforcement folks involved. The basic drill was that we had the offload site fixed, and surveillance was to be set up on the tiny island in the river where the shrimp boat was to offload the dope.

A group of locals were supposed to then take the load in bits and transport it by small boats to waiting trucks. We were going to let them take the dope to the trucks, then do the takedowns. Seemed simple, but things seldom end up being that way.

Cops had come from every law enforcement agency on the planet, it seemed. GBI, Customs, Glynn County, State Department of Natural Resources (Game and Fish, or the Rabbit Sheriffs as they were locally known), Georgia State Patrol, DEA and the McIntosh County Sheriff's Department. That latter unit was there because the new sheriff in McIntosh County had greatly cleaned up that county's reputation in the law enforcement community.

Tom Poppel, the previous sheriff, had a reputation as nasty as any cop I ever heard of. No one, and I mean absolutely no one, had trusted him. The mysterious death of an FBI informant in his front yard at two thirty in the morning added to his image of corruption and general sleaziness.

During the current wave of vessel smuggling the new sheriff was attempting to get more cooperation in that porous piece of coastline real estate.

"Phil, we are going to have a genuine Chinese fire drill on this one. There ain't no way we're going to be able to coordinate this with all these people and radio systems."

"Don't be so sure. Mikey has brought down every portable radio the GBI has, and we're gonna do this one right if it kills him. No screw up this time. Too many people watching. The Director had to go to the Governor to get the DNR people to bring their new helicopter and all the Rabbit Sheriffs from up north to help. The man's watching, and Mikey knows he's got to do good on this one."

△ △ △ △ △ △ △ △ △ △

THE BRIEFING WENT on for an hour and a half, and a lot was said, but the wary agent who was running the snitch, the agent in charge of the Savannah unit, was unspecific in his portion. Promises were made about more to come later. The final stroke was to assign us to go check into motels away from the coastal area, one team to a motel, and call in and give locations to the coordinator.

Looked like we'd be watching a lot of Rockford Files reruns. We were not to leave the hotel except for meals, on standby till the deal went down. The snitch was listening to the shrimp boat on shortwave radio, and that would be the key to going into action.

"Hey, let's stay at that Howard Johnson's close to FLETC. There's a new place that sells cop stuff out at the front gate. If we get a day off, there's a buddy of mine teaching driving over there now. Used to be a Trooper."

FLETC, the Federal Law Enforcement Training Center, is sited on the old Glynco Navy base. The Treasury Department runs it, and thousands of Feds pass through every year getting basic and advanced training.

"So what's this Trooper going to do for us?"

"Maybe get a ride on the pursuit track."

Phil lived to drive fast, had mastered most of the pursuit tricks, and would demonstrate them at a moment's notice. I had been through more than one u-turn at high speed in his car. I was comfortable with his driving but wasn't all that interested in doing laps at Glynco. The old runway was flat as a plank, and skids were something to be looked forward to. I had been involved in enough traffic accidents in my career and had already been thrilled way too many times to do it on purpose.

209

Since Phil and I had rooms on the same hall, we watched TV together for the two days we waited. It had begun to seem the case wasn't going anywhere. Then we got a call.

"This is Harry. Come in now."

Short and to the point. We both changed into camouflage BDU's, put our gear in bags, and drove to the meeting place on the river. We stood in groups, while Harry talked to Mike Eason about the arrangements. It was early dusk, approaching eight in the evening. I got assigned to ride in a DNR boat with a Customs guy, a Glynn County cop, and a GBI agent I didn't know.

I introduced myself to the others, and the first question came immediately.

"We were told that DEA wasn't involved. Why are you here?"

"I'm assigned to the GBI Smuggling Unit in Atlanta. I go where they go. I don't think Savannah DEA is playing on this one."

"So why is Savannah not working it? It's their territory."

"Beats the hell out of me. I'm just a grunt agent. I don't get involved in that administrative crap."

I strapped on my web gear, pistol, magazines, flashlight, knife, and all the other crap I could pack on the belt. You can never have enough light or too much ammunition. Trying to live by that maxim, I had at least one extra set of batteries and loaded magazines in the pockets of the BDU's. If I fell in the river, I'd sink like a rock.

It was late October, and I had brought my field jacket. It wouldn't go on over all the gear, so I carried it along to the boat in case it got colder during the night. I had no idea how long we'd be out in the boat, and I knew too well the cold that creeps in during those last hours of dark. In the early evening cool the bullet resistant vest made me sweat, though. Thank goodness we weren't doing this in the summer.

210

As I was walking toward the boat, I heard a familiar voice in the background. I turned, and there, bald head gleaming under the parking lot light, was Ludlow Adams. Lud had once been my partner, and our paths were as intertwined as kudzu. I turned and walked toward him.

"Mudhole, what the hell are you doing here?"

"Well, I could say the same to you. The boss told me there weren't any DEA folks playing on this one."

"You know me—I'm wearing my GBI hat tonight. What's the deal with Savannah sitting this one out? What are you going to do?"

"I'm flying the 210. I'll be up there with the DNR helicopter, looking for the shrimper. Savannah? I was told that Gordon's not going to work this deal. I was not told why. Sounds like a pissing match of some kind."

"I know he and Harry don't get along worth shit. That may be it."

"What're you doing tonight?"

"I'm riding in a DNR boat with a pick up crew. We'll be out on the mouth of the river to start."

"Well, stay out of the water."

"You too."

△ △ △ △ △ △ △ △ △ △

I GOT INTO the boat with the other officers, and we pushed off into the river. The DNR guy driving the boat was Charles Reynolds, a local living in McIntosh County. After a few minutes of getting away from the lights, we settled into the evening and moved slowly along, the engine barely above an idle.

The walkie talkie crackled, and Ludlow came through.

"Flint Three Fifty-Seven. I'll be up at about five thousand. Keep me advised."

211

Ludlow could not stand to have a radio nearby and not talk on it. He had a monster unit in the airplane that was user programmable, and he was able to transmit on about half the law enforcement frequencies in the country. As much as Harry had stressed low radio usage, he must not have gotten the message to Ludlow. When no one answered, I was afraid that Lud would keep shouting till someone told him to get off. Then I heard Harry.

"Ten three, ten thirty-three."

That boiled down to emergency in progress, stay off the air. Lud didn't answer, thank God.

We drifted on the river, slowly moving in the general direction of the offload island. The occasional radio update was vague and done over low powered handheld radios. After about three hours, we got the word that the shrimper was entering the mouth of the river.

It was Ludlow, of course, who spotted the fishing boat first and quietly relayed the info. He was being a model of propriety.

Things went according to plan for a while, then came slightly unglued.

Some of the local smuggling participants came to the island early in their small boats, and the surveillance team waiting there had gone to ground, radios silent and hidden. Then one of the locals had stumbled on one of the team, and the takedown was on. It was a very, very small island, and in a matter of minutes, the team had grabbed up all the offloaders, before they had an opportunity to radio out.

The problem was now that the surveillance team already had six people in custody, and the shrimper had not gotten to the island. Other offloaders were expected, and there was no way to relieve the ground team without stirring up a mess. SNAFU.

Charles offered a suggestion.

"We could head over there and take the bad guys off the island."

"We got our assignment. I don't know if they want us wandering around over there. Hell, we're liable to get shot by mistake. You know this river, how far away are we?"

"I've lived on this river all my life. Fished, shrimped, and run around here since I was old enough to walk. I ain't sure exactly which island they're talking about. He didn't tell me, since we weren't supposed to go there."

Our job had been to tail one of the load boats leaving and to make the arrest when they docked. We were depending on the two aircraft to direct us when the offloads began. One goal had been to keep all the arrest teams in boats away from the island to prevent tipping our hand to the opposition.

"Flint Three Fifty-Seven to the units. He's moving north, way into the mouth."

"DNR One. I got him."

Ludlow had an eyeball on the shrimp boat, and now the DNR helicopter had him as well. We were set, unless the melee at the island had totally screwed it up. The shrimper had VHF marine radio, and we had been briefed that the load crews were carrying handheld radios on the same channels. If nobody tipped him, he would dock at the island, and at least we'd get the load, if not the offloaders.

"Flint Three Fifty Seven. There's a big fog bank rolling in. I may have to get higher."

△ △ △ △ △ △ △ △ △ △

FOG WAS NOT a good thing. If it covered the sound and the river, we'd lose our air cover and be on our own as to finding these guys.

This was turning into the typical drug deal. Always something screwed up, sometimes minor, sometimes major, but always something. We drifted on, moving generally northward in the general area of the offload island.

There was chatter on the radio, units moving to cover, the aircraft giving positions of the boat, but nothing major.

"Flint Three Fifty-Seven. The fog is moving in."

I took the radio from Charles and called Ludlow.

"Flint, how's it looking for the target area?"

"Eight Zero, it's closing in all around. Gonna be a foggy morning."

It was quiet on the radio for a few minutes, then Ludlow came back on. Someone was going to have his ass if he didn't shut up.

"Flint to DNR One."

"Flint to DNR One."

No answer.

Seconds passed like cold syrup.

"Flint to DNR One."

"Flint to Eight Zero."

"Go ahead, Flint."

"Wayne, it looks like the DNR bird went into the fog bank. I can't raise him."

"Lud, get the boss. Let them know."

Ludlow began to tell everyone he had lost sight of the DNR helicopter. It was a brand new Hughes 500, with all the tricks. I scrabbled in my ditty bag and came up with my old DEA portable. I borrowed the DNR radio again and called Lud.

"Eight Zero to Air One. Eight Zero to Air One."

"Air One."

"Air One four, copy four."

214

Lud recognized the code we had personally worked out years before. He turned on his DEA radio and switched to channel four. We now had some privacy.

"Eight Zero to Air One on four."

"Go, Wayne."

"Lud, can you give us a heading on the last sighting?"

"Where are you?"

"North of the area. I'll point the spotlight straight up."

Charles turned the light up without a second's hesitation.

"Gotcha. Turn due south from your spot."

"We're moving."

△ △ △ △ △ △ △ △ △ △

THE DOPE DEAL WAS forgotten in less than a second. The spotter on the helicopter was Carl Alexander, head of the Glynn county narc squad and a hell of a good guy. Finding Carl and the DNR pilot had become the only priority.

"Flint to DNR One."

"Flint to DNR One."

Minutes had passed since Lud's first call. There had to be a problem, and it had to be serious for the chopper not to respond. We were at speed now, heading south toward the area where Ludlow had directed us. Suddenly everything turned grey.

The spotlight on the boat penetrated the fog for only about three feet in front. We were in the soup, as heavy as I had ever seen, but I was no expert on the river.

"When this shit comes up like this, does it stay long?"

"I've seen fog like this last till noon. Can't ever tell."

215

The Customs guy, a rookie from Atlanta, was not comfortable.

"We need to get out of this."

"We are *not* leaving here till we know they're okay. Don't even start about leaving."

"Air One, we hit the fog. Any clues?"

"Put your spot back vertical."

"It's up."

"I think I see you. You need to go about two more miles, dead south. It's getting fuzzy up here."

"Lud, get some altitude. We can't lose you, too."

We moved on, slower, wrapped in cotton. The lights reflected back so badly that we could run over the missing men before we could see anything.

"I'm going to cut all the lights. If they're here, our lights ain't gonna help. Maybe they got a light."

Charles, the DNR agent, was cool. He hadn't gotten excited and was handling the boat like lives depended on it.

We moved on, now totally dark. We couldn't see anything, but at least now there was no light reflecting back in our faces. There was the sound of the Cessna engine high above us and occasionally the throb of a boat motor. We were as alone as it was possible to be, and all eyes were stretched looking for any hint of light.

"Look there! Just a point off the bow to the left."

A dim glow, like a five watt bulb covered with gauze, sat on the water.

"Look, it's somebody in the water."

Charles had the best eyes in the boat, cause I still couldn't see shit. There was a glow, but it was so faint, I couldn't see any details.

216

He eased the power off, and we drifted up to the light. It was Carl Alexander, floating in a Mae West, a tiny light fastened to the flotation device.

Carl wasn't looking our way, and he was still in the water. As the engine died, we drifted to his position. I reached into the water, and grabbed him, trying to drag him into the boat. He was a large guy, and getting him in wasn't easy.

"Godamnit, be careful! I think I got a broke shoulder!"

Well, now I knew he wasn't dead, at least.

Carl had never been subtle. He was cold, wet and shivering. I grabbed my field jacket, and tried to wrap him in it as best I could. One of the other agents on the boat spotted another dim light, and we moved quickly to pull the DNR pilot out of the water as well.

"Air One, Air One!"

"Go, Wayne."

"Lud we got 'em both. Repeat, we have recovered both people from the water. No sign of the helicopter. They are okay. Copy?"

"Wayne, I copy. I'll relay to everyone. What are you going to do with them?"

△ △ △ △ △ △ △ △ △ △

IT SLOWLY DAWNED on me that I didn't have a clue of what we were going to do. I looked at Charles, and he looked as blank as I felt.

"Can you get us out of here?"

"I can get out of here, but I ain't sure where I can take you. Ain't nobody can navigate in this stuff. I'll try as best I can."

We headed north, with our new passengers lying in the bottom of the cabin, shivering and moaning. They were not happy. Carl suddenly sat bolt upright in the boat.

"I had my M-16, and it's gone. That's the county's gun, and I'm gonna have to pay for it. I signed for it."

The DNR pilot slowly turned toward Carl, a look of horror on his face.

"Tough shit. I signed for that Hughes that's on the bottom of the sound, so I don't want to hear any shit about some pissy rifle."

Carl got very quiet. I could tell he was in no mood to argue about anything, and it was apparent that the DNR pilot was about to have to stand in front of a panel and explain just how he put a half million dollar bird into the sound.

Charles maneuvered on north, till the fog got even thicker. There was not a light to be seen. We had darkened the boat totally, and we might as well have been on the dark side of the moon.

"I'm going to ease over till we can see the bank. If I can get us alongside the bank, I can keep us going somewhere, keep us from getting lost even worse."

"Charles, these boys are cold as hell. If we don't get them somewhere to warm up, they're liable to go into shock or something. You know, hypothermia."

"I'll find us something."

We worked on, Charles keeping us headed north, but slightly to the east, trying to find the river bank. When the tips of weeds showed through the water, it was like sighting heaven.

"We're okay now. I'll keep us just off the bank. We'll see a dock, or a house or something."

Within ten minutes, Charles made good on his promise. We came upon a rickety dock sticking out into the river. The fog was still so thick we couldn't see what might lay beyond the dock, but it was the first sign of civilization we had seen since we had driven into the fog bank.

"Let me run up there and see what we got."

Charles jumped from the boat onto the dock and disappeared into the fog. I didn't like it. He was our only hope of finding our way to help, and we were now alone.

"It's a fishing cabin. Nobody home. Get them out of the boat and get 'em up here. We'll get 'em warmed up."

The two men from the helicopter, shivering and stumbling, half crawled the fifty feet to the cabin. As we walked up, I saw Charles in the beam of my flashlight, breaking into the cabin door.

"Got to do what you got to do. We'll leave a note explaining it. These river people will understand."

An hour later, we had the oil heater going full blast, and the two downed airmen had dried off and wrapped themselves in blankets borrowed from a chest in the house.

As we later walked back to the boat, the fog started to dissipate, and as suddenly as the stars had gone away, they came back. We learned that Charles had immediately recognized the cabin, and he told us he knew the owner.

After he assured us there would be no problem with our little breaking and entering, we all boarded the boat for the quick ride upriver to the dock in Darien. A radio call to the Sheriff had produced a warm car waiting at the dock and a short ride to the office and hot coffee.

The long night was over, and it seemed strange to me that I wasn't even interested in how much dope was seized or how many arrested. I

219

sat on the floor in the corner of the office and tried to warm up. I kept thinking about how lucky we had been that night.

How very lucky.

Cataclysm
Atlanta, 1980

JIM SWEAT AND I got along like brothers. I had worked with a lot of partners by this time in my career, but Sweat was unlike most. We had a lot of the same tastes, we were both Southerners, and I appreciated Jim's truly great sense of humor. Well, I say Jim was a Southerner. He was actually from Florida, and I'm not sure that really qualifies.

Jim loved lab cases, and we had gotten on a streak. Everywhere we turned, we got more involved in chemicals. Labs had become big business, and we had hit a gold mine with a bunch of Georgia Tech students. These Yellow Jackets were sharp, and we had played the game with them as best we could.

For a week, I had crawled up into the attic of a church just west of downtown Atlanta and lay watching one of these mutts. It never got us anywhere on the lab, but we saw enough drug dealing to give Metro probable cause to hit the place with a search warrant.

We then turned to another lead, watching an older white male come into one of the bigger chemical wholesalers in Atlanta, buy a few solvents, and then ask about isosafrole, the principal precursor of MDA, or 3, 4-methylenedioxyamphetamine. Jim and I were riding together, since office economy had reduced us to the one old green Plymouth that we shared.

I was sitting in the car, watching the gold Cadillac that our prospective chemist had arrived in, while Jim had gone in to check with the manager.

Jim ambled out just behind our guy, so I slid over, started the engine, and pulled out. Jim jumped in, and we got in position behind the guy before he hit the end of the block. The surveillance was uneventful, if long, until the Plymouth started making noise. Really, really loud noise.

"What the hell is that?"

"Damn, Jim, how am I supposed to know? It sounds like the whole bottom is falling out of this junker."

We drove on, becoming aware that passersby were staring at us. Even the jackass in the gold Cadillac started looking around, and although I'm sure it was paranoia, I became convinced he was looking straight at us.

The noise got louder.

We eventually turned into a subdivision just south of Atlanta, near Jonesboro and watched the Cadillac pull into the drive of a modest home, unlike the residences of most of the lab rats we had been dealing with. We drove on to the cul-de-sac, turned around and came back out.

The driver was standing at his mailbox, staring at us as we drove by. The noise had gotten even worse, and it sounded like we had a garbage can stuck under the car.

"This ain't cool. We're attracting more attention than a circus parade. We might as well have given him a business card."

"Jim, you know they won't let us have business cards. We ain't management."

I drove back toward the expressway, and with every mile Jim got even more tightjawed. Little kids started crying when we drove by.

The noise was wearing, and Jim was not handling it well. I tried joking about it, but he got red faced and wouldn't speak.

"Stop! Stop the goddamn car now!"

I had just pulled onto the down ramp to I-75, so I moved onto the grass shoulder and stopped.

Jim didn't say a word. He jumped out of the car and dropped onto the ground on the passenger side. I heard him curse once, scream twice, and then saw him stand up. He threw a piece of sheet metal onto the grass, even more red faced than before.

Then without a word, with no warning, the blue steel .38 came out of his waistband, and the sound of six high velocity rounds echoed off the pavement. Again, without a word, Jim got into the car, looked at me, and shoved the Model 10 back into his waistband.

I pulled back onto the ramp and started to drive off.

"Well, I guess you showed it!"

Jim started laughing, tears welled in his eyes, and he began to roar. It was contagious. I was laughing so hard that I had difficulty keeping the Plymouth in my lane. We presented the perfect image of two federal special agents who had just murdered the heat shield from a catalytic converter.

Repeat Offender

Atlanta, 1980

I HAD BEEN lying in the ditch, covered with leaves for the better part of the morning. Every known insect in the northern hemisphere had crawled across me, and quite a few had stopped and taken a bite.

It was another lab case, some goofball making meth. This one was truly crazy, as one of the neighbors had pointed out when he showed us the bullet holes in his mailbox. Apparently when our budding chemist got high, he liked to do a little recreational handgun shooting across the front yard. He lived in DeKalb County, about two hundred yards off I-285.

From my uncomfortable vantage point I had seen enough to relay sufficient information to Chris Brown, sitting in an air conditioned car, to develop probable cause for a search warrant for the house. Jim Sweat was at the Magistrate's office, doing the paperwork, and flirting with the various clerical employees there. We all do what God endowed us to do, and lying in a ditch was my special talent.

"Eight Zero to Eight One."

"Eight One. Go ahead."

"We getting anywhere with the paper?"

"Sweat says he'll have it finished in thirty minutes, and he's got hizzhonor waiting to sign it before he goes to lunch."

"That's mighty white of him. Ask Jim to ask him if he wants to take the next turn in this damn ditch."

I had seen the resident of the cottage measuring liquids, stirring containers of liquid, and weighing out portions of powder. That along with his purchases at Van Waters & Rogers was enough to convince even the liberal magistrates we had to deal with that we had probable cause to think Mr. Lorenz was doing something illegal and that he was doing it in the residence in question. Oh, to be a Mountie and carry a Queen's Writ that avoided all this search warrant nonsense.

"Eight Zero, Jim's got paper, and he's on the way."

"I guess I'll wait."

Twenty minutes ticked by on my Seiko.

"Seventy Eight to Eight Oh."

"Go, Jim."

"We're ready."

"I'll take the front door. I can get to it before he can get it locked. Give me a shout when you leave the car."

"Wayne, we're moving."

I jumped up out of the ditch, crossed the road, and built up speed as I headed to the concrete stoop at the front door. Two steps and I was on the stoop, looking through the louvered glass door into the living room.

A bunch of things then happened in sequence, with me doing some, and Mr. Lorenz doing some. We coordinated well.

I could see him, sitting on the sofa, looking right at me. I was wearing camouflage fatigues, with a badge clipped onto the chest pocket. He was wearing a white t-shirt and jeans. Enough of the fashion comment.

As I stepped to the door and grabbed the handle, Lorenz picked up a Thompson Center single shot pistol that had been lying on the coffee table between him and me.

I grabbed the door knob and twisted.

Door was locked.

Lorenz opened the action of the Thompson. I drew my Colt and slashed down the louvers, breaking as many in one swipe as I could.

Lorenz picked up a single .30-30 caliber cartridge and placed it into the chamber of the Thompson.

I reached through the broken glass, with only one minor cut, grabbed the inside knob and opened the door.

Lorenz closed the action of the Thompson, grasped the grip in his right hand and began to bring the muzzle to bear on me, all the while trying to cock the hammer.

I pulled the door open wide and dived across the coffee table, landing on top of the table, Lorenz, and the Thompson Center pistol.

The table collapsed, Lorenz screamed, and I started looking for the Thompson. I grabbed the barrel and twisted the weapon from his hand. As we both struggled to sit up, Jim and Chris came storming into the living room from the back.

"DEA with a search warrant! DEA! Search warrant!"

Chris was screaming at the top of his lungs. Better late than never.

△ △ △ △ △ △ △ △ △ △

WE SORTED OUT the mini-lab, poured out the nasty residues, took samples of what we considered evidence, boxed it all up, stuffed it in the back of Jim's car, and took Mr. Lorenz to the office for processing.

The U. S. Attorney's office was not interested in prosecuting a single defendant for a small lab. They had major cases to prosecute for the FBI, and it appeared we might be interfering with their hunt for Jimmy Hoffa or some other real criminal.

Taking Lorenz to the DeKalb county jail, we, along with a couple of county detectives, booked him for violations of the laws of the Sovereign State of Georgia. The county DAs were glad to get the case, and Lorenz seemed glad to get the light sentence passed out on his guilty plea.

He'd be out in less than two years. The DAs weren't interested in pushing the business about him trying to shoot me. They told us to refer it to the United States Attorney.

I gave up.

△ △ △ △ △ △ △ △ △ △

ALL OF US at DEA were interested in trying new things, and Agent Steve Starling, who had a degree in pharmacy, had come up with a plan. The other big offices with lab problems had tried it, and they were having success.

We rented a small warehouse with an office in front and put an ad in *High Times*. We instantly became chemical entrepreneurs in a big way. The ad headlined, "Hard to get Chemicals."

Over a year and a half, we had a lot of cases, selling the mutts chemicals and then busting them when they tried to make candy from our sugar.

We did Meth labs, MDA labs, and even a PCP lab.

We did labs in Philadelphia, Denver, Chicago, and all around the state of Georgia.

This was a going concern, and one big problem had been weeding out the wannabes from the real dopers. We had more than our share of kids try to buy enough chemicals to make one PCP cigarette or enough isosafrole to make a little MDA for the weekend.

"Wayne, you got a call from Steve at the storefront on line three."

"Stevie, what you got?"

"I ain't gonna tell you, but you got to come out here this afternoon. Tell the old man that we got a lead here that you got to work on. Get your ass on out here. You got to see this."

I was looking at a ton of paper, stacked on my desk. I needed to organize it, do at least two travel vouchers and status reports on a dozen cases. I hated status reports. We had to write reports saying that during the past month, nothing had happened. I hated writing reports, but doing a status report on a case where the defendant had been arrested, released on bond, and the United States Attorney just could not find time to take it to trial seemed a greater waste than usual.

All I needed was a hint of an excuse to leave the office. I closed up my briefcase, stuck the Colt in my waistband, and headed for the door.

"Mark me as out at the storefront. Steve's got one that I've already dealt with, and I got to be there."

The receptionist looked at me, her expression screaming, "Liar, liar, pants on fire."

△ △ △ △ △ △ △ △ △ △

I GOT TO the storefront and went in the back door. Steve was sitting at a table in the back, staring over a mountain of opened mail. He was holding a Miller Lite over the pile.

"Hey, it's happy hour somewhere."

I looked at my watch.

"Yeah, it's after dark in London."

I pulled a beer from the cooler and plopped down on the other side of the table.

"So what's so all important?"

Steve pulled a packet of paper off the top of the pile and handed it to me.

"Your buddy Lorenz."

It was an order for a complete set of chemicals to make methamphetamine. It was a large order, as our orders went. Enough to make at least a pound of meth.

"Well, he didn't learn much. Where is the bastard?

"Look at the check."

The check was drawn on Mr. Lorenz' inmate account at the Georgia prison where he was serving his time.

"I called the state. He gets out Monday of next week."

Just Another Smuggling Deal
Atlanta, 1980

JOYCE IS RIGHT. Every time I tried to fix something around the house, she ended up taking me to the emergency room. I had always thought I could do almost anything, but garage door openers, sharp tools, hidden hot water pipes all plagued me. I couldn't seem to start a project without creating more havoc.

This weekend chore was all too simple. A new handle for the ax. Everything went okay till I started driving in the wedge to secure the handle to the head. Missed that sucker and crushed the trigger finger on my left hand.

Doc at the emergency room said the bone between the first joint and the tip was broken. Wrapped it up and put on one of those aluminum splints that look like a frog that has been run over on the highway.

It hurt like hell, but I was getting used to it when the phone rang.

"Wayne, it's Mike Eason."

Mike was head of the GBI Air Smuggling unit, and my boss at DEA had assigned me as a liaison. I was working closely with Phil Price, and we had become fast friends.

We had done a lot of woods crawling, navigating overland to clandestine air strips to lie in wait for an offload crew or an airplane. Mostly we had waited, with little to show for the hours in the dark, being eaten by every insect known to man.

"Hey, Mike, what's up?"

"The Anderson County thing is back on. The snitch says it's tonight for sure. You ready to go?"

"Mike, I broke my finger about two hours ago. I really ain't in no mood to go poking around in the woods at night."

"This is the one we been waiting for. The snitch says they got the sheriff paid off, and he's going to be there to get his final payment with the load."

△ △ △ △ △ △ △ △ △ △

THEY ALWAYS SAY that. If every sheriff we had heard about was really on the take, there would be no law south of Macon, Georgia. But I could not take the risk of the high sheriff actually being there and my being home watching TV.

My relationship with the current office management was shaky at best. I didn't fit the pattern of a successful agent, one who ran a thousand snitches, wore a three piece suit to work every day, and was not from the South. There appeared to be a huge bias against Southerners in DEA, and there was absolutely no top management from any of the states south of D. C.

One of my agent buddies, Tom Stafford, said that if your name didn't start with or end with an "O," you weren't going anywhere in this outfit. While I suspect Tom was exaggerating, it's true that there was no established method of advancement in DEA at that time. Later, in the 1990s, when the agency took appropriate steps to ferret out agents likely to be good management material, my high scores came a little too late to compensate for my Southern drawl.

While I was never actually in any real trouble, I always felt as if I could easily find myself at odds with management. At any rate I seemed to spend a lot of time trying not to get on the wrong side of those wielding power in the agency.

"Mike, I'll get saddled up and meet you on I-85 south. I don't think I'll be any good in the woods, but I can handle anything else."

I went into the bedroom and started changing clothes. I didn't plan on going woods crawling, but I pulled on a set of camouflage pants and an OD t-shirt along with my boots just in case. I hated to be the only one wearing regular clothes. All my gear was in the bag in the trunk of the G-car, so as soon as I was dressed, I was good to go.

△ △ △ △ △ △ △ △ △ △

"YOU ARE NOT going to work with that finger!"

"Babe, I got to go. This is one of those I got to do. If this goes down and I ain't there, I'll be in deep shit with the man. I'm on thin ice with that new Group Supervisor anyway. He's got a contract to do Chris and me and a couple of other guys. We're all on his shit list, and I don't need to give him any excuse to break one off in me. All of us that were close to Bill are walking a chalk line."

"That's ridiculous! Why would anyone be upset that you were close to the guy that had the job before? That doesn't make sense."

"They seem to have run him off for nothing, and I think they may be looking to do the same to the rest of us. We don't fit their pattern, and it's been made clear that we ought to be looking for a place to go. I wish I had gotten that San Francisco job a few years ago. We'd be in way better shape now. I keep getting told I've been here too long, but I've volunteered for transfer a dozen times and got shot down every time. I can't go if Headquarters won't send me."

"Well, at least be careful. And keep that finger up like the doctor said."

△ △ △ △ △ △ △ △ △ △

THAT SAME GROUP supervisor had sent me off on wild goose chases, way out into the sticks of South Georgia, then called my house late at night, asking Joyce if she knew where I was, as if he hadn't sent me. There had also arisen the small matter of obscene calls that Joyce had been receiving on nights when I was out of town for the G.

I found it difficult to believe that they were totally coincidental. On top of that, there was the incident with Internal Affairs. Headquarters notified me that I was the subject of a corruption allegation concerning the theft of drug money during the service of a search warrant with South Metro, and I learned that it had been made by the snitch of the ASAC's fair haired boy. The snitch had no way of knowing I was even involved in the matter in question unless the boy had told him. I had the feeling I was on a short list, prepared by a couple of three piece suited assholes.

△ △ △ △ △ △ △ △ △ △

I HAD THE Chevrolet up the driveway and on the way to the interstate in a few minutes. Since we had both missed lunch during the trip to the emergency room, Joyce had made me a sandwich. Except for keeping the wounded finger pointed at the roof, driving with the left hand and eating with the right was an activity I was accustomed to. I ate way too many meals in the car, always on the way somewhere.

"GBI Atlanta to GBI Zero Nine Ten."

Looking for me already. I had a GBI radio installed in the DEA car in addition to the DEA radio. Damned nearly filled the trunk, and with both radio control heads in the glove box, storage room was short.

"GBI Zero Nine Ten. GBI Atlanta, go ahead."

"GBI Zero Nine Ten, GBI Zero Nine Oh One is looking for you on car to car."

"GBI Zero Nine Ten. GBI Atlanta, I copy that. Going to car-to-car."

I tried for a few minutes to raise Mike on the car-to-car channel and had no luck.

"GBI Zero Nine Ten to GBI Atlanta."

"Go ahead, Zero Nine Ten."

"Couldn't raise Zero Nine Oh One on car-to-car. Advise him I'm on 285, approaching 75 south, headed to 85 south."

"GBI Zero Nine Oh One advises that he and GBI Zero Nine Oh Seven are south bound on I-75, just approaching I-285 on the north side."

"GBI Zero Nine Ten. Advise those units I'll be south on 85, on channel three, listening for them."

It was Sunday afternoon, and traffic was light. I held my speed down, easing along and waiting for Mike and Phil to catch up. Poor planning on my part. I knew they both lived near Canton, way north of me. I could have waited a half hour to start and still be up with them.

The case we had been working had been based out of a little town in Alabama, just across the line from the Georgia county where the clandestine strip was located. The case agent figured it was less likely to alarm the locals and possibly tip off the load crew if we stayed across the line. It was a long drive, and I didn't expect to get settled till way after dark. About the time I got to Columbus, Mike and Phil caught up, and we traveled together across into Alabama and on to the motel where the case agent was waiting.

"Snitch says it's on for sure tonight. They went out today and bought tent stakes, flashlights and pie plates. They are getting ready to do this one. I got a good feeling. We're gonna get us a load tonight."

△ △ △ △ △ △ △ △ △ △

GBI AGENT JOHN "Possum" Willis was good at reading snitches and was a solid guy to work with. He had been working this snitch for months, and he rarely polished up the information he got. When he said tonight, I believed him.

"What the hell have flashlights and pie plates got to do with this?"

U. S. Customs heard from!

We had a couple of young Customs Patrol Officers assigned to work with us on these smuggling deals so that we would have border search authority. Solved search problems when you didn't have to have probable cause.

The Customs guys were eager, if a little unsure of themselves. I had accused one of them of having never walked on anything that wasn't paved till he started to work with us. They were not woods walkers, but they tried.

"They super glue the plastic flashlights to the tent stakes, with the bulb pointing up. Then they put the aluminum pie plate around and over the flashlight, so the light is reflected down onto the ground and in toward the center of the strip. Makes perfect markers for the strip boundaries. Looks like a real airport from above, but you can drive within a couple of hundred yards and not see the light from a car."

"We need to write that up for a teletype to headquarters. I'll bet nobody else has ever heard of that."

At least these Customs humps were admitting that they were thieves—stealing ideas as well as cases. I doubted that the information would do any good, since every smuggling group did it differently. Chemical light sticks were the current fashion—they required no work, and the bad guys were professionally lazy. Gluing and molding would seem like too much work.

"Possum, we have any idea of who the opposition is on this one. Any names or any personal info?"

"Wayne, all the snitch knows is that they're not from around here. He says they sound like they are from down South, but not local. A couple of older redneck types is all he's met. They don't sound like our run of the mill pot smugglers."

All kinds of folks were getting into the marijuana transportation business. We'd had out-of-work airline pilots, Vietnam era helicopter pilots, and at least one active duty military pilot.

When caught, almost to a man, they said it was either their first load, or it was to be their last. The offload crews were usually long haired pot dealers, moving up in the business. They were also broke.

None of them ever had the money for lawyers or bond. At first I thought they were afraid to let the money show, but when they went off to prison after being represented by an appointed attorney, I had begun to wonder if anyone was really making any money in this trade. The markup on the product should have insured that someone was cleaning up, but I never met any that did.

△ △ △ △ △ △ △ △ △ △

THE GROUND TEAM began to make preparations for the trip into the dark. We were amateurs at this woods crawling, but were getting better. Taped flashlights, military surplus night vision goggles and face nets to keep the mosquitoes out were all standard. Some went even further, including one of the guys who had a phobia about having to defecate in the dark swamps.

Afraid of getting bites on his privates, he went to extremes not to have to go, including altering his diet to exclude fiber. One of the others had read a health magazine that recommended sulfur to keep away insects. He ate so many tablets of a sulfur compound that his bowel movements could clear the entire floor of the motel.

One older guy was in the reserves and had a lot of military skills and training. Pops, as he was called, was a great help, and his experiences in the soggy areas of Southeast Asia went far to aid the rest of us in preparing for these excursions. Although I had lain out on air strips for many, many nights, all I had to show so far was an impressive array of mosquito bites and the ever present little red chiggers.

Twice before I had crawled in on this strip, and I knew the three mile walk in was not a pleasant one, especially in the dark. There had been no rain in several weeks, so the bug population should be minimal, but the possibility of snakes was real and never ignored.

At dusk the woods team loaded into the back of a pickup to be taken out to the drop off spot. I saw them off and then crawled in the car with Mike. I hated sitting this one out, but my finger was throbbing since I hadn't taken the meds the doctor had given me. I didn't want anything that would slow me down, or worse put me to sleep on surveillance. I get groggy enough around four in the morning without hydrocodone.

We rode around the little town for a few minutes, stopped at a Waffle House and got coffee to go, and then rode out to the general area of the strip.

We waited for a couple of hours before even trying to contact the ground team, since we both knew the last thing they needed while trying to navigate to the strip was idle chatter on the radio. There was also the fear that we might be monitored.

The GBI frequency we were using was well known to the local cops, and many of the Sheriff's cars in many counties had illegally installed crystals that covered the channel. With the snitch having said the high sheriff was taking money on the deal, we were going with as much communications security as possible.

Phil had a handi-talkie that had the frequencies used by the GBI in their bugs, and he planned to use it as much as possible for communicating with us, since it was far less likely to be monitored. We would be able to hear him, but couldn't transmit on the frequency. One of the ground crew was monitoring the regular car to car channel, but it was reserved for emergency traffic only.

"Phil to Mikey."

The channel that received the bug frequency rasped out the weak signal.

"Phil to Mikey, give me a click."

Mike picked up the microphone off the car floor and clicked the transmit button twice on the car to car channel.

"Phil to Mike, gotcha."

The agreement had been that Phil would check in as soon as the team was in position, and now we were settled in for the night. I was almost hoping that nothing would happen, since I wasn't going to be there.

An hour went by. The dark had become complete, and we sat in the stifling heat of the Middle Georgia night, waiting for something to happen. Possum had been so positive that we had all gotten expectant.

"Phil to Mike, we got activity."

Mike clicked twice in response.

"We got two bodies in a Blazer, on the ground."

Now I was pissed at my clumsiness. If I hadn't smashed my finger, I'd be there, watching the two mopes. I could imagine the sweat and bugs, imagine the two guys getting out of the truck and smoking in the dark, walking around the air strip. As much as I wanted the deal to go, I hated that I was not there, on the line.

"Mike, they got a ground to air set up."

The blue battery powered VHF aviation transceivers were a common tool of the smugglers. I opened my war bag and pulled out my scanner. Already had it programmed to scan the aviation frequencies, so all I had to do was plug it into the cigarette lighter and punch a couple of buttons.

As soon as they got on the air with the airplane, we'd be able to hear them. This was beginning to look like the real thing.

"Phil to Mike, they're putting out the lights. Turned off."

Two clicks.

240

A hot, stagnant, sweaty hour passed. We couldn't run the engine to operate the AC, so we just sat and dripped into the seats.

"Mike. Mike. Mike. We got trouble!"

The silence that followed that transmission was painful. Mike and I both sat on edge, waiting for the next call. We had code words worked out to call in the three other cars parked further away from the strip, but we didn't want to waste them.

△ △ △ △ △ △ △ △ △ △

"MIKE, THE SHERIFF is on the strip."

Just what we didn't want to hear.

"The man is in his county truck, got his radio on."

There was not one damned thing we could do at this point. If the sheriff was playing law dog, he had the best back up he could ever hope for. If he was truly a bad guy, we had the best witnesses we could hope for.

We sat.

"Mike, he's talking to the guys. Sounds like he wants more money."

The scanner opened squelch, and the burst of static made me jump.

"Skyhook. Skyhook. Skyhook."

"Mike, they're calling on the VHF."

What a creative call sign. They must have spent days working on it. I looked at my watch. It was exactly two in the morning. They must have had a time schedule on this thing.

They picked a hell of a time to start calling, with the sheriff there, unless the sheriff had known the time schedule and had come out to watch and collect.

"Skyhook. Skyhook. Skyhook. Come in!"

No response. Their airplane should have been able to hear the call for many miles, depending on his altitude. They were using a frequency not used by any of the local airports, and that fact, combined with the late hour, meant there was little possibility that anyone would overhear this little drama.

"Mike, they're getting into an argument. The sheriff is screaming at them."

Four clicks.

Mike, as the squad leader, had a few perks. Long before the day of the cell phone, his car had the only car phone that the GBI had in the field. It filled his trunk. There wasn't room left for a change of drawers.

Mike turned the phone on, and started through the process of placing a call. He got through to the GSP radio operator at the patrol post in Cuthbert.

"This is Special Agent Eason with the GBI. I need you to call the Post Commander at home, and tell him we have an emergency. I'm going to need a lot of help real fast, and it needs to be off the air. This is a ten-three, ten-thirty-three situation."

Mike held the phone for a few minutes, listening.

"Call GBI headquarters and verify who I am. This is an emergency, and you need to get moving. I'm going to need every trooper you can get in, as quick as you can get them. No radio traffic, remind them. No ten-eight, no nothing."

The bug channel relayed static for a minute.

"They're taking the sheriff down. Sounds like they're handcuffing him. We can hear his car radio, so keep the traffic down."

This wasn't getting any better. Mike clicked twice, and we continued to wait.

"Skyhook. Skyhook. Skyhook."

242

They were still looking for the airplane. As long as they were waiting, we would be okay. If they decided the deal was off, we were going to be facing a real problem. The bad guys were going to have to do something with the sheriff, and since they had already handcuffed him, I doubted if they would just let him go.

The sheriff was not going to be happy with them, and this could get ugly fast.

Mike made the car phone do its thing again, and he spoke with the radio operator again. Since the Georgia State Patrol did not hire idiots, their radio operators were carefully selected. This one had done his job well. The post commander was on the way in, every trooper from the post had been called, and each was in process of coming in as well.

We rolled out, driving to the location we had left Possum.

"Possum, get in close so you can hear Phil on the walkie. They have the Sheriff on the ground, handcuffed. Me and Wayne are going to GSP to get some help on the way out here. That fucking Sheriff drove up into the field and haggled with them about money. Now they got him, and they got to do something with him. Phil is on the bug channel, transmits but can't receive. We're clicking on the car to car to respond. We'll be back."

We sped to GSP, and met with the Troopers, briefing them on the situation, as well as we could. Mike was careful to keep much of the info from the CI out of the briefing, since he didn't want to start a problem with having to flat out lie to the Post Commander. We got a quick agreement that they would get into position, as close to the strip as possible, quietly, without any radio traffic.

The Post commander was willing to do as Mike requested without any hint of inter-agency friction. He was a little upset that GSP was not aware of the operation, but seemed to understand, or at least tolerate, the situation.

We got back to the point location as quickly as Mike could drive and pulled alongside the other GBI car.

"What happened?"

"Mike, Phil has called three times, mostly same old, same old. The sheriff is still on the ground, and they are still calling for the airplane."

That flight was now over an hour late.

△ △ △ △ △ △ △ △ △ △

"HAS PHIL GOT a plan?"

"We ain't been able to ask him, and he ain't volunteering much."

Another half hour ticked by.

The GSP cars were in place and knew the drill. The simple plan from the briefing at GSP was for them to flood in to the strip the minute we called for help. They were aware that the ground team was dressed in fatigues and probably looked like a bad group photo from *Soldier of Fortune*. From there, we were going to play it by ear.

"Mike, they're giving up on the plane."

Two clicks.

The offload crew had apparently decided that Skyhook wasn't coming.

Silence.

"Mike, Pops moved in close, and they're talking about killing the sheriff."

Two clicks.

"Mike, we're going to start shooting the minute they decide to kill him. We'll shoot at hip level, full auto."

That sounded like a plan.

"Mike, two clicks to approve."

Mike looked at the windshield, then at me.

"Any ideas?"

"Mike, Phil has the scene. He's got to make the decision."

Two clicks.

"Mike, gotcha."

A very long ten or so minutes dragged by. We sat, unable to even guess what was going on. Not knowing was killing me.

"Mike, get ready. They're leaving. They're leaving the sheriff on the ground. He's alive."

"Phil, get the sheriff. Now!"

Mike switched from the GBI car to car channel to the GSP car to car channel, telling the GSP in the clear what the situation was. They went to blue light immediately, and as the Blazer bounced out of the pasture onto the dirt road, there were two blue and grey Crown Victorias right behind them. The chase was on, and the GSP did what they do best.

△ △ △ △ △ △ △ △ △ △

WE GATHERED AT the patrol post, with the ground team bringing the Sheriff along. He was confused at being rescued so quickly, and the gears in his mind had begun to turn slowly. He wasn't talking to anyone. Mike had taken him into a quiet room, where he tried to interview him with no good result. The Sheriff couldn't even think of a good cover story, just mumbled about being kidnapped.

The Troopers had chased down the Blazer and now dragged both the occupants into the Post in handcuffs. They had made a run for the Alabama line, but the Blazer was no match for a GSP Trooper. They chased hard, and they almost always caught their quarry. These two had taken more than a little subduing at the time they were stopped, and it showed.

Some of the damage may have been due to the abbreviated briefing, since we hadn't told the Troopers that the Sheriff might be cooperating with the smugglers. They tuned the two up because they had put their hands on a Georgia law officer, period. Turned out the two were from Mississippi, a long way from home.

"Mr. Eason, I got something for you."

It was the radio operator. Mike had enthusiastically thanked him for the job he had done, and the young man seemed eager to help. I wondered if he had the GBI in mind for a future. Many GBI agents had started their careers as GSP radio operators.

"Whatcha got?"

"I ran those two in NCIC."

"Yeah?"

"One of them's got a record for drugs, but the other one is the real deal."

"What'd he do, rob banks?"

"He was arrested in Neshoba County, Mississippi, for killing those three civil rights workers back in 1966, you remember. He beat the case, but he's a real killer."

We all went back home after doing the paperwork to have the two charged with kidnapping and attempted murder. We weren't sure how it would work out, since the sheriff would have to testify, and with what we knew, he wasn't going to make much of a witness.

Maybe Phil and Pops could make the case without him, but I doubted it. A good defense lawyer would make hash of the sheriff on the stand.

△ △ △ △ △ △ △ △ △ △

TO GET TO Columbus, the largest city near his rural home county, the sheriff had to travel through Ft. Benning. We got the word when the Ft. Benning MPs arrested him for DUI the first time, and then the second time.

Apparently our little smuggling case had driven the sheriff to excessive drink, and since no one in his county had the legal authority to arrest him, it fell the lot of the MPs to deal with him. At that time, in Georgia, no law enforcement officer could arrest the sheriff of a county. Only the coroner had the legal authority to make such an arrest, and I'm not sure there even was a coroner in the county.

Eventually the sheriff became such a disgrace that the Governor removed him from office. Without the sheriff's testimony, the two smugglers-kidnappers were never tried for the night's activity.

And we went on doing what we did.

Bainbridge
Atlanta, 1980

I HAD SEEN film clips of folks getting off airplanes, then bending to kiss the concrete or asphalt or whatever the runways were made of. I had always considered them a little hokey.

No longer.

It all started with a deal I had done with the Georgia Bureau of Investigation down in Bainbridge. We had snagged a planeload of pot, the offload crew, and all their attendant vehicles. We had been lucky, and all had gone as planned. Although the snitch had floated a tale about the group paying off the locals to provide security, we sure as hell hadn't run into any of them the night that deal went down. I was, as usual, the only DEA agent on scene. I was assigned to work with the GBI Air Smuggling unit, and since the boss considered the arrangement mostly a political sop, he wouldn't waste any more manpower on it. Besides, crawling through the mud on a summer night to lie on a dirt strip would have ruined the suits and shoes of other downtown agents.

Actually, I wasn't the only DEA agent. My old ex-partner, now DEA Special Agent/Pilot, Ludlow Adams had flown surveillance and air cover on the operation, coordinating everything from the Cessna 210 that served as his private office. The little guy, dressed in his usual Goodwill finery, was the best at what he did. He would never be near the cover of *GQ*, but he worked a deal from the air like no one else alive.

One of the Georgia State Patrol pilots had flown the seized Beechcraft Queen Air to the Albany airport and stored it in the GSP hangar there. I had gone back to Atlanta to do paperwork, wash my fatigues, and put cortisone on my mosquito bites when Ludlow called me.

"Wayne, I just got a call from Chumley, and we have to move the Queen Air today. I've called Lawson and got permission to store it there, but we've got to move now."

"Ludlow, what the hell has Chumley and the Highway Patrol got to do with moving the Queen Air? The GBI seized it, and they are damned well in charge of where it's tied down. I just talked to Eason, and he didn't say anything about moving it. That ain't my job."

Lud slowed down and started to fill me in on the details. Although he was hell on the telephone, sometimes he assumed the receiver was more well informed than was the reality.

Seems the Sheriff of Decatur County had come to the GSP hangar in Albany with a piece of paper that entitled him to take possession of the airplane. The Corporal at Albany resisted, and the situation got to be contentious real fast. Maybe there was something to the local protection story after all.

"Lud, I'll get back to you as soon as I talk to Mike. It's their airplane, and I ain't doing squat till we get them on board. Call you back in five."

That would give Lud a chance to give himself another of his Norelco haircuts. It wasn't that he was cheap — he just didn't see spending money on a hair cut when he had virtually no hair.

△ △ △ △ △ △ △ △ △ △

SINCE I HATED paperwork, any excuse to put it off for another day was good. Mike Eason, the GBI Narcotics Squad commander, was heavily involved in the anti-smuggling initiative. The airplane drivers were running up from Colombia with everything that would fly, bringing anything from a hundred pounds of pot to a C-114 loaded with counterfeit Quaaludes. I was assigned there mostly to keep the GBI from crawling totally into bed with Customs.

I walked across the big workspace of the GBI in the office tower adjacent to Hartsfield Airport and stepped into Eason's office.

"Mike, I just got a call from Ludlow. He's out at Charlie Brown in Chumley's office, and they just got a call from the Corporal in Albany about the Queen Air. Looks like the High Sheriff is trying to get his hands on the airplane."

"How long ago did Chumley get this call?"

I could see the hackles rising, and the absolute last thing I wanted was to get in the middle of a pissing match between the GBI and GSP. Chumley should have called Mike directly, and Ludlow and I should not have been in the loop till the honchos had conferred.

"Mike, Chumley was still on the phone with Albany when Lud called me. He's a little ahead of himself here, and I knew I had to get this to you right away. I hope the Sheriff's motives are pure here, but you know what we were told about this deal."

Okay, so I lied a little. Ludlow had already had time to call Lawson Army Airfield at Ft. Benning and start the dance to get us permission to land and store the bird there. I'm probably going to hell for a lot of other things, so one more little lie won't make it any hotter.

Mike retreated behind the thick glasses for a moment, then emerged.

"Will you seize the Queen Air?"

Straight to the heart of the matter, no frills. Mike had just defined the whole issue with that question.

If the Federal government seized the Beechcraft, then the Sheriff would be out of the game, and the GBI wouldn't have to take the political heat that would follow. This would, of course, cause me to have to do a ton of paperwork, but the seizure stat would look good for the DEA office, and it might even get me a little more breathing room with the boss.

"Hell yeah, Mike. You know I'm here to help, and if that's what you want, that's what you got."

Jeez, what an ass-kisser I'd become.

"You know what the snitch said about the Sheriff. He sat right there in that Waffle House in Albany and told us what a crook the Sheriff was, and that we would have to shoot it out with them if we took the load down."

"Mike, the CI had good info on the deal, but I don't know about his stuff on the Sheriff. I got a feeling the snitch was just putting a little icing on the cake for us."

△ △ △ △ △ △ △ △ △ △

TOO MANY SNITCHES, too many meetings. I was trying to bring the exact words back, but I wasn't getting anything. Way too many people assumed that local cops were compromised by the dopers, passing money around like candy, and sometimes they were.

"Seize the Queen Air for us, and that'll solve this one. Even the Sheriff won't screw with a DEA seizure sticker."

Time to cover Ludlow.

"Mike, I already asked Lud to call Ft. Benning and see if we could store it there, if you need us to. He may have that taken care of, and if he got a green light, we'll go down tomorrow and get it done."

"Good thinking. That ought to do it."

I walked back to my desk, patting myself on the back all the way.

Before calling Ludlow, I called the DEA office, and told the boss that we were seizing the Queen Air. His only question was the market value of the bird, which I assumed would go into a teletype to HQ.

△ △ △ △ △ △ △ △ △ △

IT WAS ALREADY after lunch, and I didn't want to work late, yearning to spend time at home with my wife and family, rather than sleeping in another cheap motel in South Georgia.

When I got to my desk, Phil Price looked up. Phil and I had become close friends, despite our age differences. It amused him that I had put the father of one of his classmates in prison when he was still in junior high.

"Ludlow's called three times while you were in Mikey's office kissing ass. You better call him back before he strokes out."

"He tell you what he was having such a fit about?"

"That Queen Air. Chumley's scared that he's gonna have a war on his hands down in Albany. He's talked with Confederate Avenue, and they are hot to get out from under this. They have to live down there when this is over, and that Sheriff has some good politics. Chumley don't want be to doing midnight shift in Ware County."

The reference to state politics was pointed, and I knew that while Lt. Chumley would never be sitting in a GSP Crown Vic, patrolling rural South Georgia in the dark, I also knew he was a good friend of DEA, and we had to take care of our friends when we could. I punched in Chumley's number and started the ball rolling.

"Lieutenant, this is Wayne. I hear we got a problem with the Queen Air."

"You know the drill. Y'all got to do something to get this off my plate."

"Well, I talked it over with Mike, and I've talked him into letting DEA seize the Beech. That'll get the Sheriff off your ass and keep you from looking like the bad guy. I know you got to live with these guys after we pull one of these deals. Will that help?"

"Wayne, that will absolutely solve my problem, but you got a bigger one. Have you talked to Lud?"

"Not since the first call."

"He's right here. Let me put you on the speaker phone. By the way, Shaw's here too."

△ △ △ △ △ △ △ △ △

"LUDLOW, WHAT'S GOING on now?"

"Wayne, Chumley just got another call from Albany. The Sheriff has gone to get a Superior Court judge to sign some sort of seizure

254

authorization. If he gets it, the Corporal down there is going to have to give up the Queen Air. He can't fight a judge."

"Lud, I'm going to slap a DEA sticker on that sucker and shut all this down. Lieutenant, how much time we got before the judge signs something and the Sheriff gets back to Albany with it?"

"The Sheriff and the Judge are not exactly on good terms, so the Sheriff is gonna have to talk him into signing this. Since it's got to be served in Dougherty County, the Judge will want to make sure he's on good ground. I figure about three or four hours. In any case, he'll try to do it before tonight."

"Lud, can you do a trip in the 210 today? If we can get there and do an official DEA seizure notice, we'll be ahead of the game."

"Way in front of you. The 210 is on the ramp, ready to go. Just waiting on you. The Lieutenant and Shaw are going to fly down in the 172 to help us if we need them."

Sounded like an out of town trip for the Troopers, complete with a night on the town.

"I'm on the way."

It took almost no persuasion to get Phil to drive me to the Charlie Brown Fulton County Airport where GSP headquartered. He loved blue lights, and he got me there in near record time. I had grabbed my GI tool bag out of my G-car, and I had seizure forms, stickers, and my other junk.

"Wayne, you got a state radio in your bag?"

Phil was a techie and always had the best, most up to date stuff the state had. He was horrified at the junk the federal government issued us. We never had the newest toys.

"I've got a flashlight, a box of .45's, and my other stuff, but I don't have a good radio. Got two screwdrivers, though."

"Here, take mine. It's charged up, and if you got room in that junk bag, I'll loan you another battery. Y'all can at least talk to Chumley on the way."

"Thanks. I'll get them back to you safe and sound."

"You'd better! That's my radio, not the Governor's."

A true techie. When the state wouldn't buy it, Phil would. He had more contacts in Motorola than God.

At the Fulton County Charlie Brown Airport, we piled into the 210 and rolled out. Lud had already talked to the tower, and we were put in front of the other light traffic. The 210 was southbound in no time.

△ △ △ △ △ △ △ △ △ △

"WHERE ARE CHUMLEY and Shaw?"

"They left as soon as you got off the phone. Chumley wanted to get down there so he could get some backbone into that Corporal, just in case."

We flew on, and Ludlow talked to everyone on the planet as we flew. I got an education from riding with him.

Although my first partner had been a pilot, Ludlow virtually worshipped at the throne of aviation. His airplane had every gizmo known, and he used them all.

We were hardly underway when he called Atlas on the High Frequency radio and checked in. They were a contractor for all the communications in the DEA Aviation Division.

Lud then talked to several airline pilots about the weather. His military call sign assured him conversation with the mostly ex-military pilots.

We flew on without a problem, landing at Albany just behind the GSP Cessna 172.

As we taxied up to the GSP hangar, we saw four troopers in crisp uniforms standing in front of the locked hangar, along with the pilot Corporal in his flight suit. The looks of relief on their faces were obvious.

Turned out Lt. Chumley had done a little psychological warfare, in that he had announced the arrival of the Feds on the state radio frequency, which was also monitored by the Sheriff's department. At least they were now on notice that we had arrived and were taking charge.

△ △ △ △ △ △ △ △ △ △

I HAD FILLED out the seizure documents as we flew, and as soon as we got out of the Cessna, I placed a DEA seizure sticker on the Queen Air. The extra Troopers got back into their Crown Vics and faded into the sweltering evening.

During the ensuing conversation, the possibility of the bad guys breaking in and stealing the airplane arose. The possibility seemed a little over the top to me, but the bird had a strange registration, and it didn't seem to be the usual leased or rented smuggling vehicle. A new coat of paint, some new frame numbers, and this Beechcraft could have a new life in the global south.

"I have a PPL number, and the commander at Lawson assured me that we could store the bird there."

"You got a what?"

Ludlow constantly amazed me by using terminology that no one but him knew. He never bothered to explain.

"PPL. Prior Permission to Land. If you come into a military base after normal op hours, you gotta have a PPL or they won't let you land."

I would have assumed this was something Ludlow had learned today and was just making us all feel stupid, except he wasn't really like that.

"Lud, that's just fine and dandy, but how are we gonna get this thing to Columbus? Lieutenant, is the pilot who flew it up here from Bainbridge available?"

"Wayne, he's on a detail flying the Governor. He's the only pilot we got that's rated in the Queen Air."

△ △ △ △ △ △ △ △ △ △

DARKNESS WAS FALLING in Albany, and we all stood, looking for an answer.

"Wayne, I have a multi engine ticket. I've flown a bunch of two motored airplanes. This one can't be that different."

Ludlow had spoken, and for reasons known only to the almighty, I didn't even object. Both Chumley and Shaw were primarily helicopter drivers, who flew the little Cessnas when they were in a hurry. I sure as hell couldn't fly it, so it was left to Ludlow.

Everything I should have said went away, and I looked into the darkening sky. I had seized the damned thing, and now we had to do something with it. The thought of explaining to the deskbound boss that I had lost a valuable asset was the final straw.

"Hell, let's do it."

Famous almost last words.

△ △ △ △ △ △ △ △ △ △

WE OPENED THE hangar doors, and started pulling and shoving on the big airplane to get it outside. It didn't look all that different from the other airplanes I had flown in with DEA. I reassured myself repeatedly that this would be a piece of cake.

Ludlow assumed that I would fly to Benning with him, just as naturally as I had assumed we could do this. We sat in the cockpit, strapped in and idling. Ludlow was struggling with a checklist that was new to him.

I pulled my flashlight out of my GI tool bag and offered to read it for him. I still had perfect sight, and my night vision was excellent.

I worked through the checklist, reading each item and getting a satisfactory — or so I hoped — answer.

We got the engines started, and all seemed well till I hit the item about the electrical power output on the right engine. The answer was not what I wanted to hear. Apparently the generator, or was it an alternator, on that side was out.

Ludlow then assured me that one was enough, and the left side was putting out full power. Ludlow spoke briefly with Lt. Chumley over the VHF as we watched him roll out in the 172. The plan was for him to fly to Lawson ahead of us, hover while we landed, and then pick us up for a ride back to Albany.

"Lud, how's he going to land without one of those PPKs or PPL thingies?"

"I'll explain it to the operations officer after we land. There won't be a problem."

Great. We may or may not have a ride home after this is over.

259

Check sheet finished, we rolled out after the GSP Cessna. The big Beechcraft easily broke the surly bonds of earth, and we headed toward Lawson.

△ △ △ △ △ △ △ △ △ △

IT WAS A lot later than I had imagined. As I looked at my watch, I was amazed that it was way after ten in the evening. This was turning into a long day.

I realized that I had not gotten authorization to stay overnight and would have to do some fast talking to get per diem money approved. It occurred to me that I could just sleep at the GSP in Albany, and it wouldn't cost the G a dime.

Lost in financial reveries, I looked out the window at the strobe flashing on the wing tip. Strange, it wasn't firing regularly but had become erratic.

"Hey, Lud, what's up with the strobes?"

The question received no response from the headset. Maybe I hadn't pressed the right button to talk to the pilot.

I worried about pushing the wrong button in the cockpit, so I turned to look at Ludlow. His face was tight with concentration, and he stared out across the cowl into the night.

"Hey, Lud."

This time I was looking right at him, and I saw a flicker of response in his face. I also saw that it was way darker in the cockpit than it had originally been.

Maybe he had dimmed the lights.

Ludlow then jerked off the headset, and shouted, "We got a problem!"

260

Oh shit. Not what I wanted to hear.

"Looks like the other alternator has gone out. Went sudden. Maybe a broke belt."

"We okay?"

"Yeah, motor's good. We're okay. Magnetos on engine don't need juice. We got power, we're okay."

As we flew on, Ludlow didn't say much, which was unusual for him, but all things considered, I wasn't in the mood for a lot of talk.

Lud was a damned good pilot. I had been with him in other touchy situations, and he always stayed cool. He didn't worry me, but the aircraft damned sure did. I knew enough to know that the engines would keep running without any electrical power, but I also knew we had a lot of other problems.

△ △ △ △ △ △ △ △ △

"LUD, WHERE WE going to put down?"

"What do *you* think?"

Why was it suddenly a passenger's decision?

"I think we go back to Albany. Less fuss, and they already know us. Hate to start over with the Army in this mess."

"Me, too. Let's turn around. You see Chumley out there? He was going to hang off our wingtip."

I stared out into the black Georgia night. I couldn't see a thing that looked like the GSP Cessna. As a matter of fact, I couldn't see a damned thing. It was black out, and now the strobes were barely firing at all. I hoped Chumley and Shaw had a fix on us.

261

"Lud, try them on VHF, cause I don't see shit."

Lud put the headset back on, and I saw his thumb on the PTT switch on the yoke. I grabbed my headset and held one earpiece to my head.

Nothing. No static, no squelch, nothing.

"Battery's gone. I left the landing lights on after I broke ground so they could get a fix on us. Forgot to turn them off."

Ludlow was back out of the headset, and his face betrayed the calm of his voice.

Great. Now we couldn't even talk to them. This was not getting any better fast.

"How much fuel did we have on takeoff?"

"Chumley said the Corporal put a good bit on from their fuel truck, just in case. We got at least three hours on board."

△ △ △ △ △ △ △ △ △

WE WEREN'T GOING to run out of gas, but just what the merry hell were we going to do? Sort of like the cartoon character, a light bulb suddenly popped on in my head. Phil's radio.

I pulled the bag from between my feet and pulled out the Motorola. Phil had set it up himself, and I had no idea which channel was GSP car to car, and even less idea whether Chumley was actually monitoring that channel.

My assumption was that Phil had set the first channels like the standard GBI radio, and then I remembered that he had set GSP car to car as channel six on his car radio. I tried to recall Chumley's radio number, but it wouldn't come to me.

I held the walkie-talkie to my mouth and started.

262

"GBI Zero Nine Ten to GSP Air One."

Nothing.

"GBI Zero Nine Ten to GSP Air One."

Air One wasn't original, but I doubted if anyone was listening, and I knew for sure they weren't giving out prizes.

Chumley's voice suddenly drawled out of the Motorola.

"GBI Zero Nine Ten, say your ten-twenty."

Nothing could have sounded better, and I looked out to find a landmark. There wasn't one I could describe.

"GBI Zero Nine Ten. We're airborne, can't give you a position. We have total electrical failure. I'll start looking for a landmark."

"GBI Zero Nine Ten, say again on failure!"

"Lieutenant, we've lost all electrical power. We got engines but no lights, no radio but this."

This was no time for long explanations.

"GBI Zero Nine Ten, what are your intentions?"

To get the hell down on the ground would have been just a little too smartass.

"Lieutenant, we're heading back to Albany. Can you report our situation to Albany tower?"

"GBI Zero Nine Ten, I'm on the VHF with them now. We're turning back too."

△ △ △ △ △ △ △ △ △ △

WE FLEW ON into the night, and it was pretty quiet in the cockpit. I was holding my flashlight so Lud could see the compass. No need to light the instrument panel which didn't work without electricity.

We hadn't been outbound that long when this situation arose, so going back shouldn't take too long. I was straining to find a bright landmark that we could relay to Chumley, so at least we could regroup.

Then it occurred to me that maybe we didn't want to regroup. With our plane totally dark, it suddenly got to be a bad idea to have them fly anywhere near us. Electrical failure was one thing, but a mid-air collision was really something to avoid at all cost.

"Lieutenant, we're heading back to Albany. Can you try to get on the ground and give us a hand with the tower? This may turn into a problem."

"GBI Zero Nine Ten, sounds like it already has! We'll head straight back and try to stay out of your way."

Chumley was a mind reader.

△ △ △ △ △ △ △ △ △ △

"LUD, HOW'RE WE going to do this?"

"Line up on the primary. Do a long straight in."

The calm answer showed Ludlow had already been thinking about just how to get this thing on the ground in one piece. Made me worry a little less.

We had gone through a lot together, and I trusted him. I knew if anyone could do this, he could. Actually, since I didn't have any choice, I decided to just accept the thing I could not change.

I continued reading through the checklist, looking for any other problems. Lud would occasionally ask for the light, and I was always ready to share.

"Lud, does this thing have electrical landing gear or hydraulic?"

It was a question that an amateur like me could ask, since I had absolutely no idea what made the wheels go down on one of these monsters.

I really wish I hadn't been looking at him when I asked. He looked blank.

I quickly realized that I had asked an important question. Made you look good in a history class, but here it rocked the pit of my stomach.

"I don't know. This may be a problem. Does the list have anything about emergency gear lowering?"

"Can't find anything."

It got very quiet in the Beechcraft.

"Tell Chumley we're going to do a racetrack around the water tower off to our west till he gets the ground stuff straightened out."

The lighted white tank sitting atop the stilts was the first really identifiable landmark we had seen. With this information, the tower could keep other airplanes, if there were any, away from us till we got down.

I relayed the info to Chumley, who advised me he was descending to land at Albany. With him on the ground, we at least had some comms with the airport.

We did the long oval around the water tower, sitting about five thousand feet up. If no one ran into us, we were okay.

"Lud, you ready for this?"

"Wayne, to tell you the truth, no. I ain't. "

We continued the racetrack pattern till we heard from Chumley.

"GBI Zero Nine Ten, you guys gonna need fire equipment?"

That was an inconsiderate question!

My stomach rolled, and the seat suddenly got very hard and uncomfortable. I looked over at Lud, and he was studiously interested in something out in the black hot night.

"Well, what do I tell him?"

"Tell him to stand by."

Ludlow was looking at the dark panel. He asked for the light, which wasn't making anything any better. We continued our pattern, as he studied the mute instruments.

"We got to check the gear. If we don't have any wheels, we're going to have to sit up here and burn fuel till we get nearly dry. No fuel gauges, so we're gonna have to guess. I'm not putting it in on the runaway with fuel on board."

With that, Lud leaned forward and pulled the gear handle. The second or two of silence was horrible, but then the noise started, and the gear started to extend. It was hydraulic after all, and our immediate problems vanished.

"We got wheels!"

Ever the pilot, Lud shook his head, and said, "I *hope* we got wheels. No electricity, no gear-down lights. Too dark for the folks on the ground to tell us if they're all down, and we ain't gonna know if they're locked till we put weight on them."

Why the hell couldn't he just humor me and say it was all okay?

"Lieutenant, tell them to keep the fire trucks in the shed. This is going to be an absolutely normal landing. There is no emergency."

I hoped Chumley believed it, cause I wasn't as sure as I sounded.

"Well, GBI Zero Nine Ten, come on down. We're ready when you are."

"Lieutenant, we're going to swing out, and make a straight in approach from about ten miles out. We're coming down."

△ △ △ △ △ △ △ △ △ △

I HAD RELAYED Ludlow's instructions as well as I could, and now I resumed the duties of the guy in the right hand seat. I ran through the check landing list by flashlight, touching on the items I knew we could do with no electrical power. When I got to the part about flaps, I heard the bad news.

"Oh, shit! Electric flaps."

We were coming in a little hot, and now we realized that we had no flaps. Well, the Wright brothers didn't have flaps either.

"We're too fast."

I really wished he wouldn't tell me this shit. I wondered if he wanted me to put my arm out the window to slow us down.

"Did you tell Chumley to have them dim the runway markers?"

This hadn't come up before. I thought I was doing pretty damned good in my first stint as a co-pilot on a twin-engine aircraft, but I surely didn't remember him saying anything about dimming the damned lights.

△ △ △ △ △ △ △ △ △ △

WE WERE VERY short. I could barely see anything over the nose, but I saw the problem. We had been in the dark so long the brilliant markers alongside the runway would blind Lud for sure.

In seconds Lud put the nose wheel on the runway about six inches past the numbers. He was looking to get all the concrete he could. He was standing on the brakes, and they were screaming.

We whizzed past hangars and parked airplanes on the taxiways and shot down the runway. Lud was putting all his weight on the brakes, and I was pushing dents into the floor. We shot by the main building and continued down the runway, going way too fast.

The beast was beginning to slow but not in a time frame that would make us relax.

We got way past the buildings and past the taxiway before Lud got the thing stopped. He powered one engine and swung around in the middle of the runway. We taxied back to the pool of light in front of a hangar where the GSP Cessna sat.

I was stuffing my junk back into the bag when Lud killed the engines. We both sat for a moment of silence.

 I guess we would have prayed but for the Supreme Court and this being a government airplane and all. I unfastened the harness, crawled my bulk out of the seat, and went aft to open the door.

I heard Lud coming behind me and catapulted down onto the concrete. It wasn't intentional, my bad knee just folded up, and I sat on the hot taxiway.

Lud jumped out and walked over to where Shaw and Chumley stood. I just sat on the concrete. Nothing ever felt better.

The three of them walked over to the spot where I sat. The burned brake pads filled the air with a stench I will never forget.

"What are we going to do with this thing now?"

Chumley laughed and said, "Well nobody's going to steal it now. Hell, they won't be able to get it started. I'll lock about ten feet of logging chain around each prop, and we'll just leave it here. It'll be okay till morning."

"You hungry?"

We drove across town to the same Waffle House where Mike and I had talked to the snitch. There wasn't much else open this time of day, and Ludlow loved the chow at Waffle House.

We sat and ordered, and while we were waiting for the food, we were unusually quiet.

Thinking to break the ice, I asked, "Hey Lud, I did finally see the problem with the bright runway lights. Sorry about that. Did they bother you?"

"No. I just kept my eyes closed till we got stopped."

Busted

El Paso Intelligence Center, 1986

THE EL PASO INTELLIGENCE Center was, and continues to be, the joint center for the collection and dissemination of intelligence concerning drug trafficking, and especially drug smuggling. All of the Federal agencies involved in combating drug trafficking participate at the center, with state and local agencies using its services as well.

EPIC runs twenty-four, seven, and as those of us who worked there remember, "We may doze, but we never close."

When the following incident happened, I had been working at EPIC for about four years.

I had first started working the rotating shifts, designed by the wife of one of the agents to maximize weekends off, but the rotation seemed more designed to drive the employees crazy. Over a five week period, each employee rotated through the three shifts, never having sufficient time to be able to adjust to the next one. I averaged about three hours of sleep a day when I worked the midnight shift.

Now, I worked days, six a.m. to two p.m. in Special Operations. It was heaven, a regular job playing narc by remote control and cooperating with Feds from other agencies rather than fighting with them. Instead of running around with the bad guys, we were able to locate and follow them electronically and then disseminate information out to the various agents of several different U. S. law enforcement organizations.

Although I corresponded with agencies all over the United States and in other countries, I had found myself working most closely with the DEA office in Bogotá, Colombia. I was on a first name telephone basis with most of the agents and analysts and spoke with them regularly.

One of the issues that had developed in my relationship with Bogotá concerned coffee. Since coffee seemed to be the only legal export coming out of the country, I looked for the possibility of acquiring a quantity for my personal use.

△ △ △ △ △ △ △ △ △ △

"HEY, JIMMY, YOU guys ever ship any coffee to the offices up here?"

"Hell, we get asked to mail coffee over every day. It's got to be a real pain in the butt. We have a driver who handles it for us. I don't like to mess with it, but if you 're looking for a couple of cases, I can fix you up."

"I'll ask around and see if anybody else is interested. What does it run a pound?"

"The damned shipping is more than the coffee. It seems to me that the last I messed with ended up costing the guy about a dollar a pound, delivered."

"I'll let you know in a day or two."

I'd come a long way from my noncoffee-drinking youth. I ran through at least eight or ten cups a day at work, and when I was home for breakfast, we always finished a pot. A dollar a pound sounded good.

Then I screwed up.

I printed out a note and posted it on the bulletin board in the break room. Before I got it stapled up, I had requests for ten pounds. Over the next three days, agents, analysts, secretaries, and the security officer all approached me, dollars in hand, asking for one or two pounds.

I had already decided that I was going to get a case for myself, and before the second week was up, I had orders for an additional nineteen cases of Colombia's finest. This was getting to be a problem.

My first rule was that the money had to be fronted, as I wasn't about to pay for all the stuff myself. All the coffee would be shipped to me, and I would make distribution when I had it all in hand. I kept a list of who had paid, how much, and in what order. I didn't want anyone getting their feelings hurt by someone else getting their delivery first.

It began to sound a bit like a dope deal.

△ △ △ △ △ △ △ △ △ △

A COUPLE OF weeks rolled by after I had mailed the money order to the embassy in Bogotá. I had been assured that the money was received, and that the Colombian native was accumulating the coffee, and would ship the twenty cases as soon as possible.

It turned out that the driver bought postage stamps from the embassy and sent the packages out in the embassy mail run.

I got asked about the delivery date at least once a day, and I was getting tired of answering questions. More than once I had been approached by a rather indignant coworker, asking if anyone else had gotten their coffee, and just where on the list his or her delivery lay.

I assured them all that the coffee would be distributed to everyone on the same day. This was turning into the good deed that never goes unpunished.

△ △ △ △ △ △ △ △ △ △

ONE DAY THE receptionist at the front desk called me on the intercom to tell me that I had a package there.

"You better bring the hand trucks, cause it's a big package."

Since I got tech equipment from Headquarters on a semi-regular basis, that was what I expected to find when I went forward. The mailman was standing there with two brown cardboard boxes with what looked like half the stamps at the post office stuck on them.

I walked out, picked up one of the cases of coffee, stuck it inside the receptionist's area, and went back to get the second.

"Don't be quick to run off. I got three more of these in the truck."

I waited for the mailman to bring up the three boxes, then carted the lot to my work area. There was a small tech space at the side, and I tucked the boxes there. Within an hour, people began to drop by, asking if they could pick up their coffee. I held them off, reverting back to my rule that none would be distributed till all had arrived.

This scenario was repeated in about two days, this time with six cases arriving in the afternoon mail, for a total of eleven cases. With luck the others would arrive soon, and I could get this albatross off my neck.

Every day, someone called on the intercom or casually dropped by in hopes of getting their portion of the load. By the first of the next week, I had most of the coffee, missing only three cases.

△ △ △ △ △ △ △ △ △ △

WEDNESDAY ROLLED AROUND, and no more coffee had arrived. Late in the afternoon, I got called by the receptionist to tell me that I had a call on the main administrative number. She said it was from Customs. We got calls from Customs every hour, but they always called in on the operational numbers. This must be a newbie who had the wrong number.

"Wayne Smith, Special Operations."

"This is Inspector Johanssen. Are you expecting a shipment of goods from Colombia at this address?"

I was a little baffled, and I stumbled for a second. The coffee didn't immediately come to mind.

"Well, I'm not sure. We get shipments of documents and stuff from Bogotá all the time. I don't know of a specific item."

"This is not documents. This is trade goods. It's in your name, I guess. You are Wayne H. Smith, right?"

"Oh, it must be the coffee."

"Well, it's marked coffee. You need to come down here and get this straightened out."

Straightened out? This was beginning to sound like a problem.

"Okay. Where's down here, and what needs to be straightened out?"

"Down here is U.S. Customs at the entry bridge, you know the POE. The customs declaration needs to be finished, and you need to come down and pick this up."

We had several local Customs inspectors working on short assignments at EPIC, so I looked one up after I got off the phone.

275

"What the hell is the POE?"

"Port of Entry. It's down at the main crossing to Juarez. It's where all the commercial shipments from Mexico get cleared into the country. I've worked down there a lot."

△ △ △ △ △ △ △ △ △ △

IT DIDN'T OCCUR to me to get him to call ahead, since I couldn't imagine there'd be a problem with the coffee. After finishing work for the day, I got into my little pickup and drove across El Paso's downtown to the Customs facility at the international bridge. I stumped around for a few minutes, asking everyone if they knew an Inspector Johanssen.

I finally got directed to an office, where I knocked on the door.

"Come in."

"Inspector Johanssen?"

The young, very buff Customs inspector sat at a table, his uniform pressed with creases sharp enough to cut.

"Yes, how can I help you?"

"My name is Wayne Smith. I work at EPIC, and you called about a package."

"Mr. Smith, it's not *a* package. It's *three* packages."

I looked on the table, and there sat two of the brown cardboard boxes, identical to the ones delivered at the office on Montana. Where was the other one?

"Mr. Smith, this is a lot of coffee."

"It's not all for me. A bunch of people at work ordered coffee, but it was simpler to have it addressed to me."

"So this is not all yours."

"That's right. It belongs to several other people at work."

276

At this point the door opened, and another young, buff Customs inspector, similarly uniformed, walked in carrying the missing case of coffee. The case had been opened, and one of the half kilo packages was lying on top. Although the package had been taped closed, it had obviously been opened as well.

"Mr. Smith, this needs some explanation."

First, I didn't like the young man calling me Mr. Smith. At this point, I was Special Agent Smith, and I was about to remind him of that fact.

"*What* needs an explanation? It's coffee for people at work."

"So now, *none* of it is yours?"

"Yes, a portion of it is for me. The rest is for people at the office."

I did not like the way this was going. At that moment, however, the tide turned. I have always felt like I'm lucky, and there has to be someone up there looking out for me.

At that point an older Inspector who had worked with me in Special Operations for several months walked into the office.

"Wayne, goddamnit, what the hell are you doing down here? Slumming?"

"Charles, it's good to see you. How's Janice?"

"She's mean as hell, like always. Wife and kids doing good?"

"Yeah, Joyce's staying busy at UTEP, and the kids still haven't adjusted to the border, but they're working on it."

Inspector Johanssen was staring at the exchange and my arm across Charles' shoulder. I could tell he wasn't at all happy with this turn of events.

"So what are you doing here?"

"I got called down about a couple of boxes of coffee that I had shipped from the office in Bogotá. Inspector Johanssen sent for me to get it cleared into the country."

Charles snapped a look at Johanssen that was not at all friendly.

"You *what?*"

"They told me I had to come down and do something about a Customs declaration to get this coffee."

Charles's vision shifted to the now three boxes of coffee on the table in the center of the room. The box closest him was the one that had been opened.

"Johanssen, do you mean to tell me that you intercepted a shipment from the DEA office in Bogotá to the DEA office here at EPIC? Did you actually open the package?"

"It looked suspicious, and we did a normal inspection. That's what we get paid to do."

"You get paid to use your goddamn head and to occasionally think about what you do. Don't you have a lick of sense? If DEA finds out you're opening their mail, you'll be out at Sierra Blanca for the rest of your career."

"It was personal stuff, not official."

"Yeah, but you didn't know that when you opened the box. Wayne, get that box, and I'll carry the other two. Where're you parked?"

We walked out into the hot El Paso sun and over to my little pickup truck.

"Wayne, I'm sorry as hell about that. That boy is new here, and he ain't got enough sense to get in out of the rain. He wants to be Port Director next year, I think. He'll be lucky to still have a job if he keeps this up."

I unlocked the truck and put my opened package on the seat.

WAFFLE HOUSE DIARIES

"Charles, just throw those in the bed. They'll be okay."

I reached into the opened box and pulled out a half kilo package.

"I remember you'd drink a cup if somebody else would make it. Here, take one of these."

"Wayne, you don't have to do that."

"Hell, I know that. Good friends are hard to find."

I drove off, coffee firmly in my possession. I figured I ought not tell Charles and the prim Mr. Johanssen about the other seventeen cases he had missed.

79

The Road to Chimore

El Paso Intelligence Center, 1986

I WAS FINALLY there. Roger had told me that if I'd hang tight, he'd get me back to Bolivia. The flight from El Paso had been uneventful till U. S. Customs in Miami decided to x-ray outgoing luggage on the flight to La Paz. I know there are rules about guns in luggage, but I wasn't about to put a big sticker on my bag that said "STEAL THIS!" I figured what no one knew, no one would care about.

I grabbed the nearest Customs guy, badged him, and told him that they might see something in the big silver Halliburton suitcase on the belt in front of the x-ray machine.

"What will we see?"

"Well, there're a nine millimeter Smith, three magazines, and a box of Federal Hydro-Shock ammo, to start with. There're also five jars of Yuban instant coffee and a bottle of Herradura tequila, but that's another story."

The customs guy was great, just stepped up to the x-ray operator and whispered something that slid my bag on through.

A few hours later I was through Bolivian Customs in seconds, and Roger drove me down the mountain to La Paz and the Plaza Hotel. The embassy got us a rate just below per diem, and the rooms were immaculate. Since I was alone, the rather short bed would do, with me sleeping corner to corner.

Roger had been my boss in El Paso, and we had talked several times about me coming to La Paz after he took over as the Assistant Country Attaché. He knew I had some skill in tech equipment, and he and his boss were looking for someone to take over the firearms training program and the tech equipment program for both Bolivia and Peru. It sounded like a great gig, with cost of living and danger pay bonuses, and government paid housing. The Country Attaché himself was a little off-putting, but I soon learned that he was under a considerable amount of pressure, both from our agency as well as the boys on the seventh floor of the Embassy.

The CIA had taken a sudden interest in the cocaine business in Bolivia and had been heard way too often telling folks just how much better they could handle the country operation. The State Department types were impressed with the gentlemanly CIA reputation, and in way too many embassies, we of DEA were considered a little dirty and blue collared for State. We were, after all, just narcs.

△ △ △ △ △ △ △ △ △ △

I SETTLED IN at the plaza, and I walked the few blocks to the Embassy every morning. I had been somewhat mystified about the request to bring instant coffee to Bolivia, but after breakfast in the Plaza, the explanation became obvious. I soon learned that the Bolivian idea of coffee was alien to the American palate, and even the dreaded instant began to look good.

That morning my waiter brought a tray with three pots, each looking like a restaurant cream pitcher. I watched as he poured a black, tar like substance into my cup, looking at me as if I was expected to "say when." He then added hot water from the second vessel, and offered milk from the third. I declined the milk, only to stir and drink the worst brew I have ever encountered. I apparently had waited too long to stop the coffee syrup because the stuff in my cup would have raised the dead, or at least taken the enamel off their teeth.

In the cafeteria at the embassy, the coffee was passable, but I was amused to find in the center of each table a container similar to the ones that hold sugar or other sweeteners at home. These were present, but some of the little racks also held white envelopes marked *Mate de Coca* or, in English, coca tea. Each envelope held a tea bag, containing the dried shredded leaf of the coca plant. I was repeatedly offered the pale green brew as a cure for altitude sickness common at the 12,000 foot level in La Paz. It had the taste of privet hedge leaves, and I was no fan.

I worked in the embassy for several days, trying to get the satellite communications system DEA had bought from General Electric to work. It was a simple system, using some borrowed bandwidth on a weather satellite. We had bootlegged onto the system, and our limited use was not noticed by the folks who actually owned and controlled the bird. The problem was that in cities like La Paz, where the electronic noise level was high, our weak signals often could not get through. I was there to try to fix the system, and I was in way over my head.

My knowledge of electronics was rudimentary, but I had picked the brains of everybody in our tech shop in DC, and had spent over a week at GE trying to get into the head of the guy who had developed the system.

My other task was to get the High Frequency radio system in the out offices up and running, or at least running better. HF, or what I had always known as short wave, was the communications lifeline in South America, and it was critical to our mission. Again, I was trying to prove my usefulness, but was not as proficient as I needed be.

"Hey, Wayne."

Roger was calling me away from the satellite terminal, which had been frustrating the merry hell out of me with its lack of usable information. Any break would be a good thing.

"Yeah, boss. What'a you need?"

"Come on in my office when you get a chance."

"I got the chance right now."

We walked into Roger's corner, and I was introduced to a guy I had seen in Headquarters the year before.

"Wayne, this is Steve Casteel from DC. He's down for the operation in Chimore. Steve, Wayne Smith from EPIC."

We shook hands, then sat down. I had a feeling I wasn't being invited in for another cup of hedge tea.

"Wayne, Steve is going down into the Chaparre, taking a load to Chimore. He's got two trucks to get down, and I thought you might like to take the run down with him."

My head almost burst. Getting out of the office and into the real world where people do things sounded like a great deal. I was way more than ready. A chance to get away from the damned radios.

"It'll work out real good, too. They got a problem with the HF at the base camp in Chimore, and maybe you can hook up one of those directional antennas you were talking about yesterday."

Me and my big mouth.

"Wayne, I could sure use the help with the other truck, and you'd get to see the real Bolivia. We'll take a run to Cochabamba, overnight, and then shoot on down to Chimore. Two days there. And you can take whatever you need. We'll have room in the trucks."

Steve was a headquarters guy for sure, and he had me on board in a New York minute.

"Roger, anything else I need to do? And how do I get back here?"

"We'll deal with that as you go. You may have to fly LAB back, or maybe you can hitch a ride on one of the DEA birds."

Steve told me we would leave the next morning, to come dressed for work. I had been wearing slacks with a dress shirt and tie in the embassy, and it was killing me. Jeans and hiking boots sounded like a much better deal.

△ △ △ △ △ △ △ △ △ △

I WAS UP and ready the next morning. I packed a set of fatigues and some other necessities in a small bag, put my other stuff in my main suitcase and checked it with the concierge, assuring him I'd be back in a day or two.

I met Steve at the embassy, and we then met a Bolivian Army colonel who was going on the trip with us. The colonel was driving a Ford Bronco II, a gift from DEA to him, and he was rather proud of his new toy. We went out to the embassy motor pool, where Steve and I picked up two brand new Toyota trucks. These were unlike any I'd seen before, built on the Land Cruiser chassis, a version never imported to the States.

The three of us then drove up the mountain to the airport, where I finally learned about our cargo for the trip. In a small metal building on the cargo side of the airport was a stash of ammonium nitrate fertilizer. We loaded about a thousand pounds of the smelly stuff into each of the Toyotas, and our journey began.

I knew about ammonium nitrate. The stuff was great for crops, but it had a dark side. It was the cheapest high explosive on the market. A little difficult to detonate, but it was perfect for cratering the clandestine runways the cocaine traffickers used to ferry supplies and finished product around the lowlands. You just cut the corner off the plastic bag, pour in the requisite amount of diesel fuel, and you had a very significant explosive charge. A team out in the boonies flew into the trafficker's strips in helicopters, dug a hole in the center of the runway, heaved in a sack or two of AMFO along with a detonator and a booster charge, and put a really huge hole in the runway. Since a lot of this area was very low, even below sea level, the holes quickly filled up with water, rendering the strips unusable, and often irreparable. Since they needed a lot of ammonium nitrate to do this, the ton we were taking out would be used quickly. The trucks were then destined to be used by the DEA/UMOPAR teams working out of Chimore to disrupt the cocaine traffic.

Steve and I quickly established that the two Toyotas had two-way radios installed and soon found a car to car channel that we could use for the trip. The Colonel's Bronco had no radio, but he showed little interest in talking with us anyway. We were stalled for an hour or so, waiting on a Bolivian who worked in the American embassy to ride out with the Colonel. He showed up so late that our arrival in Cochabamba by dark was now out of the question.

In the early afternoon we headed out, our two Toyotas following the Bronco. The roads near La Paz were well paved, and we made good time. Steve and I were on the radio constantly, chatting about the countryside. I had never driven outside La Paz, even though I had flown over most of the country in my previous temporary assignments there, so this scenery was new to me

"Steve, how you doing on fuel?"

"Doing okay. Got over three quarters of a tank."

We had started with full tanks, but I had not seen a service station since we left La Paz. I always worried about gasoline, since I had run out of fuel more than once in my life.

"Is there a place to top up on route?"

"Wayne, I've never driven this route, but the Colonel assured me we wouldn't have a problem. We'll just stick on his tail till we get to Coch."

I eased into the afternoon and found I really liked driving the big Toyota. It had a large six cylinder gasoline engine with plenty of power, even at the high altitude. Some of the American cars that agents had brought down really struggled at the La Paz elevation, and quite a few of them ended up parked when no one could work on the engines with the tacked on pollution control devices.

△ △ △ △ △ △ △ △ △ △

WE CRAWLED ON, finally making the first real turn of the day, moving off the well paved road and turning left onto a road that was partially paved at best. There was a service station at the turn, and I felt a sudden need for gasoline.

287

"Hey, Steve. Blow the horn or something and see if we can get the Colonel to stop. I think we ought to grab some gas while we can."

"Wayne, I've been flashing my lights ever since I saw the station, but he ain't looking back. I'll try the horn."

Steve surged ahead, and I could hear the horn blasting. The Colonel speeded up, and Steve couldn't catch up close enough to wave him over.

"Hell, he can't hear me. That damned Bronco has a stereo tape deck, and he's probably got it turned all the way up."

Broadcast radio left a lot to be desired in Bolivia, and tape players were very popular with the embassy personnel. Country and western tapes were the most in-demand, closely followed by Mexican Norteño music.

"Hope we see another gas dealer soon. I don't think we're gonna make it on what I got."

"Me neither. Wayne, I'll try to get him to stop next time we hit a wide spot in the road."

We drove on, eventually into the sudden dark of the tropics. One minute it was evening, the next it was black. We had moved off any semblance of pavement and had started climbing even higher into the Andes. The road had narrowed, and the dirt was growing softer from the misting rain falling from the clouds we were driving through.

"Hey, Steve, are you sure we're on the right road? I thought we were taking the highway to Cochabamba."

"You got me, buddy. I'm just following the Colonel. He's supposed to know the way. I was told this is the only road, if it is the right one."

We had been climbing steadily for a long time. It was almost 14,000 feet above sea level at the airport, and it seemed we had come up several thousand feet since we had started. They make you use oxygen when you fly at these altitudes. I had turned the heat on in the truck, and I suspected it was really cool outside.

"Wayne, how's your fuel?"

"Not good. I'm down below a quarter. These hills are eating up the gas."

"These ain't hills, these are mountains. I'm way below a quarter. I gotta get this guy to stop. We're gonna have to push these Toyotas to Coch if we don't find a station soon."

We were meeting a steady stream of traffic coming toward us. Little Japanese trucks, bigger two and a half ton trucks loaded with God knows what, and the occasional tractor trailer rig, slogging through the soft dirt of the road. I was getting more and more uncomfortable with the trip. This wasn't the fun ride I had been led to expect. The traffic flow prevented Steve from getting alongside the Colonel, and he began to flash his lights.

"Damn, I wish I knew Morse code."

"Even if you knew Morse, the Colonel probably doesn't. Especially in your half-assed Spanish."

I had just been through a quickie Spanish cram course in El Paso, and could order from a menu, ask for the bathroom, and get a hotel room. Morse code in Spanish was out of the question. Steve had taken Spanish classes from the State Department in Washington and was a little better than me, but he wasn't getting any response from his headlight flashing.

△ △ △ △ △ △ △ △ △ △

WHAT HAD BEEN merely a problem was quickly turning into a disaster. It had been misting rain softly, but now it had begun to snow. This was not good. It was summer here below the equator, and I was running out of gas in a snowstorm, at an altitude where breathing is a chore.

"Wayne, look ahead to your left. Is that a store or a service station?"

I strained to see through the fine snow that was whishing around my headlight beams. There was something up ahead, but I couldn't tell what it was. There sure as hell weren't any Gulf Oil signs.

"Steve, it looks like some kind of truck stop. Make this guy stop!"

Steve charged ahead, slewing around in the mud, and finally pulling alongside the Bronco. I kept waiting for one of the tractor trailer rigs to push him off the side of the mountain, but he blew past the Bronco, and pulled off to the left, into the parking lot of some sort of business where there were trucks of all descriptions parked, big and small.

I breathed a huge sigh of relief, cause where there are trucks, there has to be fuel. I pulled in behind the Bronco, which was just behind Steve. I jumped out into the snow storm, in a T-shirt and jeans, and suddenly realized that it was really cold outside.

Steve was at the driver's window of the Bronco, working in his best new Spanish. The embassy employee hitching a ride to Coch came out his side of the truck and walked around to us. He spoke fluent English, and he immediately grasped the problem.

"They do not sell gasoline here. They may have some diesel in drums, but it is not clean, and has to be strained through cloths before you can use it. They will not have any gasoline at all."

I learned a lesson here. All the rest of the world operates on diesel fuel, but not the USA. In my travels over the next twenty years, I saw more and more countries where diesel was the common fuel and gasoline a luxury.

△ △ △ △ △ △ △ △ △ △

"WELL, WHAT ARE we going to do? How much further is Cochabamba? How are we going to get fuel?"

Steve had lots of questions, but the Colonel looked away, in obvious disinterest. He wanted to get home, and he wasn't particularly concerned about us. Hernando, the embassy employee, on the other hand was very concerned. He seemed to think that we gringos were simple children who had to be taken care of and that it was his job to do that.

"Sirs, I will go with the Colonel to Cochabamba and stir up the people at the consulate. I can get someone to get a barrel of gasoline and come back here with the fuel. If it is as you say, you do not have enough gasoline to make the trip down to Cochabamba."

Hernando and the Colonel pulled off, leaving Steve and me shivering in the dark, in the snow.

"Let's pull the trucks over to the side, out of the way. We don't want to get blocked in here."

That sounded practical enough to me, so we backed over to the edge of the rough parking lot, headed out toward the even rougher road. It was going to be a long night. I got out and joined Steve, and we walked to the low building that appeared to be a truck stop. Having worked drug dealing truck drivers in another life, I felt I knew truck stops as well as anyone.

We got to the door, and both of us had to bend way over to get through the low entrance. Inside it was a truck stop, after all. Large

291

numbers of drivers, very short drivers, were loudly talking over the noise of a battery powered tape player. It was dim in the low room, and Steve and I stood out like Gulliver in Lilliput.

We walked to the rude bar, and in our best classroom Spanish obtained something in a bottle that was intended for human consumption. It was so dark, I had no idea what it was, couldn't read the label, and didn't at all recognize the taste. It was wet and cool, and that was good enough for me. The smoke from a million cigarettes and four kerosene lanterns swirled about, and I nudged Steve.

"Let's get out of here before I asphyxiate."

He said something, but I couldn't tell what, and we walked back out the low doorway into the cold night.

"That's a great night spot. They ought to open a branch in Georgetown. Go over real big."

"Yeah, I don't know whether I was getting poisoned or just smothered to death. If the smoke don't get you, the cancer will."

I walked to my truck and opened the nylon bag I had packed before leaving La Paz. One of my most treasured possessions lay inside. Not the Smith & Wesson, but a genuine Georgia State Highway Patrol flight jacket. A few years back I had run a training program for GSP, teaching their pilots to spot marijuana, and when it was over, I was given a set of GSP pilot wings and the navy blue nylon flight jacket.

I wouldn't have taken anything for it, because the pilots I had worked with were some of my best friends. It meant a lot to me, and tonight, it meant even more. It was warm. I was freezing, and the snow was coming down even harder. We were afraid to run the trucks much, so the heater was out. I bundled up, and sat and shivered.

△ △ △ △ △ △ △ △ △

IT WAS WELL after midnight when the snow stopped. I got out of my truck and walked out away from the little truck stop hut. The sky was clear and the stars looked so close that it seemed you could reach out and touch them.

It came on me slowly. All my life seemed to assume a new meaning. Here I was, a linthead cotton mill boy from a nowhere place in North Georgia. I was standing on top of the world, sixteen or seventeen thousand feet above the nearest ocean. I was transporting high explosives across the top of the world to do important things in a country thousands of miles from home.

I was someone. I had made a mark. I had, by God, accomplished something. I had been voted Most Likely to Succeed in my senior high school year, and by my own reckoning at that moment I had.

And I had run out of gas *again*.

Hiring Jeannie
Chattanooga, 1989

WHEN I HAD taken the opportunity to open a new office in Chattanooga with my old partner Kelly Goodowens, not to mention to move from El Paso back to the South near our aging parents, I knew we would be short of manpower. Our two-man office would need all the help we could muster.

We didn't actually hire Jeannie. She was, and remains, a Chattanooga Police Officer. We just picked her out and sort of borrowed her. When Kelly and I had opened the Chattanooga DEA office in 1988, we were the only federal agents. To accomplish any real law enforcement and combat drug trafficking in the area, we formed a task force staffed with representatives from local police organizations.

"Hey, Wayne. You want to look at these women's police personnel files, I got 'em here for you."

"Uncle Pat, I got to go see Steve Cook at court, then I'll come over to your office. Be there in about an hour."

Since CPD was willing to donate another officer, we had indicated that we'd like to get a female, and Inspector Pat Rowe had arranged for me to look at the files of a group of qualified women. Kelly and I needed to make a decision before the powers that be changed their minds and we got nobody.

"Well, whatcha think?"

I had read the six or seven files, and they all seemed about equal, nothing standing out strongly about any of them. They all had about the same experience level and were all working as patrol officers.

"Nothing jumps out, Pat. What do you know about them?"

"Not much. I don't actually know any of them. We ain't ever had a woman working dope here. Ain't sure it's all that good an idea. One of 'em has some undercover, though. That Larkin girl."

"Yeah, what'd she do?"

"Vice has borrowed her a couple times to work johns. She done good enough."

Pat got on the phone with the Vice commander, and in about five minutes, we were watching a VHS tape of a prostitution sting. Officer Jeannie Larkin was wearing tight jeans and a puffy nylon parka to hide the bug she was wearing, talking to the drive-up johns looking for a little love.

Then came the thirty seconds that made up my mind.

Jeannie leaned into the cab of a pickup truck and quickly negotiated just what she would do and for exactly how much. That done, she started to step back to give the bust signal, which called for her to raise her hands above her head.

"Yeah, girl, I gotta be careful. Last week, right over there, bitch come up to me, we talk, and then she raises her hands up, and the whole damned police department shows up, and I ended up in the county jail. I ain't going there again."

For a split second time stood still. You could hear the gears grinding in Larkin's head. Not wanting a violent confrontation, or a car chase, she stood for that split second, then said, "I'm coming around to get in."

As she walked behind the truck, she did a stutter step, thrust her arms high above her head out of sight of the driver, then continued to walk to the passenger door of the truck. Before she got the door opened, the driver, who had his attention fastened on Larkin, was dragged from the driver's side by two stout uniformed officers.

Thinking on the move.

I was convinced she would be an asset to our office.

After a few years at the DEA Task Force, Jeannie went to patrol as a Sergeant, then to Internal Affairs as a lead investigator, then to Narcotics as the Lieutenant in Charge, and on up the ladder. I've rarely been as proud of any of my team.

Incredible
Chattanooga, 1990

W E WORKED WITH the Chattanooga PD narcotics squad every time they asked. With our limited crew in the DEA office, when we had a job to do, we had to call on our friends for help. In turn, when our friends asked, we went.

The stuff they did wasn't big time, but it was working on the crack problem in Chattanooga, a fire that was consuming black neighborhoods. I personally felt that fighting it was the best use of our limited resources.

African-American neighborhoods were being terrorized with drive by shootings, home invasion robberies, and outright planned executions. The crime rate had shot up, and homicides were way out front. The city narcs were doing search warrants and using other techniques as best they could, and I was always with them when I could be.

The procedure was simple. We grabbed a street rock slinger and replaced him with an undercover cop. When the UC made a crack sale to a drive up, we let the car move away from the sale, then stopped it, and arrested the driver for possession.

We weren't getting kingpins, but we were making the street corners a little less of an open air drug market. On occasion, a buyer would just walk up to the UC, and we would end up chasing him down on foot.

I was too old and slow to play in that league. Only the best and fastest were eligible for the foot race.

△ △ △ △ △ △ △ △ △ △

JIM BROCK WAS a monster. He worked out with weights on a level that most mortals never dream of approaching. His arms were like tree trunks, and his feats of strength were legendary.

Mike Williams, SWAT team commander, told me a story about Jim. When Jim applied for SWAT, they played a trick on him. He had been so good in the physical portion that he totally overshadowed all the others.

The general consensus was that Jim was not the brightest star in the sky, something I soon learned was not remotely true. At the end of the routine physical testing, Jim was brought in and told that a part of the test was mathematics and that he had to hold his breath during the exam.

The test was actually used to measure endurance and patience. Normally a simple, but lengthy, math problem was supposed to be done while holding the breath. In Jim's case, the simple test was replaced by a division problem that involved dividing a seven digit number into a twelve digit number.

Jim sat at the table and took several deep breaths. The sheet bearing the problem was turned over, and Jim began working on the division problem. When the stop watch was well over one hundred seconds, the team commander began to worry. At just over a hundred and ten seconds, he slapped Jim to get him to breathe.

Jim protested and immediately responded that if he had only been given a little more time he could have completed the math.

△ △ △ △ △ △ △ △ △ △

THE NARCOTICS SQUAD had borrowed Jim and several other SWAT members for the street crack arrests. All went well till a walk up bought off the UC, and began to stroll away.

The UC gave the bust signal, and officers began to approach the buyer.

He was skinny, but well over six feet tall, and must have had a forty-inch inseam. When he realized what was going on, he broke into a high speed gallop.

Jim Brock jumped from the surveillance car and gave chase. It was like watching a cheetah chase down a gazelle.

The crack buyer never had a chance. Jim hit him at full stride, swinging his meaty right arm like a baseball bat, knocking the miscreant to the ground.

Jim stopped, grabbed the runner by the back of his shirt, and carried him like a rag doll back to the marked unit that would transport him to the processing center at the PD.

I walked over to help put the buyer into the car and get his name for transmission back to processing. He sat in the car with a look of disbelief on his face.

He turned his head and looked at Jim. Then he looked at me with a question.

"Do he turn green?"

Jumpout

Chattanooga, 1990

T HE VAN SMELLED new, and it had real seats along the sides, so we could all sit, instead of crouching on our knees on the floor. My knees aren't what they used to be, and crouching just doesn't work for me anymore. I've been doing this, in one fashion or the other, all my adult life. Riding around with a bunch of smelly armed men, looking for someone, waiting to scream, shout, arrest and handcuff some citizen. Like a terrorist carrying out a kidnapping—riding to find the perfect victim, screeching to a halt, jumping out, pointing guns, grabbing the poor soul, dragging him into the vehicle, and disappearing in a cloud of exhaust smoke.

Sure, things are better now. We have a new truck, better equipment, we are safer, smoother, but we are still arresting strapped drug dealers. We always treat them like they were armed to the teeth.

How can you do otherwise? It only takes one easy approach to the crackhead with a Glock in his low rider pants to send you to the emergency room instead of home for dinner.

△ △ △ △ △ △ △ △ △

IT WAS HOT, early spring but already in the eighties during midday. So far we had picked up about thirty of the indicted dealers from the undercover operations.

The processing center at the Police Service Center was moving smoothly, Polaroids and FD-258's stacking up in the brown file folders filling the liquor boxes on the floor. But it was liberating to be riding in the jump out van.

My age and my seniority and my ability to roll near perfect fingerprints usually doomed me to work in the processing center, taking histories, rolling the aforementioned prints onto the FD-258's and listening to the incessant drone of "You got the wrong dude, I ain't sold no dope."

Today I was sitting in the last seat in the back. I knew I shouldn't be in front of Sully and Stretch and the other younger, fitter and way faster city officers in the truck. I needed to be there, but I knew better than to slow them down. Although they were laughing and joking, they were deadly serious about what we were doing.

The lead car, a Firebird with the snitch inside, was cruising along slowly in front.

Sully called on the radio, asking for a break.

"We got to go get something to drink. It's hot in this truck."

The reply, muffled from the undercover officer driving the Firebird, was, as usual, unintelligible. Afraid of being burned talking on the radio, the UC held the unit low, between his legs, and spoke softly. We couldn't hear a word he said.

Sully shouted over his radio, "Talk up, fool. We can't hear shit from you."

In a moment, the silence was broken by another mumble, as the Firebird sped up, heading out of the neighborhood we were working. The undercover cop and the snitch moved rapidly across town to an area where they hadn't bought any crack.

We all pulled into a convenience store near Moore and Shallowford, and bailed out. We pulled bottles of Gatorade or one of its clones from the coolers and walked them up to the counter. The clerk never broke stride at the sudden invasion of heavily armed men, dressed in fatigues, or bib overalls, descending on her register.

After she cheerfully calculated the police discount, most of the local guys left with the drinks for free.

The bibs probably need a little explaining. Stretch wears hickory striped bib overalls. Never seen him in anything else He's at least two inches taller than anyone else in the group, and his flaming red beard and shaved head make him stand out like a torch.

He has been called Stretch so long that I doubt if anyone knows his real first name anymore. Tough as nails, this Sequatchie farm boy knows the street names of the dealers, who they're shacked up with, where their mamas lived, better than anyone in the squad. His soft drawl and slow manner belie his temper, which flares early and often.

Back in the truck, we cruised toward the area where we had been working. The UC and the confidential informant rolled past a knot of young men on a corner, and the radio mumbled back into service. The two voices crowded over the air as we picked out a description of one of the bunch.

△ △ △ △ △ △ △ △ △ △

JOHN IS DRIVING, and he has the arrest packages next to him in the front. We stop, and as John mulls over one of the folders, our team begins to tense up.

It is ritual. We roll up to the corner, the doors slam open, and everyone flows out onto the street. Immediately, one of the crack slingers begins screaming, "Five O, Five O," and all begin to move.

It is a ballet in slow motion.

As the group breaks into singles, Jim Brock picks out the red shirt and baggy blue jeans, as already identified by the CI, and moves like a hawk striking a rabbit.

The dealer starts moving and has about a three-step lead, when Jim hits him, going full speed. The hours and days Jim spends at the Sports Barn have produced a combination that is awesome to witness. At about two hundred and eighty pounds, with a body fat level so low as to be immeasurable, Jim is as fast as he is strong. We'd borrowed him from the SWAT team, another tool in our bag.

Jim grabs the dealer in full stride, swooping him up in a clothesline maneuver that leaves him hanging in mid air, his legs pumping. Down onto the concrete, hands in back, the doper's head bounces off the sidewalk. The nylon disposable cuffs go on, and the dealer is dragged into the maw of the truck, forced to the floor, now to become a foot rest for the trip back to the Center. His protestations, muffled into the floor of the van, are not listened to.

We have struck again, one more to process, one more off the list to catch. A scuff on the forehead, and a stream of mucus running down the face, combined with the tears of rage and fear and realization, and we

306

deliver him to be dealt with by those who don't get to ride with the catchers.

△ △ △ △ △ △ △ △ △ △

THE TEAM IN the truck talks about everything but what we're doing. Motorcycles are the big topic. Everyone wants a Harley, and more than one of the narcs have one in a garage at home. The bikes have caused more financial friction and divorces than the motorcycle dealers have ever thought of. Harley has franchised everything else, and we wonder aloud if maybe they should have a Harley legal firm to handle the divorces.

We are cruising again, and the UC and the CI are out front in the Firebird, looking for more meat. It is getting late, and the Captain wonders over the radio if we're going to get our limit today. He has the media on stand-by, to release the statistics of those caught, the monetary seizures, the drugs bought.

The media jump on the news of arrests, but they never stick around to go to court and see the cases pled down, down, down. A hand to hand sale of crack to an undercover policeman suddenly becomes simple possession, and the dealer gets a misdemeanor conviction, serves thirty days at the work house, and goes back to a new street corner to sling again.

The lawyer gets his fee, and justice triumphs.

The UC who sees himself as risking his safety and even his life to serve and protect his community soon learns it is a game only lawyers win.

The radio mumbles again, and we pull over.

The Firebird is taking a run by another street corner, this time on the edge of a housing project. This time, the message comes through clear. Big Boy is on the corner.

Of all the cases the UC has made, this one has the most promise. This guy is selling bargain basement crack. His rocks are big, his prices small, and he has held out the notion of an endless supply from out of town.

△ △ △ △ △ △ △ △ △ △

NARCS ALL WAIT for the big one, the small dealer that takes the UC to the real big time. The real kingpin behind the street slinging. The guy that runs the business, that has the connections, that makes the real money out of all the misery that this slave trade brings.

We tense again, but this time with some promise, some hope that we're going to get something going that will make some real difference. I'm riding with the city cops hoping to find that trail that leads out of town, out of state, maybe to that one big thing.

We get the description, and we brace to go. I sit tight on my rear seat, back against the wall, and dream of how this could be the one we have waited for. The plain white van begins to roll again, and we are all straining for a look out the front, trying to see the prey before we stop and jump out.

It's quiet in the truck, and we roll evenly to the corner, braking to a gentle halt.

Then the tumult begins, as everyone, hurriedly but orderly, rushes to get through the door at the same time. As usual, I'm last, and as my knees pop when my feet hit, I remember a line from one of my favorite movies, *To Live and Die in L.A.*, "I'm getting too old for this shit." I move to the front of the truck as everyone outside moves to the right of the van, toward the small group of youths standing in amazement at the herd coming toward them.

As I move past the front bumper, something catches my eye to my left. I turn my head away from the action and see a YBM, on my left, standing on the sidewalk, holding in his left hand a black object.

△ △ △ △ △ △ △ △ △ △

THIS YOUNG BLACK male is five seven or eight, maybe a hundred and sixty pounds, wearing the uniform of the day. Baggy shorts with the crotch near his knees and a Lakers jersey. I hear myself screaming, "Gun! Gun! Gun!"

I turn to face the young man and get my bulk in gear, moving toward him. "Police! Police! Drop the gun!"

I'm on automatic now, not looking back to see if anyone is following me, not even thinking about what I'm doing. It's pure instinct. As I move on the guy, he turns and begins, in slow motion, to run away from me.

" POLICE! POLICE! DROP THE GUN!"

Across the yard and into the rear of the area behind one of the shotgun houses lining that side of the street. I have unsnapped, drawn, and come to the pistol ready position as I turn the corner behind him.

The guy stops. Dead still.

I continue to scream.

"POLICE! DROP THE FUCKING GUN."

309

The young man turns, the black object pointed toward the ground. I now see the slide, the trigger guard, clearly the outline of a semi-automatic handgun.

"DROP IT! DROP THE FUCKING GUN NOW!"

He looks at me, and slowly starts to raise his hand, the hand with the pistol. I have the S&W .645 locked into the firing position, finger inside the guard, feeling the smooth trigger with my fingertip.

I carry a .45, as one of my co-agents once said, "Because they don't make a .46."

I like .45's, always have. They make big holes in things, but I've never shot a person with one. I begin to think I'm a millisecond away from doing just that.

Suddenly I have tunnel vision. I am unaware of anyone in the world besides him and me.

His hand continues its upward path, his face beaming. Why is he smiling?

Is he actually going to shoot me?

Am I going to shoot him?

Then I see it.

The gun is not a gun at all. Well, not *really* a gun.

It is a Marksman brand of BB pistol. Looked a lot like a Glock long before there was a Glock. When I was a kid, one of my buddies had one. We used to shoot tin cans with it.

I *know* that BB gun, and I know the kid in front of me isn't really going to shoot. He continues to look at me. His hand turns palm down, and he drops the BB gun onto the grass at his feet.

I continue to do what I do best in situations like this, I scream. "DOWN! DOWN! ON THE GROUND."

I look behind me for the first time. I am alone, in the back yard, with no help and no witnesses. The young man drops to his knees, and I take one giant step to him and throw him onto the grass on his face.

I kick the BB gun away, and then all hell breaks loose.

A stout black lady rushes out the back door of the shotgun house and begins screaming at me.

I can't hear the words, just a shrill roar from the porch. In a moment, I look up as she charges down, raging at me.

I am trying to figure out why she is so pissed, what she is screaming about. I have one foot planted squarely in the back of the young man on the ground, pistol at the ready, and slowly, I start to hear her.

She is, not very patiently, explaining to me that I am in trouble for messing with her son. Her twelve year old, mentally challenged son.

I try to explain about the BB gun, about the drug arrests, about my being a big time federal agent, but all this means nothing to her. I have messed with her son, and I am about to pay the price. I hear about lawsuits and complaints to the chief and calling the NAACP.

I realize that I have lost the battle and that no amount of explaining will ever satisfy her. I want to tell her just how close she came to losing that son to this war on the streets paved with crack rocks. She is now in full rant, and I holster and walk away.

311

△ △ △ △ △ △ △ △ △ △

HOW CLOSE? A COUPLE of pounds on the trigger, one more second before I recognized the BB gun. How close?

I walk back to the van, where Big Boy is trussed up, lying on the floor, awaiting his ride to the center.

John looks at me, "Hey, Wayne, where the hell did you go? We been waiting, and we need to get out of here with this package."

I start to explain my side trip, where I had been, why I was making us hang around in an area where we could only make things more uncomfortable, but the words wouldn't come.

"I got lost."

Intruders

Chattanooga, 1992

W E WERE working a crack case with the TBI, not a normal experience. A lot of the other agents working dope in Chattanooga preferred to work white defendants. It avoided problems. I had other ideas, but this one was going as usual, all screwed up. The snitch had fronted money to the black defendant, who had promptly left the area. It was beginning to look like he wasn't coming back.

We had followed him into a predominantly African-American neighborhood in the area of the Summit Landfill, north of the city. The defendant had driven to a single family dwelling and gone inside.

The area was small, and it was difficult to watch the house from a car without stirring up the curiosity of everybody living within a mile.

"Hey, Joe. What do you think about me going into the house across the street and watching from there?"

Joe Copeland of the TBI was slow in responding. It crossed my mind that he probably thought I was crazy.

"Wayne, you think that'd be cool?"

"Be better than heating up the whole neighborhood. I'll do it if you think it's okay."

"We sure as hell ain't getting anywhere like this. Go ahead."

△ △ △ △ △ △ △ △ △ △

I PUT MY radio in a paper bag that had previously held some sports drink or something else for nourishment while sitting long hours in the car. Then I walked the three blocks to the house I had picked because it was clean and the yard seemed to be well cared for. Looked like the house of someone who would not want a crack dealer living across the street. I walked up to the door and knocked.

"Yes?"

The ebony grandmother who opened the door didn't look exactly happy to see the big white guy on her porch.

"Ma'am, could I speak to you a second?"

She stepped back, and I stepped in, showing her my badge.

"Ma'am, we're watching a drug dealer, and I need to sit in your front room for a few minutes. That be all right?"

She looked at me with a lack of trust. She hesitated a couple of moments before okaying my request.

I walked into the living room of the small home.

In a way it was as I had expected. The furniture was spotless, everything dusted and clean.

What I had not expected was to see two rosy cheeked young white women, sitting in this living room in this all-black community. They

314

were deep in conversation with three black women, one older, and two younger who appeared to be her daughters.

The grandmother clarified the inhabitants, "I'm here with my daughter and my granddaughters. These other two's just visiting."

I quickly introduced myself as a Special Agent with the Drug Enforcement Administration and briefly explained why I was there.

"I bet you watching that trash across the street. He ain't no damned good."

The grandmother had spoken. I didn't agree or disagree, but moved to a position where I could see the house across the street and radio Joe.

"Hey, Joe. I got the eye."

"Everything okay?"

"Yeah, it's cool."

△ △ △ △ △ △ △ △ △ △

MY CURIOSITY ABOUT the other two visitors was palpable, and I was waiting to be introduced.

Several minutes went by, and no one made any attempt to tell me who I had joined in this visitation. The quiet conversation between the two young white women and the three black women continued.

I strained to hear what they were saying, as I strained to see the house across the way.

The conversation ceased, and the two white girls stood, as if to leave. One walked over to me.

"It will be safe for us to go out, won't it?"

"Yes ma'am. We're just watching these people. There's no danger at all."

"I've seen all these things on TV, and I don't want to get hurt."

"No, ma'am. Nobody's gonna get hurt. There's no problem."

She turned to the three seated on the sofa, and said, "We'll see you at church Wednesday night."

I wondered just what this was all about. Some kind of religious pep talk, I supposed.

The young woman then turned to me, and said, "We're doing our missionary work this summer. Where do you go to church?"

"Grace Episcopal."

"Oh. If you'd like to know about the Church of Jesus Christ of Latter Day Saints, we'd be glad to talk to you, too."

"Lady, I'm just a little busy right now, and I already know quite a bit about Mormons. Thanks, anyway."

She produced a card, identifying herself, and told me to call if I was interested.

△ △ △ △ △ △ △ △ △

Sometime later when I stepped outside, I laughed to myself at the weird gathering of people that had occurred in that modest living room.

Grandma had been right when she'd answered my earlier question about coming into her house with a shrug of her shoulders and a feeling of having lost control of her territory, "Hell, yeah, why not? You might as well come in. *Everybody else has.*"

My Other Son

Chattanooga, 1994

VAN GOT TO be such an important piece of the Chattanooga DEA office I wasn't sure what we would have done without him. When Kelly retired in 1993, we had hit hard times with the local cops.

A urinating for distance contest within the Chattanooga PD administration had resulted in the loss of both their officers from the Task Force, and the other locals had pulled away as well. The year turned into 1994, and with it my fiftieth birthday. That made me eligible for retirement at about fifty per cent of my high three years average salary, and I was thinking about it.

The Division seemed to have forgotten about Chattanooga. No word on a replacement for Kelly, and the office was down to me and Hamilton County Deputy Sheriff Van L. Hinton, who had just come from Patrol and had absolutely no experience in the dope business. Gloomy days.

△ △ △ △ △ △ △ △ △ △

"Wayne, this is Mr. Hammond's secretary. Please hold."

Garfield Hammond was the Special Agent in Charge of the Atlanta Division, and he had never called me before. Garfield and I had been in Washington at the same time.

He had attended BNDD Class III while I was in Class IV. My remembrance of him ran to his El Dorado convertible, his numerous suits with matching shoes, a room of his own at the Sonesta for his extensive wardrobe, and his great guitar playing.

"Wayne, how is everything in Chattanooga?"

"Mr. Hammond, we're down to me and one Task Force officer. I am not accomplishing much with so little manpower, but we're working with the TBI and the other locals, and I'm doing my best."

"Well, your stats look good, and I hope we can have a replacement for Kelly within the year."

Great! Within the year. That may as well have been forever.

"Wayne, the reason I called was to ask about your intentions."

"Sir, I don't understand."

"Wayne, I see from your file that you will turn fifty in January. That's not a month off, and I need to know if you're going to retire when you get your age."

"Sir, I've been thinking about it, but I'm not at all sure. Why is this an issue?"

"Wayne, if you retire in January, I'm going to have to close the Chattanooga office. We can't get anyone up there in time to keep it open, and I got surprised by Agent Goodowens's retiring when he did. We can use the resources somewhere else."

"Mr. Hammond, I'm not going to let this office go down the tubes that easy. You got my word that I'll stay on board till we can get a replacement for Kelly."

"Then I'll plan on that."

△ △ △ △ △ △ △ △ △ △

NO THANKS, NO heartfelt encouragement for my sacrifice, just that it would be put into the plans.

After that, Van and I got close. I got to the office first, made the coffee, and then he showed up. He worked hard, did everything that a DEA agent with ten years experience would have done. I never worried about him handling phone calls from DEA offices all over the world, making agreements, committing us to do things. I trusted him as I have few police officers.

He never let me down. He was always ready to work, always ready to ask me just how a thing should be done. I never worried that he would go off half-cocked and do something out of his range of experience. When he didn't know, he said he didn't know, and then he learned how for next time.

Van had a great sense of humor and enjoyed a good laugh. One of his favorites was introducing me to people as his father. Van loved his father greatly and worshipped his mother. That he was close enough to me to even joke about me being his father was great.

We got called to come over to Coffee County to work a case with the Sheriff's Department. They had a snitch who was supposed to be able to buy high quality California meth from some people in the trucking business. The names involved were interesting, so we ran over and soon had a simple deal turn into a nightmare.

Their snitch, currently in custody, was also the son of a dealer we were about to indict. My greed to do a case got over on my good judgment. After the deputies checked their snitch out of the Coffee County jail, we wired him up and sent him into a trailer to talk to his supposed connections in the trucking business. We loitered nearby in our car.

The conversation inside the trailer lasted a few minutes. Then we began to get static on the wire.

"He's dumped the wire. We got to go in, *now!*"

I sped into the gravel in front of the trailer ahead of the others from the Coffee County Sheriff's Office.

Van grabbed my shotgun as we got out of the car, explaining in a word or two that he had left his pistol in the office.

We burst into the trailer to see the two inhabitants sitting on the sofa, smoking a joint. No sign of the snitch, who had obviously planned this escape, apparently without the prior knowledge of the inhabitants.

Van was suddenly in charge.

"Up against the wall, muthafuckas! I'm yo' worst nightmare, a nigger with a shotgun!"

One of the rednecks promptly pissed himself.

I couldn't have been prouder of my other son, Van Hinton, a natural narc.

Aftermath

Chattanooga, 1998

I PULLED INTO THE DRIVEWAY AT ABOUT 12:30 in the morning. The motion-sensor lights came on when I drove the G-car to the end of the drive. Trying to be as quiet as possible, I eased the car door closed and went in through the back entrance of the house. This wasn't going to be easy, like sneaking dawn past a rooster. As I walked in, I drew the little .38 from my ankle holster and put it on the top of the bookcase. The house was still, as I went into the kitchen and had a bowl of granola with skim milk. My stomach was churning, and it felt the granola would help.

Up the stairs and into the bedroom. With the kids grown and gone, the only one not to wake was my wife. She seemed to be sleeping soundly, and after undressing, I crawled into bed without waking her.

I stared at the ceiling for a few minutes, and then remembered to get up and set the clock radio for 6 a. m. Had to get up and get back at it early. My crew was on the street, working, and it always made me feel guilty when I wasn't there. I prepared to stare at the ceiling again, when I heard the clock radio come on.

Damn it all, I had set it wrong. No, I hadn't. The sun was peeking in, and my watch was dead on six. Slept much better than I thought I would.

I was dressed and ready in about fifteen minutes, and had cut myself shaving only once. I was worried that the bathroom fan would wake Joyce, but she was still dozing when I finished dressing. I leaned over and gave her a quick kiss, hurried down the stairs and out to the car.

As soon as the G-car was out of the driveway, I called on the radio, "Fourteen Oh Two to surveillance. You guys awake?"

"Fourteen Oh Eight. We're awake. How was your beauty rest?"

"Two to Eight. I'm so pretty I can't stand it. I'm en route. Be with you in ten."

"Eight to Two. Bring coffee!"

Hardee's provided breakfast, along with three cups of black coffee. If they wanted it light and sweet that was their problem. I'd been drinking it straight black so long I couldn't even consider it any other way.

The night team gave me a quick rundown on the activities of our suspects, and we began to relieve them to go home for a little sleep. The rest of the group arrived in a trickle, took their places, and we started my eleven millionth surveillance.

I had been doing this job for almost thirty years, and it was getting me down. One of my partners used to say that nothing ever changed but the names and dates, the work was always the same. We spent the rest of the morning following two guys who made it painfully obvious that they weren't going to do a damned thing we would be interested in.

322

I broke off about noon and headed to the office. The boss was going on annual leave for a week, and was leaving me in charge. I needed to talk with him before he got out of the office, so I was glad he came in for half a day, even though I couldn't understand why anyone would waste the time.

△ △ △ △ △ △ △ △ △ △

"*JEFE*, I HAD a little problem last night. I need to run it by you, cause I think I may have to do some paperwork, and you know just how happy that's gonna make me."

"Wayne, you didn't wreck the car, did you?"

"Naw, I ain't wrecked a G-car in years. Last night, while we were watching the mopes from El Paso in that hotel on 23rd, I sorta, almost got carjacked."

"What happened?"

My boss had been in the Office of Professional Responsibility before coming to Chattanooga as the RAC when we expanded from the two-man post Kelly and I had first opened to a Resident Office with several agents, and he hadn't got the ramrod out of his back yet. OPR is DEA's version of Internal Affairs. It became OPR at about the same time that Personnel became Human Resources. Bureaucratic crap. The sort of thing Jimmy Carter loved to do. Make a meaningless change in the name of something and call it progressive management. The boss loved doing things by the book, and he was already staring longingly at the Agent's Manual on his desk.

I told the story again, how the two black youths had come up behind the car, stuck a gun in the window, in what appeared to be an attempt to separate me from the government's car, or at least from my money, or in the absolute worst case, from my life. Jim was wide eyed, as nothing this exciting had ever happened to him in the line of duty.

"I think this requires a teletype to Headquarters, and it needs to go out immediately. There's a section in the manual that lays out the procedure."

Somehow I knew there was going to be a section in the manual. I hated that book. It had dogged me my whole career. No matter what I did, at least some part of it was always in violation of some section in the manual.

"Since I'm on leave, as of about five minutes ago, you'll have to do the TWX to Washington. Try to get it out as soon as possible. I've got to go now."

And he was gone, leaving me to do the dirty work.

Going back to my desk, I dragged out my manual and looked up the section on assaults and threats to Special Agents. Dull, dry reading, but at least it gave me a clue of what I had to do. In the old days, I wrote teletypes on a yellow legal pad, and the crypto clerk typed them into the machine. I was the crypto officer here, as we didn't have the clerical support we had been promised for way over three years, and I required everyone to do their teletypes on computer so I didn't have to type their stuff in. I can't type worth a damn. Now I had to type my own story.

In about an hour I finished the message, making sure I had touched all the bases and spelled all the words correctly. I always tried to use at least one word that no one would know the meaning of, even if I had to make it up. I loved to think of the headquarters humps looking for a dictionary in the hope that I had used a word incorrectly.

Saved on a floppy and stuck into my shirt pocket, the TWX was soon ready.

Going to the radio console, I called the surveillance team. They were still camped on the boys from El Paso, and the wire tap in New York and the cloned pagers in El Paso weren't telling us anything. I wondered if the dopers were just doing a training exercise, giving their troops a little workout before annual evaluations. Probably not.

I used to kid other agents that if we made the drug dealers do the same kind of paperwork we had to do on every undercover buy and surveillance, they would all quit, and get jobs at Wal-Mart.

The surveillance was dead, and I suggested that the team might want to ease off and get some rest.

Before leaving the office I went into the crypto room, stuffed the floppy into the terminal, and made the machine do its magic. The teletype went out in a matter of a few minutes, a great improvement over the older system. Then I hurried out of the office and into my car. I couldn't stand for my troops to be out working with me sitting in the office.

I heard them on the radio, tailing a taxi toward the mall. The surveillance went past me, as I fought with a little slow traffic, but I eventually got onto the interstate behind them. At the mall we watched as the two flunkies went inside, bought clothing, and then hopped another cab to the Airport Shuttle.

When we saw them walk out, get into the van, and head for the expressway toward the Atlanta airport, I officially gave up. New York reported in shortly thereafter, telling us that the two guys were returning to El Paso. So much for another big dope deal.

After sending everyone else home for the day, I went back to the office. We had done more than our share on this job, and it all had come to nothing. Like I said, nothing changes but the names and the dates. I came into the office through the back entrance, went into my little cubicle and closed the door.

The phone was ringing off the wall. No one seemed to be answering it, so I walked up to the front to see if Barbara, our contract asset forfeiture specialist, was in. She had paper stacked up to her eyes, and was on one line, with another holding. I listened for a moment, and was able to determine that it was a computer problem concerning seized assets. That was her principal job, keeping up with the cars, money, and the occasional house that we seized. Our agency shared most of the seized proceeds with local law enforcement, and there was a constant struggle to make sure everyone was happy with their share.

Barbara looked up, waved, and then handed me a stack of telephone messages. I had only been gone a couple of hours, and there were already several messages. I went back into my cave at the back of the office and sorted through the messages.

"Trash can. Trash can. Hold for the boss. Trash can. Call next week."

And a couple I didn't know what to do with. I put them in the pile of other messages on my desk. I'd get to them later.

Barbara slid into my office and just stood. I waited, and she waited. I gave up.

"What's up?"

"That Mr. Gonzales from Washington really needed to talk to you."

I looked at the stack of messages, picked them up, and looked at her.

"In here?"

"Yeah, he was very sort of excited about you getting back to him in a hurry."

If it was all that big a deal, why hadn't she called on the radio, the pager, the cell phone?

"Did he say what he wanted?"

"No, just that he had to talk to you as soon as you got in."

I looked through the stack and found the call, I guess. It was from a Mr. Gutierrez, with a 202 area code. The prefix was that of our masters in Headquarters. I dialed up the number and waited. After about six rings, a breathless young lady answered, and I asked for Gutierrez. She advised that she would get him.

△ △ △ △ △ △ △ △ △ △

I SAT AND held the handset for five minutes of dead silence. At least I didn't have to listen to Barry Manilow during that stretch.

"Gutierrez. Can I help you?"

I doubted it.

"Yeah, this is Wayne Smith from the Chattanooga RO. I got a message to call you. I have no idea what this is about."

"Oh yes, Agent Smith, just a second. You sent this teletype about the assault on the agent."

No question, just a statement. I didn't see the need to respond, so I waited.

"Well, did you?"

"Yeah, I wrote the message after lunch today. Is there a problem?"

"Yes, there most certainly is a problem. That message should have been in here first order of business this morning. We needed it for the

Administrator's briefing this morning. That assault occurred yesterday, and there is no excuse for the teletype to be this late."

"Well, I did it as soon as I could. The guy tried to jack me about 10:30 last night, and I had to get some sleep, and we still had the surveillance to do. I got to it as quick as I could. I figured it wasn't as important as the case.

△ △ △ △ △ △ △ △ △

"THE MANUAL SAYS that reports about assaults are to be filed with this office immediately. You didn't get it in here till four or five hours after the office opened and over twelve hours after the incident. Don't you realize how serious this is?"

Since it was my head that the little punk had stuck the gun next to, I did sort of realize how serious it could have been. I also realized that I was talking to some HQ desk jockey, who was scared that he was going to get in trouble if the Administrator found out that something had happened yesterday and he wasn't briefed on it over coffee. Not that the Administrator cared. He was just the sort of asshole who would raise hell with a peon if he caught him out on something like this.

"Look, Gutierrez, I was almost shot last night. I got maybe five hours sleep, and I've been running this surveillance since early yesterday. The boss left town, and I'm in charge. I had to write and send the damned teletype myself, in between doing real police type work. If that ain't fast enough for you, I'm sorry as hell."

I figured he could read between the lines and know that I wasn't sorry at all. Actually I didn't give a rat's ass about it.

Then it came. The line I was expecting. I could have written it out ahead of time.

"I know how it is out on the streets. I've done my share of work. Don't think just because I'm here in headquarters that I don't know how it is."

△ △ △ △ △ △ △ △ △ △

ALL THE HQ humps, getting their tickets punched to become managers, think they are God's gift to law enforcement, and they all know what field agents think of them. They see themselves as making some great sacrifice by spending a year or two in the puzzle palace, but underneath they are not proud of what they end up doing.

Kinda like a story my old first partner once told. We were going to the Narc squad at the Atlanta PD, riding up the keyed "POLICE ONLY" elevator. The thing stopped, and a guy in a sage flight suit and shoulder holster got on, punching the button for the roof.

Joe looked over at me, gave a wink.

"Wayne, did you know that flying a helicopter is just like playing with yourself?"

Being the designated straight man, I just looked at him.

"Yeah, it's fun while you're doing it, but you're sort of ashamed of it later."

The APD helicopter pilot started to flush, just as the elevator hit our stop. I moved off smartly, only to see the grin Joe gave him as he sauntered off.

△ △ △ △ △ △ △ △ △ △

"I KNOW. LOOK, I'm sorry about getting it out late. We're shorthanded here and don't even have a secretary. I'm the crypto officer, and here that means I send the TWX's myself. If you get any heat about it being late, put them on me. I'm far enough away not to give a shit. What are they going to do to me, send me to Chattanooga, Tennessee?"

Gutierrez laughed, made nice, and hung up. I could see him, in my mind's eye. He's telling someone else in the closet of an office he shares just how he made that jackass field agent toe the line.

"I, by God, straightened him out, believe me!"

△ △ △ △ △ △ △ △ △ △

OVER THE NEXT few weeks, I found that I was required to tell the story of the attempted carjacking again and again. It was *not* one of the stories I pulled out, after having a glass or two of wine, to bedazzle and entertain friends.

I kept having to tell this story to people who claimed to have a need to know. I began to have unpleasant dreams, odd for me. I never seemed to let this sort of thing bother me before, but now I was seeing the ugly muzzle of the little Llama .380 automatic more and more.

Over and over, people who had heard the story from someone else would ask me the same question.

"Why didn't you shoot the little bastards?"

I had seen the muzzle shoved near my head, I had seen the "little bastards" run up Willow away from me. I had put the front sight blade of my Smith and Wesson directly in the center of that bright white back as it ran away. Why hadn't I shot?

I had carried a handgun on my person for over half my entire life and had been in at least one situation in my career where I had discharged a firearm in the general direction of another person. I had fully intended, on that occasion, to use deadly force. Was I getting old and soft and unable to close the deal? Had I been hamstrung by the tidal wave of paper we were drowned in after the FBI's escapades at Waco and Ruby Ridge?

Our simple deadly force policy had gone from one paragraph, which rather succinctly stated that we should "only use deadly force in the defense of our lives or the lives of another" to a bloated missive, some fifteen pages long, with reams of footnotes and citations that boggled the mind. In the quiet of my office I re-read that tome several times after this incident. I called a friend in OPR and asked what the decision would have been if I had capped the kid. No one seemed to have an answer.

△ △ △ △ △ △ △ △ △ △

THEY WERE ALL entertained to hear my story, as much as I had grown tired of telling it, but they had no answers. Sleep was slower coming, and the dreams got more and more tortured. They were never about the incident but were often about my father, which made no sense at all. I saw that blue Llama .380, not in dreams, but in the corner of my eye at lunch, at my desk, or at home in my living room.

Finally I called Atlanta, and talked with a Patti in Admin. She was our Employee Assistance Representative, and when I told her what was going on, she suggested that I get in touch with a counselor that DEA had on retainer in the city. This calling bothered me. I wasn't the guy who called for help. I often kidded that they could never make a movie about me because John Wayne was dead, and nobody else could do me justice.

Now I was going to talk with a shrink. Clint Eastwood never needed a shrink. When Harry Callahan whipped out the most powerful handgun made and strewed bodies all over San Francisco, he slept okay. They told me it was a good thing, that everybody did it, that it would help me. I decided that if it would help me sleep, it would be worth the ribbing I would get if anyone ever found out about it.

The really weird thing is that it did help. The even stranger thing is that now I cannot remember a single thing the guy said to me. I'm sure he told me that everyone has these reactions, that it is normal, that I would get over it. All I really remember is that he took my wife and me out to dinner, for which I'm sure DEA paid.

In a few weeks I slept better, and now I don't even mind telling the story anymore.

Looking back in the mirror, I saw something that piqued my interest, something out of place. Two young black males, not unusual, dressed in what appeared to be school uniforms, unusual for 10:30 at night. They were walking west along the front of the strip mall with the Dollar Store on the corner, white long sleeved dress shirts with tails out in the breeze, khaki pants. These were not the low rider khakis with crotch at knee level, but very traditional slacks. Why school uniforms that late at night? My kids could never wait to get home and shuck the Catholic school uniforms they wore. Some of the public schools in the city had instituted the white shirt and khaki pants uniforms recently, but I was surprised to see them at night. The two strolled directly down the front of the building, walking purposefully, but not in a hurry.

I looked back in the rearview, and the two kids had reached the corner and stopped. One reached out and took the handset of the payphone on the wall, put it to his ear, and then dropped it in what appeared to be disgust. That same phone that was working well for the prostitutes. Both then stepped off the curb and started walking directly toward my car. Their line of travel would take them between my car and the utility pole on which my payphone was mounted.

This was a minor job, just a surveillance for other offices, and I hadn't brought all my gear. My SIG .45 was locked in the trunk, and I had a small five shot .38 in an ankle holster as my only weapon. I may never know why I did it, but I reached down, pulled the Centennial from the elastic sheath, and held it inside the fishing vest I was wearing. The two kept walking, approaching the rear of the car. The lead YBM said something to me as he moved to the front of my open window. Damn these electric windows, you can't close them like the old roll up kind. I assumed he wanted to use my phone, but then I saw what was really going on. A small blue steel automatic handgun appeared, as if by magic, at the upper rear corner of my open window. It looked a lot like a Spanish Llama .380. Amazing what goes through your head, beside the ninety grain jacketed bullet in the .380.

I dropped back onto the console between the bucket seats, trying to lie as flat as possible. My revolver came up to the window, and I screamed.

"I"LL KILL YOU MUTHERFUCKER!"

Nice talk for a Federal Agent!

The kid with the pistol was slightly behind me, and the wide center pillar of the car blocked any shot I might have had. It seemed like minutes went by before the two began to run. I jumped out of the car, screaming epithets of various kinds, raging in the dark. I came around the front of the car, and looked north on Willow. The two white shirts stood out in the center of the street, and I went into a perfect combat stance and put the front sight blade right in the middle of one of the retreating white blobs. I could have easily made the shot, but my brain began to tell me what not to do. Which blob had the gun? The internal debate over dropping the shot downrange was going furiously in my head. I could see headlines, "Narc murders 15 year old black youth." Good sense overtook me, and I stuck the piece in a vest pocket, and got back into the car.